The Creative Writer's Survival Guide

The Creative Writer's Survival Guide

Advice from
an Unrepentant
Novelist

John McNally

UNIVERSITY OF IOWA PRESS, IOWA CITY

University of Iowa Press, Iowa City 52242
Copyright © 2010 by John McNally
www.uiowapress.org
Printed in the United States of America
Design by Richard Hendel

The University of Iowa Press is a member of
Green Press Initiative and is committed to preserving
natural resources.

Printed on acid-free paper

Library of Congress Cataloging-in-Publication Data
McNally, John, 1965–
The creative writer's survival guide: advice from an
unrepentant novelist / by John McNally.
p.   cm.
Includes bibliographical references and index.
ISBN-13: 978-1-58729-920-9 (pbk.)
ISBN-10: 1-58729-920-8 (pbk.)
ISBN-13: 978-1-58729-949-0 (ebook)
ISBN-10: 1-58729-949-6 (ebook)
1. Authorship—Handbooks, manuals, etc.   2. Creative
writing—Handbooks, manuals, etc.   3. Authorship—
Marketing—Handbooks, manuals, etc.   I. Title.
PN147.M478 2010
808'.02—dc22   2010006337

This one's for Amy.

If I have anything to say to young writers,

it's stop thinking of writing as art. Think of it as work.

If you're an artist, whatever you do is going to be art.

If you're not an artist, at least you can do a good

day's work.

— Paddy Chayefsky, Academy Award–winning

screenwriter, from an interview in *American*

Film

Contents

....

PART SIX: The Writer's Life

The Writer's Wonderland — Or: A Warning

I like warnings.

In a preface titled "To Be Read Before Purchase" in the "complete and uncut" edition of *The Stand*, Stephen King warns readers who had bought the original version that they might not want to buy the new edition because it was simply the unedited version of the old one. "If this is not what you want," he writes, "don't buy this book." Fair enough.

I also like warnings for prescription drugs. Will you risk hives, itching, swelling of the tongue, hallucinations, agitation, and vision changes in order to get a good night's sleep? Sure! Why not? Warnings are good; they're useful, sometimes even life-saving. And yet we ignore them.

The reissued version of Stephen King's *The Stand* has probably outsold the original version since the one with the warning is the only one available in paperback these days. Meanwhile, people are still popping prescription drugs like Pez candy, warnings be damned. For the record, I own both versions of *The Stand* and have prescriptions to three medications, one of which is for asthma with a possible side effect of "worsening asthma symptoms." Is it human nature to desire the very thing that's pushing you away? If so, I urge you not to read this book.

While this book won't swell your tongue, I do think a warning is in order. If you've picked this up looking for an objective book about what it takes to be a writer, you've come to the wrong place. If you have writer's block and want to be inspired, this probably isn't the right book either. If you're searching for a book so that you can learn how to write a short story, a novel, or a poem, you definitely need to look somewhere else.

This book is a highly subjective and idiosyncratic take on the writing life. You might agree with most of it or find something of value in each chapter, but it's entirely possible that you won't agree with me. In any case, I set out to write an honest book about what it takes to be a writer today, using my own life as well as the lives of other writers I've known as anecdotal support for my opinions on a wide range of subjects.

Why am I writing this book? For more than twenty years, I've worked with thousands of students at nine different universities, and I have become friends with hundreds of writers. I've published books with university presses, commercial houses, and small presses. I've edited six anthologies, and I've worked with a collaborator on a handful of projects. In short, I've been doing this long enough and have had enough highs and lows (plenty of lows) that I thought I might have something useful to offer the lonely soul who's thinking about becoming a writer, or the person who already is a writer but isn't sure what to do next. I'm aware that I'm on shaky ground here because, at the end of the day, much of what I offer up is my opinion. Hence, this warning.

Years ago, a student of mine who was interested in attending an MFA program showed up in my office, angry with me, after attending the reading of a famous writer. The famous writer, who hadn't attended an MFA program, told my student that she didn't need a degree to become a writer. According to the student, the famous writer had told her not to do it. (For the record, I never tell my students that they should or shouldn't get MFAs or PhDs. This is a decision they need to come to on their own.) In this particular case, I had been advising this student because she had *wanted* an MFA, but now that the famous writer had told her she didn't need one, she looked at me askance, as if the degrees I held were shams and I had been trying to pull a fast one on her. I'll confess that I was irked by how star-struck the student was and by how she was equating success with supreme knowledge, but the student wasn't the object of my ire. No, I was pissed off at the famous writer for offering blanket advice to someone the writer didn't know based on . . . *what?* Her own success? Disdain for something with which she hadn't had any experience? The writer's advice was not only self-serving but irresponsible.

If you do decide to plunk down your hard-earned cash for this book, please don't shake it in defiance at your creative writing teacher if she offers different advice. I believe firmly in what I offer up in these pages, but I am also willing to concede that this book shouldn't be a template for everyone. One size *doesn't* fit all. In a talk delivered to students in a course titled "How the Writer Writes," in which a different writer was invited each week, Flannery O'Connor said, "The only parallel I can think of to this is having the zoo come to you, one animal at a time; and I suspect that what you hear one week from the giraffe is contradicted the next week by the baboon."

I also stated that I wanted to write an honest book. I've been to too many writers' conferences where faculty are advised to be gentle and upbeat (the conference, after all, needs recurring customers in order to stay afloat). I've also seen creative writers put spins on their lives that aren't quite accurate. I'm sure I've done this, too. You don't want your readers to know that you're driving a car that's twelve years old or that you still have student loan debts, do you? The writer who radiates a sense of success probably has a better chance of selling books than the one who's always talking aloud about how he's behind on his VISA payment. Also, the subtext of many writing magazines is that you, too, can be a successful writer if you just follow these twelve simple steps. Reassurance is the key to any successful enterprise, which is why some writing conferences, most magazines, and many books put positive spins on the would-be consumer-writer. I may be in the minority here, but I find truth reassuring. If it's going to take me thirty years to pay off my mortgage, I don't want to be told that I can do it in a year. In this regard, I have attempted to be honest—brutally so, in parts—so as not to sell you a bill of goods.

Erskine Caldwell, in his slim autobiographical book *Call It Experience*, writes, "The purpose of this volume is to set forth some of the experiences of an author which may be of interest to curious readers and would-be writers who seek visions of the wonderland in which all authors are believed to exist."

So it goes for this modest book as well. I'll leave it for you to decide whether or not it's a wonderland.

Don't do it—unless every cell in your body insists and keeps insisting. (Ditto: marriage.)
— Julianna Baggott, *The Madam*

1

The Decision to Become a Writer

This Writer's Beginnings

I started writing my first book when I was in the seventh grade and finished it shortly before I entered high school.

It was a nonfiction book about old-time film comedians, and I spent a great deal of time sending letters to anyone who had ever been in movies with, or who had personally known, Abbott and Costello, Laurel and Hardy, the Three Stooges, Charlie Chaplin, or the Marx Brothers. I was stunned when people actually began to respond.

Margaret Hamilton, whose most famous role was the Wicked Witch in *The Wizard of Oz* but who also appeared in an Abbott and Costello movie, sent me a polite, handwritten note along with an autographed photo of herself. Charles Barton, who directed a number of Abbott and Costello movies, including *Abbott and Costello Meet Frankenstein*, sent a letter with his phone number, asking me to call him. (Afraid my voice would reveal I was a child, I never called.) Lou Costello's daughter, who had recently written a book about her father, sent a letter wishing me luck on my project. Moe Howard's son-in-law wrote back warning me not to use the name "The Three Stooges" in my book's title. Moe Howard's son-in-law! Never mind the menacing threat of litigation. I was beside myself.

I also wrote to a number of authors to ask technical questions, and, amazingly, they wrote back, too, including Leonard Maltin, who had yet to gain fame on *Entertainment Tonight*. I wrote to movie studios to inquire about permissions fees to reproduce photographs for my book; envelopes stuffed full of contracts began appearing in my parents' mailbox, and although the studios were asking for too much money, I was excited nonetheless to be receiving daily mail from Universal Studios, MGM, and even the defunct Hal Roach Studios, which must have been nothing more than a rented office in L.A.

During breaks from pounding out manuscript pages on the cast-iron Royal typewriter I had bought at a flea market in the sixth grade, I wrote to every major publisher in New York and asked for their guidelines. I sent letters to publishers in Illinois, too, figuring that I had an in with them since, minus three miserable months in Houston, I had lived my entire life just outside of Chicago. In no time at all, envelopes bearing the names of famous publishing houses began appearing in our mailbox. It was as if editors had been doing nothing but waiting for a letter from me! Using their royalty rates as my guide, I calculated how many books I would need to sell before I could buy a house for my parents. I tried not to let anyone know what I was doing, but a few days before graduating from eighth grade, I couldn't help telling girls I'd had crushes on, and so in my autograph book they wrote, "I can't wait to read your book!" and "Don't forget me when you're famous!"

Oh, no, I thought, *I won't forget you. Ever!*

I finished the book during the summer of 1979 and promptly began writing query letters to publishers, asking if they would care to see my book. I imagined bidding wars; I imagined my photo on the cover of *People* with the headline, "Young Author Secures Enormous Advance"; I imagined all those girls in grade school who'd ignored me calling me up to apologize for dismissing me as a snide, fat kid instead of seeing me for what I really was—a sensitive, misunderstood intellectual with a love for words. (In truth, I *was* a snide, fat kid, but I was willing to play the sensitive misunderstood intellectual role, if necessary.) What I hadn't imagined were letters from publishers telling me that they did not accept unsolicited manuscripts, and yet this was what I received, day after day: form letters (not even personal responses) informing me of their companies' policies. Having no idea what "unsolicited" even meant, I looked it up in the glossary of one of my books on publishing: "A story, article, poem or book that an editor did not specifically ask to see."

Unsolicited? If publishers didn't want to see my book, why were they so damned eager to send me their guidelines?

Before full-blown despair crushed me, a letter arrived from an editor at Harmony Books, asking to see the manuscript. This is it, I thought. Solicited! All you needed was *one* person who wanted your book to negate all those rejections. Who cared what Warner Books, Random House, or William Morrow thought? Harmony Books understood what I was trying to do; they saw something in my query letter that had piqued their interest; they knew, in short, that they had a goldmine on their hands. And so I waited—one week, two weeks, three weeks. It wasn't until week six that a letter from Harmony finally arrived. The first sentence began, "While your book is a fine first effort . . ."

I stopped reading, not because of the rejection I knew was bound to follow. No, I stopped because of the editor's presumption. "First effort?" I yelled, enraged. *"First effort?"* I found a draft of my original cover letter. Nowhere—*nowhere!*—did it say that this was my first effort. Let us forget for a moment that I had typed the entire manuscript on erasable bond paper that smeared with the slightest touch, or that my signature at the bottom of the cover letter looked like a child's. Let's ignore that when I wanted to emphasize a phrase, I had flipped the lever that raised the ribbon so that I could type the words in red ink instead of black. The fact remained that I had not told Harmony Books that the book I had sent them was my first. So, where did they get off suggesting that it was?

That, at least, was what my thirteen-year-old self was thinking. The forty-four-year-old me is now amazed that someone actually asked to see the book in the first place and then took the time to write back. The rejection letter went on to say that they already had a film writer on their list—my old pen-pal Leonard Maltin—and that it wouldn't be fair to him to add yet another. It was a courteous letter, encouraging even, but they had dashed my hopes. I allowed myself to sulk for a day—but just for one day and no more. The next morning, I began thinking up new angles to pursue, new books to write, and I was determined to show all of them—everyone who had rejected me—that they were wrong to have done so. I was money in the bank! I was the next number one bestseller!

By the time I turned fourteen, I had been rejected by every major publisher in New York. I honestly can't think of a more valuable education for a writer—for *this* writer, at least—than what I put myself through. In this profession, failure isn't just a fact of life; it's a necessary part of the process. What I learned first-hand at fourteen was how hard it is to get your foot in the door; I learned how insurmountable it can be to get a book published. Instead of getting discouraged, I started to view myself in a new light—as a seasoned writer, as someone already on his way up.

It was Teddy Roosevelt who said, "It is not the critic who counts, not the man who points out how the strong man stumbled, or where the doer of deeds could have done better. The credit belongs to the man who is actually in the arena; whose face is marred by the dust and sweat and blood; who strives valiantly; who errs and comes short again and again; who knows the great enthusiasms, the great devotions and spends himself in a worthy cause; who, at the best, knows in the end the triumph of high achievement, and who, at worst, if he fails, at least fails while daring greatly; so that his place shall never be with those cold and timid souls who know neither victory or defeat."

My childhood hero Evel Knievel often paraphrased the above quote at press conferences before jumping a few dozen school busses, crashing his Harley, and breaking half the bones in his body. Better to die, was Knievel's philosophy, than to live a quotidian existence. (Since Knievel could barely walk by the end of his life, you may want to take those inspirational words in stride.) As for me, I decided to keep daring greatly, all the while hoping for, in the words of Teddy Roosevelt, "the triumph of high achievement." It took a mere twenty-one years after the mass rejection of my film comedians opus and the writing of two unpublished novels before I saw the publication of my first book, a short story collection titled *Troublemakers*, in 2000. Ten years later, as I sit here typing this, I've written six more books, two of which remain unpublished as of today, but so far not a broken bone in my body, only stitches and bruises—and all of those, I'm happy to report, have pretty much healed.

Knowing Why

It's useful to know why you want to write so you can adjust your expectations accordingly. If you want to write short stories for your family and friends to read, that's great. If you want to write short stories with the hope of eventually publishing a book, that's great, too. If you want to write short stories so that you can become a millionaire . . . okay, now we're running into some problems.

You get my point. Your expectations, your plans of action, even your daily writing habits: each of these will vary based on your ultimate goals for writing.

Between fourth grade and my sophomore year of college, I had entertained the idea of being a professional writer, but I grew up in a part of Chicago where no one I knew, except for my teachers, had gone to college, let alone become a writer. Although I knew as early as the fourth grade that I wanted to write, it wasn't until I took my first poetry-writing course in college that I realized that writing was something I wanted to dedicate my life to. But what did it *mean* to dedicate my life to writing?

For me, it meant doing everything I possibly could. I would go to grad school for writing; I would start sending my work out; I would spend my spare time reading when I wasn't writing. I was, in short, going to give myself a legitimate chance to make it as a writer.

I often joke that if I knew back then what I know now about how damned hard it would be or how many set-backs I would encounter along the way, I probably would have chosen a different occupation. I'm not serious, of course—I would still have pursued writing— but there's a nugget of truth in that I would have flinched at seeing how difficult it really was. The beauty of youth is ignorance. I wrote every short story as though it were going to appear in the *Atlantic*. I mapped out books as though Knopf and Viking were going to bid for them. In other words, my optimism sustained me. And when the story in question proved not to be destined for the *Atlantic*, I was already hard at work on another, certain that *this one* would be the one.

I knew why I wrote. I wrote because my life depended upon it. Not literally, of course. I wouldn't *die* if I didn't write. But I most definitely would be miserable. Unfulfilled. For lack of a better, more tangible way of putting it, writing is what nourishes my soul. There were lean times when I took other jobs, sometimes menial, sometimes merely mind-numbing, that didn't allow for much if any actual writing time, but even when I wasn't writing, I was writing in my head: imagining scenes, committing interesting details to memory, dreaming up plots for entire novels. During one particularly dark period, I was juggling three jobs at once and not writing a word. Then I joined a gym, forced myself to wake up at 4:30 in the morning so that I could exercise for at least an hour, and then return home to write before heading off to my day job. The schedule was grueling, and I didn't write much of anything worthwhile during that period, but I knew that I needed to provide an escape hatch from these jobs that had no meaningful connection to what I wanted to do with my life. The important thing was that I was writing. For me, writing was its own reward.

Where would-be writers run into problems is when their reasons for writing don't match their expectations. Years ago, I taught a proposal writing workshop for nonfiction book projects. One student had been commissioned by the community college that employed him to write a narrative of the school's history. Somewhere along the way he got it into his head that Random House or Scribner might be interested in such a book, and that, if he could only convince one of the big New York publishing houses to accept it, Hollywood was bound to come knocking. Clearly, the man was enthusiastic about his project, but his expectations were completely unrealistic. There wasn't anything particularly unique or distinctive about his school. He couldn't understand why I didn't think the book wasn't a bestseller in the making. I honestly don't believe that this fellow—a decent and nice man, I should add—had ever entertained the idea of being a writer before he was commissioned to document his school's history. The bug had bitten him, but which bug? The bug to become a writer, or the bug for fame? I doubt he ever asked himself *why* he wanted to pursue this project. Did it mean anything more to him other than fulfilling a latent desire to become a celebrity? At some point, his expectations derailed from the project's purpose, resulting in runaway delusions. By the end of the workshop, with his dreams of offers from Random House and Hollywood shot, his disappointment was palpable, yet if he hadn't lost sight of the project's original purpose and had dedicated himself to doing a good job on it, he might actually have gained a measure of satisfaction from it.

Do yourself a favor. Ask yourself why you want to write. Once you know the answer to that question, it'll be a lot easier to determine what your goals should be.

What Have You Ever Done
That's Worth Writing About?

One night in a bar named Gabe's, while I was working toward my MFA, the drunk guy standing next to me wanted to know what my deal was. When I told him, he smirked and said, "What the hell have you ever done that you can write about? I used to jump out of airplanes. Have you ever jumped out of an airplane? How old are you, anyway?" On and on he went, until I walked away.

I have heard this same litany of questions, or a version of them, most of my writing life, the implication being that I've spent my life in school, so what could I possibly have to write about?

Few arguments get me as riled up as this particular one. I don't discount experience—experience is good, experience is useful—but what *is* experience, precisely, and what role does it play in the life of a fiction writer? The person who discounted my life experience is guilty of a fallacy in thinking that only *big* experiences, like jumping out of airplanes, constitute worthwhile experiences for a fiction writer. What about all those years of my life that preceded that moment in the bar? My mother grew up a sharecropper in the South and told me dozens of fascinating, bizarre, and gripping stories about her life. Granted, I wasn't there with her, but being raised by someone who'd gone through the things my mother had gone through certainly helped shape my sensibilities. And what of my own experiences? I lived through a trailer fire when I was four; our family stayed with relatives for over a year after the fire; I attended five different grade schools, because we moved a lot, so I experienced an almost constant fear as the "new kid"; my mother worked in a factory, and I went with her on more than one occasion to meet her coworkers; my father was a roofer, and I helped him put down fresh tar on apartment roofs more times than I'd care to remember; one of my aunts committed suicide; family members divorced and remarried; for ten years, and as early as the second grade, I spent most of my weekends helping my father sell a variety of junk at flea markets; in 1976, when I was in the sixth grade, I bought scalped tickets for an Elton John concert; I had crushes on girls in my classes; I was the second-fattest kid in the seventh grade (I wouldn't allow myself to become the fattest); I fell in love in high school and subsequently had my heart broken; for a number of years, I sold bootleg concert T-shirts and (briefly) made more money than I knew what to do with; I was in fist-fights; our apartments were broken into; I was in the hospital with my mother when she died of cancer. Are these not experiences? Are these not worthy subjects to write about? Why do I need to jump out of a plane in order to qualify as a fiction writer?

When people snottily ask what experiences you've had, they're failing to acknowledge *emotional* experience. For my money, emotional experience is more important than wrestling an alligator with your bare hands. What about a writer like Flannery O'Connor, who lived a relatively secluded life? Or Emily Dickinson, the über-recluse? Can one honestly say that they would have been better writers if they'd driven race cars, run with the bulls in Pamplona, or taken up hot air ballooning?

A book like *The Things They Carried* is a great book in part because the writer Tim O'Brien was able to marry his own experiences in Vietnam with emotional honesty. But how much of *The Things They Carried*—a fictional memoir featuring a character named Tim O'Brien—is actually true? In an interview with the *Missouri Review*, O'Brien says the following:

> Everything I've written has come partly out of my own concerns as a human being, and often directly out of those concerns, but the story lines themselves, the events of the stories, and the characters in the stories, are almost all invented, even the Vietnam stuff. If I don't know it I just make it up, trying not to violate the world as I know it. Ninety percent or more of the material in [*The Things They Carried*] is invented, and I invented 90 percent of a new Tim O'Brien, maybe even more than that.

I recently read a blog entry singing the praises of "writers with experience." The blogger was inspired by this passage from an article about the writer J. G. Ballard, published in *The Guardian* and written by John Crace:

> To generalise wildly, the career path of most young (successful) writers goes something like this. Go to university—preferably Oxford or Cambridge—and read English. While there, start writing novel and get a few pieces published in the university magazine. Move to London after graduation, start a creative writing

postgraduate degree and pick up some work reviewing books for the literary supplements while tidying up the fourth draft of your novel. You then get your novel published, which gets a few kind reviews thanks to the contacts you've made and sells precisely 317 copies.

But someone, somewhere offers you a contract to write a second novel and your career is up and running. From then on you have a meta life. You write because you write, not because you necessarily have anything interesting to say. You probably actually write quite well, but you are trading on style, not substance, because you've never actually done anything much beyond writing.

The blogger's response was a kind of "ha-ha-ha, so true, so true," while a reader of the blog weighed in with this gem: "Imagine spending your life following the publication of your first book teaching in an MFA program." Oh, yes: Imagine!

All of this strikes me as another kind of snobbery. For reasons I've already cited, I don't buy Crace's argument. As for the responder's comment, I spent several years after my MFA working crappy jobs, some of which proved to be good fodder for fiction, but am I a *better* fiction writer because of those jobs? No. In fact, during those periods when I worked those jobs, I was a *worse* writer because I didn't have the mental energy to write consistently or, for that matter, to write well. I was just too damned tired.

How does the experience argument apply to writers of historical fiction? Or what about writers who choose to write from the perspective of a race or gender other than their own? Should we write about *only* what we've experienced?

Baloney, I say.

Fiction writing is a balancing act of many things: empathy, technical proficiency, artistic sensibility (everyone has a story to tell, but knowing *how* to tell it is where the art of storytelling comes into play), insight into human behavior, and, yes, experience. But experience is only one part of the equation. And the ways in which experience translates into fiction are as diverse as all the people on this bizarre little planet who put pen to paper.

Perseverance

Is there a common denominator for writers who eventually have careers as writers?

At first glance, there appears to be no logic for who becomes a published writer and who doesn't. It can't be talent, can it? For every great book, there are many more mediocre books and even more downright bad ones. Conspiracy theorists will tell you that it's all about whom you know, but this simply isn't true. Plenty of writers out there, myself included, have worked their way up, struggling each step, without the benefit of connections.

No, the only common denominator I've ever seen among working writers is perseverance. This isn't to say that perseverance alone will get you published, and it's not to say that all those who persevere, even those with enormous talent, will eventually find publication. What many struggling writers fail to realize is that serendipity, luck, and chance are strong forces in the publishing world. The right agent needs to send the right manuscript to the right editor at the right time. And how in the world can someone plan for that?

Ted Solotaroff, who worked with hundreds of writers as editor of the influential magazine *New American Review* and as a senior editor for many years at Harper and Row, had his own theories in his essay "Writing in the Cold: The First Ten Years":

> Still, it's worth considering why some gifted writers have careers and others don't. It doesn't appear to be a matter of the talent itself—some of the most natural writers, the ones who seemed to shake their prose or poetry out of their sleeves, are among the disappeared. As far as I can tell, the decisive factor is durability. For the gifted writer, durability seems to be directly connected to how one deals with uncertainty, rejection, and disappointment, from within as well as from without, and how effectively one incorporates them into the creative process itself, particularly in the prolonged first stages of a career.

Perseverance or durability is a significant factor in a writing career. To give yourself the best chance, you have to work, and work *hard*. Come up with a schedule and stick to it. It took me ten years before writing became a daily habit, but once it did, three things happened: My writing became stronger, I started publishing short stories more frequently, and I began publishing books.

When I was in my twenties and enrolled in an MFA program, I met talented writers on whose careers I would have bet the bank. There were others I thought were long-shots at best. And you know what? I would have been dead wrong either way. I didn't factor in perseverance. Some of those writers I'd have bet on eventually quit writing, while the others kept to a daily writing schedule and now have significant writing careers.

Perseverance is a hell of a lot harder than it sounds. It's not just about putting in the daily work; it's about putting in the *years*. I used to wonder why certain writers—even those writers who had published books—gave up writing altogether, but the longer I've been doing this, the question isn't so much "why give up?" as it is "why *not* give up?" At every step of the way, building (and then sustaining) a writing career is an uphill struggle.

It's a struggle for the unpublished writer to push on while Book 1 is getting roundly rejected. And what about Books 2 and 3? What if they also get rejected? At what point do you cave in and say, Enough! But let's say Book 4 gets accepted. What if it doesn't sell as well as your publisher hoped? Do you write Book 5? And what if your publisher decides that they don't want Book 5 because of Book 4's sales?

Now, let's say you're a lucky person. Book 1 not only sells but becomes a bestseller. You're the Hot New Thing! Let's say Book 1 is a historical novel set in nineteenth-century France. Maybe you want to set Book 2 in present-day Boise, Idaho. What do you think your publisher is going to say? Oh, they'll publish it, but they won't be happy. If Book 2 had been a retread of what had made you a bestseller, they'd have pumped marketing money into the book the likes of which no one had ever seen before. But a novel set in present-day Boise? *Please.* So, let's say Book 2 flops. What do you do? Do you return to what worked so well the first time, or do you follow your heart and write what you want to write? Or, do you take the next ten years to write Book 3, maybe never completing it?

I doubt anyone reading this book is weeping for the bestselling writer, but my point is that perseverance never ceases to be hard. What makes a person persevere? Where does drive come from?

I learned a thing or two about perseverance and drive in the fall of

1988, when T. Coraghessan Boyle was a visiting professor at the Iowa Writers' Workshop and I was his research assistant.

Boyle used to stroll up to me at parties and offer this sound advice: "Bury your enemies, John. Bury your enemies, and bury 'em deep." To Boyle's credit, he always smiled when he said it, a smile that conveyed wiliness, yes, but also that he was in possession of the inside scoop. Vindication would be, I soon realized, the recurring theme of our conversations that semester.

Boyle liked me in part, I suspect, because he looked at my experiences at Iowa and saw a reflection of his own. Boyle had gone to SUNY-Potsdam; I had gone to Southern Illinois University, also a state school. According to Boyle, he, too, had been left out of the funding pool at Iowa, as I had been. My research assistantship with Boyle had come as a last-minute appointment in my second year after a visiting editor made a case on my behalf. From what I gathered, anger became Boyle's fuel at Iowa, his motivator. And maybe this was the best thing that could have happened to him. As a student, he began publishing in places most writers only dream about—the *Atlantic*, *Esquire*, the *Paris Review*.

"Bury your enemies, John. Bury your enemies, and bury 'em deep."

We were standing in some student's apartment the first time he told me this, crammed in the corner of a kitchen, drinking beer. Boyle shook his head, smiling. You could see it in his eyes: the sweetness of vindication.

But there was more to that semester than just talk of vindication. There was the sound of Boyle typing; he was *always* typing. The typewriter had been a gift from his mother, and whenever I stopped by his office, I would pause before knocking so that I could listen to those keys clacking, the bell ringing, the carriage return slamming. I want to say that it all now seems like a scene from another century, but it *was* another century. Over twenty years ago. A lifetime.

Do I ever use vindication to fuel my writing? Sometimes, yeah. Sure. And what about Boyle? All you have to do is count how many books he's published since *East Is East*, the novel for which I was his research assistant. By my calculations, as of today, fourteen. So you tell me.

At every step of the way, there are pressures, and it's always easier to give up than forge ahead. Poet and fiction writer Joseph Bathanti, who teaches at Appalachian State University, offers these wise words about the life of the writer: "It's a romantic life of deadly peril. A hard head is requisite, as well as dead aim for spitting in the eye of those who tell you you can't do it." The careers I admire the most are those of writers who've faced every possible set-back but are still here, still writing, still publishing. They are the real troopers. These are the writers whose books you should keep stacked next to you each time you sit down at that keyboard, which, I hope, is every day.

Do You Have What It Takes?

A student asks his teacher, "Do I have what it takes to be a writer?" and the teacher responds, "Do you like sentences? If you do, then you have what it takes."

"Do you like sentences?" may seem like a silly criterion, but the longer I've been teaching, the less silly it seems. All too often, I meet students who are interested in becoming writers, but when I read their work, it's clear that they don't like *anything* about sentences. They can't punctuate. Their manuscript is full of misspellings. They're not interested in learning how to control point-of-view. Frequently, their primary storytelling influence is TV, and their first stories are full of all-too-familiar melodrama or sentimentality. More disturbing is the student who takes my class but can't think of anything to write about. Why take a creative writing class if you can't think of a story to tell? I wish these were isolated cases, but in the twenty-plus years I've been teaching, it's been more the rule than the exception. Most students who sign up for my courses do so as an elective, and that's fine. But the ones who worry me are the ones who seem more interested in the *idea* of becoming a writer rather than the *reality* of becoming a writer. If this book does nothing else, I hope it narrows that gap between the *idea* and the *reality*.

Yet there are those students who clearly want to become writers from the get-go. These students are burning with ideas (and not the plot-heavy ideas of a TV series); they're eager for criticism and not defensive when it's given; they not only ask for recommended reading, they actually go out and read books I've suggested, and they read them as a writer would, paying attention to language, pacing, details, voice. Most importantly, they're always writing. And, yes, they love sentences.

Early on each semester, as a kind of test, I'll write on the board the first sentence of Gabriel García Márquez's *One Hundred Years of Solitude*:

Many years later, as he faced the firing squad, Colonel Aureliano Buendía was to remember that distant afternoon when his father took him to discover ice.

By this point in the semester, I already would have talked about how a strong opening sentence of a short story or novel can serve as a contract with the reader, and how it establishes any number of important things: tone, rhythm, scope, characters, themes, point-of-view, and so on. I'll read García Márquez's sentence aloud several times and then ask my students what it is that makes this such a wonderful sentence.

The students for whom I hold out the most hope are not only the ones who keep finding things to talk about with this sentence but also those whose eyes light up during the conversation. Here, after all, is a sentence that has a life of its own. In a mere twenty-six words, the author has given us the past, the present, and the future; he has created an entire world. It's a sentence worthy of a good half-hour discussion. I start losing hope when students, even with my prodding, can't sustain more than a few minutes or aren't excited by the discussion, because if this sentence can't excite one about the possibilities that a sentence has to offer, then *no* sentence can.

So, you want to know if you have what it takes to be a writer? Tell me. Do you like sentences?

My Own Illogical Journey

There are those lucky few whose writing careers follow a trajectory that is both ideal and enviable. She goes to a top MFA program; while there, she publishes a story or poem in the *Paris Review* or, hell, maybe even the *New Yorker*. Agents begin contacting the author, not the other way around; the story or poem gets chosen for the *Best American* series. The writer then goes on to a prestigious fellowship program, like the one at Wisconsin or Stanford; there, she lands a two-book deal with a major publisher. The first time she enters the job market, she bags a cushy teaching appointment in the region of her choice. The first book comes out and garners glowing reviews in places like the *New York Times Book Review* and *Washington Post*; the book makes everyone's end-of-the-year "must read" list; the author's first book, unlikely to win a major award, is a finalist for the National Book Critics Circle Award or the National Book Award. Movie rights sell, if it's a novel, and everyone eagerly awaits the next book, hungry for whatever this charmed writer has to offer the world.

Was there a time when I thought this would be the arc of my career? Maybe. Most likely, it was when I was an undergraduate and still smoking too much dope. Here's why my delusions, if I ever harbored any, didn't last long. Even as I wrote each short story with the hope that the *Atlantic* would snap it up, I was sending work to magazines with names like the *Old Sad Horse Review* and getting rejections. Initially, I always set the bar high, but I was also willing to adjust it accordingly once the rejections piled up.

While wrapping up my undergraduate degree at Southern Illinois University at Carbondale, I *did* (miraculously) get accepted to the Iowa Writers' Workshop. (I should note that I was rejected by two of the four schools to which I applied.) Anyway, at Iowa I first met writers who truly believed that there was an arc that their career paths should follow. I knew one guy—he was twenty-two—who, having once received a long, encouraging letter from the *New Yorker*'s famous editor Roger Angell, had decided that he would submit all of his stories to the *New Yorker* and nowhere else. This struck me as utter lunacy. What if the *New Yorker* never took anything by him? Turns out, they didn't. It's been twenty years since I graduated from

Iowa, and I have never seen a published word by this guy. Meanwhile, my classmate Chris Offutt—who has certainly made a name for himself—published his first short story in the *Coe Review*, a tiny magazine in Cedar Rapids. In his essay "Getting It Straight," Offutt writes, "The story was embarrassingly bad and the editor spelled my name wrong, but I was very proud. At the age of 32 I finally became a father and an author." Offutt went on to win Guggenheim and National Endowment for the Arts fellowships and to publish in damned near every magazine *except* the *New Yorker*. Imagine where his career would be right now if he'd held that standard for himself: the *New Yorker* or nothing!

Yes, the *New Yorker* is the Holy Grail. But it's not the only place to publish your work. Nor is it the only magazine to launch your career. Young writers can get side-tracked (and by "young" I'm not talking about age but rather the stage you're at in your career) by fixating too much on the small goal while losing sight of the larger picture. And in the scheme of things, getting a story published in the *New Yorker*—as an end-all-be-all goal—is pretty small. I would urge the young writer to keep her eye trained on two things at once: her writing (the work that's on her desk) and her longer-term goal (the work that's three, four, or five years down the road).

But what is that longer-term goal? I'm hoping it's not to win the Pulitzer or land on the *New York Times* bestseller list. Those aren't goals. Those are wishes. Those are desires. You can't work toward them. They either happen or they don't, and in all likelihood, they won't. I'm speaking from a gambler's perspective now. The odds are overwhelmingly against you. The *ultimate* goal should be to get your book published. And not by just Knopf or Random House, either. (In later chapters, I'll discuss why these aren't the only places worth publishing with, and why some books are better fits for other kinds of publishers.)

Even though there were flashes of careerism among my classmates when I was an MFA student in the late 1980s, students are a lot savvier now, and there appears to be an ideal track to follow, a right agent to get, a pecking order for publications, and little acknowledgment of serendipity, luck, and chance's role in their careers. But I guarantee you, there is also a lot of disappointment. I urge you not to buy into the illusion that a "perfect track" exists.

I'm not a household name. I've never had a story published in the

New Yorker. Oprah never mentioned my books on her show. As of this moment, I have never had a book reviewed in the *New York Times*. And yet, I have a writing career. Not Junot Díaz, Jhumpa Lahiri, or Jonathan Safran Foer's career, but a career nonetheless. And not a bad one. The path I've followed can't be charted. (Or, rather, it could be charted, but it would look like rugged terrain rather than a smooth, unencumbered ascent to an idyllic summit.)

The only consistency in my career is that there has been no consistency. If you look at my bio on my website, you'll see listed a number of published books, many magazine publications, fellowships, a lot of degrees (*too* many degrees, probably), and a few cushy teaching appointments. But that's only one side of the story—a carefully constructed biographical note that infers, via omission, that it's been a cakewalk. If I had my druthers, my bio would look more like this:

John McNally has published three novels and two story collections. He has written another five books, one of which he spent five years writing, that have never been published. He wrote what would become his first published novel, *The Book of Ralph*, against the wishes of his then-agent. His short stories have received far more rejections than acceptances, and most of the stories from his first five years of writing never found a home. He's edited six anthologies but has had at least as many book proposals turned down. Although he has held the University of Wisconsin's prestigious Carl Djerassi fellowship, he received it a full ten years after he applied for it the first time. He has never won a National Endowment for the Arts fellowship, despite applying for one over a twenty-year period, nor has he ever received an Individual Artists grant from any of the states he's lived in. He has had five different agents. He is an associate professor at Wake Forest University, but only after years and years of shitty adjunct work for which he was paid an unlivable wage. In fact, for a seven-month period, after all the adjuncts from one of his jobs were let go in the middle of the school year, he lived in a fourteen-foot camping trailer in southern Illinois. With a garden hose as his only water source, a hot plate, and a bungee cord holding the door shut, he began work on what would eventually become his first published novel, but he assures everyone that there was nothing romantic about this experience. He gained twenty pounds from lack of exercise, drank too much, and watched more bad morning TV than he ever imagined possible. He is presently hard at work on a novel for which he is not under contract and has no guarantee of publication.

Everything in the above bio is true, just as everything in my public bio is true. Let me repeat: The prescribed track for the creative writer is a myth. Oh, sure, some writer somewhere has gone from point A to point B to point C without a hitch, but she is the anomaly.

For every up in my career, there has been a down. As for the five books I wrote that have never been published, only three of them were my "first" books. One of them I wrote after the publication of *Troublemakers*, my first published book. Another I wrote after *America's Report Card*, my third published book. The publication of one book doesn't guarantee the publication of another book, unless, of course, you're making money hand-over-fist for your publisher, in which case you could probably publish your book of finger paintings. I know a lot of wonderful and accomplished writers who can't get their second, fifth, or eighth books published. I also know a lot of wonderful and accomplished writers who can't get *any* book published.

Why, you may be wondering, do I keep writing with so little certainty and so much rejection? The answer to that question, like the writer's path, is thornier than anything I can sum up in a sentence or two, but I hope by the end of this book that it will be clear.

Be old-fashioned, think of yourself as a storyteller, as a bard, as a friggin' lute player, and take some drama classes so you can learn how to passionately perform your stories and poems.
— Sherman Alexie, *War Dances*

Education
and the Writer

Learn Your Craft

Students taking their first creative writing courses are often resistant to learning craft. Why? Because it demystifies their favorite short stories and novels, and it makes the writing process less mysterious. In other words, it takes all the fun out of it for them.

Some beginning writing students, though not all, would like to believe that they're geniuses who don't need training. These students aren't taking creative writing classes to learn a craft; they're taking it for affirmation of their brilliance. I hate to admit this, but I felt this way when I signed up for my first creative writing course. After all, I had been dashing off short stories and poems for years, and all of my grade school and high school teachers had patted me on the back and told me how creative I was. By the time I stepped foot in my first college-level creative writing course, I had come to believe that I was something pretty special. When the professor introduced himself as a poet, my first thought was, *Aren't we all?*

As it turned out, my professor was Rodney Jones, who was on the brink of being a finalist for the Pulitzer Prize and a few years away from winning the National Book Critics Circle Award. What I quickly learned in his class was this: "No, we are *not* all poets." He didn't ever *say* this to me, but when my first batch of poems was returned with the words *cliché, abstract,* and *didactic* in the margins, I started to see, for the very first time, that I wasn't the little genius I had thought I might be. Nor are my students, by and large, whose recurring problems in their first short stories are often that they use clichés, abstractions, and didactic language. On rare occasions—*very* rare occasions—a student will show up with full-blown talent, turning in stories that are wholly original and devoid of commonplace issues. But I can count on one hand the times this has happened in all the years I've been teaching, and a recent student of mine whose first short story absolutely blew me away was not only accepted to nearly every graduate program to which he applied but offered their top funding as well. In other words, I wasn't the only one blown away by his work. If you're a genius, chances are pretty good that your genius will be acknowledged. If, however, you *think* you're a genius who's simply not getting recognition for being one, or if you think your professor isn't bright enough to *see* that you're one, I've got some bad news for you.

Most of us have to work on our craft for many years before we hit our stride. What do I mean by *craft?* I mean point-of-view. I mean characterization. I mean language. I mean a few dozen other things. But what I mean most of all are two things: being in control of your craft and making it second nature.

The first time I read what John Gardner wrote about "psychic distance" in his book *The Art of Fiction*, I had an epiphany. It's a simple concept, and yet it makes all the difference in the world. Psychic distance refers to the distance that the reader feels to what's happening on the page. If you write, "It was 1871," the reader is going to feel more removed from the moment than if you write, *"Holy crap,* Jack thought," which places you inside Jack's head and, in doing so, brings you closer to Jack's consciousness. There are several levels of psychic distance, and what I learned was that by carefully *controlling* the psychic distance, I could control the reader's involvement in the story. If I wanted the reader to feel cold toward what was happening, I could move out; if I wanted the reader to feel what the narrator was feeling, I could move deep inside. It's all about manipulation. Gardner points out how the sloppy writer has no control of psychic distance. I compare it to watching a film that moves from an intense close-up of a character to a bird's-eye view to a medium-shot to a bird's-eye view to an intense close-up. In other words, the filmmaker's choices would seem arbitrary to the point of inducing a migraine. The same is true of the writer who has no concept of psychic distance and who uses it willy-nilly.

Students resist learning craft because, they believe, it makes the act of writing too mechanical for them. The writing *is* mechanical at first, but eventually it should become second nature. Making it second nature is the trick—and, yes, the difficulty.

My teacher Frank Conroy would say, "You hear about three-year-old pianists who are prodigies. You hear about genius chess players who are three years old. But you never hear about the brilliant three-year-old novelist. Why is that?" His theory was that it wasn't possible for a three-year-old to write a brilliant novel because writing novels took *living.* It took life experience that a three-year-old, no matter how brilliant, doesn't have—not to mention the insight gained from that life experience. (And no: By "experience" he didn't mean jumping out of airplanes or wrestling alligators.) Conroy also believed that you needed to have read hundreds or thousands of novels and to have read them as a writer—something that a three-year-old is unlikely to have done.

Which brings me to my final point. Most of my beginning students have taken many years of literature courses but very few, if any, creative writing courses, which means that they've been taught to look at fiction primarily from the other end of the telescope. Instead of learning about craft, they learn about theme in high school (which may be the most reductive way of looking at literature and the reason why so many of my beginning students turn in heavy-handed stories at first), or they learn in college to apply some kind of theory to the "text" (notice how the story ceases to be a "story" and is now a "text"). The students of mine who are English majors, steeped in theory, have a tendency to begin their stories with abstract ideas rather than concrete situations and vivid characters. As a result, there is rarely a beating heart anywhere in these stories.

If you want to be a fiction writer, you need to start reading like a fiction writer. To do so, you need to learn about craft so that the next time you pick up a contemporary short story, you're reading it not as an abstraction floating in formaldehyde, existing simply for the theorist's dull scalpel to saw on, but as a concrete thing constructed out of words and shaped by syntax, brought to life by a writer who made several thousand choices, some large, some small, before letting that imperfect beauty, the story, walk on its own two feet.

Can Writing Be Taught?

This debate is as old as the hills . . . but a hell of a lot less interesting.

A colleague recently said to me, "But, really, how many of your students are going to be great fiction writers?" He's a literature professor who clearly has problems with creative writing as a scholarly pursuit. I replied, "How many of *your* students have gone on to be great scholars?" He had to concede not many. By his litmus test, what I did wasn't worthwhile if I wasn't producing *great* writers. His question was meant to disarm me. I was supposed to raise my arms and surrender. But when I applied the same standard to him, he couldn't offer up proof that he was producing any more great scholars than I was producing great fiction writers.

Another colleague asked, "What the hell do you do in a fiction-writing class, anyway?" *What do you think we do?* I wanted to ask. *Play the bongos? Sit in a circle, hold hands, and hum until inspiration strikes?*

I wish I could say that these sorts of presumptions are rare, but they're not. I've heard these questions or questions like them ever since I stepped into my first creative writing class in 1984. Curiously, no one ever asks, "Can physics be taught?" And why don't they? Because no one's benchmark for teaching physics is for a professor to produce a classroom full of the next generation's Einsteins. Yet people often assume that if a creative writing professor isn't producing the next Austen or Melville, then the whole enterprise of teaching creative writing is an academic con game.

The charge that creative writing can't be taught isn't lobbed by literature professors alone. Some creative writing professors dispute the ability to teach creative writing. In her book *The Situation and the Story*, Vivian Gornick writes, "This book grew out of fifteen years of teaching in MFA programs, where I have learned that you cannot teach people how to write—the gift of dramatic expressiveness, of a natural sense of structure, of making language sink down beneath the surface of description, all that is inborn, cannot be taught—but you can teach people how to read, how to develop judgment about a piece of writing: their own as well as that of others."

I couldn't disagree more. Gornick perpetuates the myth of the "born writer." Sure, people are possessed with varying degrees of talent, and, yes, some talent is innate. Yes, some people probably don't have what it takes to be a writer. But there is a wide swath of gray between the born writer and the person who doesn't have a chance. As will become clear by the end of this book, I believe strongly in the notion that all these things—the gift of dramatic expressiveness, a natural sense of structure, making language sink down beneath the surface of description—are the result of internalizing what you've read over a period of years as well as internalizing the craft you've practiced, combined with the act of writing itself.

If I didn't think that writing could be taught, I wouldn't be teaching it. I'm not a snake oil salesman. I *know* these things can be taught because I certainly didn't enter my first creative writing classes with an innate gift for dramatic expressiveness, a natural sense of structure, or the ability to make language sink beneath the surface of description. These things, when I accomplish them, are the result of years of hard work on my part, and I failed more often than I succeeded during my first ten years of writing. But whenever I've experienced a breakthrough, where dramatic expressiveness, structure, and language all fell triumphantly into sync, I *knew* it was happening, and whenever I sent those stories to magazines, those were the ones that got snapped right up and won awards. But was I *born* with these gifts? No. I was born with a *sensibility* that creeps into my work; I had certain *passions* for narrative early on; I had an *aptitude* to learn.

Look: I can't turn a young writer into the next Flannery O'Connor or John Updike any more than a math professor can produce the next Pythagoras or Descartes. In every profession, there are always going to be those whose work becomes transcendent, whose work will, with luck, endure. But most *published* writers are not Flannery O'Connor or John Updike. (Even Flannery O'Connor's early stories are labored. She tended to use phonetic spellings in her early work to replicate dialect; later on, she manipulated syntax instead, which is a good example of how a sophisticated understanding of craft can vastly improve a story.)

Like the math professor, there are certain things that I can teach. Most of my beginning students don't understand point-of-view, for instance. Oh, they may know what first-person means, but most of them don't know the difference between omniscience and limited third-person, and they haven't really considered why some points-of-view are more effective for some stories than other points-of-view, nor do most of them realize how filtering a story through the consciousness of a particular character brings the reader closer to the material than does a narrative voice that hovers outside the point-of-view character and uses generic language. How is point-of-view connected to the work's vision? How does point-of-view affect the story's immediacy? For a good part of the semester, my students continue to struggle with controlling point-of-view, but if they work hard at it, they start making breakthroughs. They're not born technically proficient.

I learned something useful from each of my writing professors, all of whom were successful writers themselves. Richard Russo, one of my undergraduate fiction-writing professors, pointed out my own sloppy use of point-of-view in one particular story and then walked me through how it could be tightened. In graduate school, Frank Conroy spoke often about "meaning, sense, and clarity," holding the language in our stories to a high standard. Allan Gurganus, whose mentor was John Cheever, took great pains to show us how our stories could be more immediate. Madison Smartt Bell was interested in story structure the semester I took his class. From all of my teachers, I learned the importance of writing every day.

I can't teach anyone to become a genius. I can't even guarantee that my most talented students will ever publish a story, let alone have successful careers. But I can teach craft, and I can lead by example. The rest is up to them—or, more likely, to the Gods of Luck, who are often cruel but sometimes generous.

Going It Alone

In an interview for the *Paris Review*, John Irving was asked how helpful his years at the Iowa Writers' Workshop were, and he replied, "I was not necessarily 'taught' anything there as a student, although I was certainly encouraged and helped—and the advice of Vance Bourjaily, Kurt Vonnegut, and José Donoso clearly saved me some valuable time; that is, they told me things about my writing and about writing in general that I would probably have figured out for myself, but time is precious for a young writer. I always say that this is what I can 'teach' a young writer: something he'll know for himself in a little while longer; but why wait to know these things?"

You could always forgo degree-granting programs. There's certainly nothing wrong with that approach. Bear in mind that the journey might take longer, and you may end up with fewer contacts, not because MFA programs are a secret cabal bent on world domination but because you simply won't have as many opportunities to forge friendships with people in your field.

If you decide that the academic route isn't right for you, I still recommend that you try to find a few good readers of your work and listen to their criticism. By "good readers," I don't mean family and friends who may or may not like to read; I mean other writers, preferably more established than you and writing in the same genre that you are. Where do you meet these folks? Perhaps at a writers' conference. Occasionally in local writers' groups. Maybe even in a short-term summer workshop, where bonds can form after a week of working together. The reason I suggest this is because it's awfully difficult to work in a vacuum. Let's face it: Few writers ever really go it alone. Many writers of the Lost Generation, none of whom had MFAs, read each other's work, made suggestions, and published each other. They were, in many ways, an ad hoc MFA program, without the university affiliation, of course.

Perhaps along the way you'll find a mentor as well. Sigrid Nunez had Susan Sontag. Melville had Hawthorne. Plato had Socrates. The writers' workshop may be a relatively recent phenomenon, but the spirit of it harks back to ancient times.

Creative Writing Degrees: What Are They?

In my office at home, on the wall to the right of my desk, hang three diplomas. One is for my BA, another for my MFA, and the third for my PhD. But to the left of those diplomas hangs an original lobby card for the movie *Bonzo Goes to College*. In the lobby card, a chimpanzee carrying a football is dressed in a football uniform, including shoes with cleats and a helmet. He is clearly pleased. The tag-line for the movie is, "He's running riot on the gridiron . . . and making *monkeys* out of the profs!" In the bottom right-hand corner of the lobby card, Bonzo wears a mortar board and holds a rolled-up diploma.

I've met people, as I'm sure you have, who put way too much stock in their degrees (or, more accurately, in the supposed prestige attached to the schools confirming their degrees). The Bonzo lobby card stays next to my diplomas in order for me to keep some perspective. The degrees are useful to have—necessary, even, for certain kinds of employment—but *where* I went to school has always been less important to me than what I'm going to do next. Right now, as I sit here typing this, I have five ideas for novels that I'd like to pursue. *That's* what I'm fixating on. (I've worked with people who can't *not* mention that they went to Harvard, Cambridge, or Oxford, and it's like watching a fifty-year-old still talking about the first time he had sex. *Please.* I beg of you. Stop embarrassing yourself.)

More than fifty years ago, Flannery O'Connor wrote, "Everywhere I go, I'm asked if the universities stifle writers. My opinion is that they don't stifle enough of them." When she wrote those sentences, you could have counted on one hand the number of creative writing programs in this country. There are now more than two hundred graduate programs in creative writing and more than four hundred undergraduate programs that offer creative writing options. For some universities, creative writing has become a cash cow. We could debate the ethics of this day and night, just as we could debate the ethics of English Departments continuing to accept PhD students when the odds of getting a job are ridiculously slim, but the fact remains: Creative writing programs are here to stay. (One can't help wondering what Flannery O'Connor would have said about the proliferation of these programs, but who knows: Had she not suffered from lupus and died at such a young age, she might have accepted the directorship for one of these programs or a sweet Distinguished Professorship position. After all, she herself held an MFA from the Iowa Writers' Workshop, so clearly she wasn't opposed enough to boycott the entire enterprise.)

What follows is a *very* general overview, one that attempts to draw large distinctions between various creative writing degrees but can't possibly acknowledge all the differences. The same degree offered at two different universities may vary dramatically. Furthermore, creative writing programs are like living organisms: they are prone to change, especially in regard to who's on the faculty, so you should seek out the most recent information possible for the programs that interest you.

The Associated Writing Programs' website is an invaluable tool for researching specific programs, offering information about most undergraduate and graduate creative writing programs. I recommend other reference sources at the end of this book.

Undergraduate Degrees
BA in English with a Creative Writing Concentration
Back when I was an undergraduate at Southern Illinois University at Carbondale, I majored in English with a creative writing concentration, which meant, essentially, that I took the core English Department requirements while also taking a prescribed number of creative writing courses. Don't be concerned about the terminology. Some English degrees offer concentrations in creative writing, as mine did, while others offer a creative writing track within the English major. Or they may call it something else altogether. The requirements vary from university to university, but the basic idea behind these programs is the same: The student walks away with a core English degree, topped off with a required number of creative writing courses.

Years ago, I met a magazine editor who, upon hearing what my degree was, zeroed in on "concentration in creative writing" and assumed that I had taken all creative writing courses at the expense of traditional courses, which, of course, wasn't the case at all. It was a rigorous degree. In fact, the total number of English courses that I was required to take in order to major in English added up to more than what's required for a traditional English degree where I now teach.

I've met numerous published writers whose most important mentors have been their undergraduate creative writing teachers, teachers who were embedded within an English Department and teaching lower-level courses. Southern Illinois University at Carbondale may not sound like the creative hub of the universe, but while I was there I studied with poet Rodney Jones (who was a finalist for the Pulitzer Prize and, a few years later, won the National Book Critics Circle Award) and fiction writer Richard Russo (who has since won the Pulitzer Prize and made a name for himself as an A-list screenwriter in addition to being a top-rung novelist). Before I attended SIU, John Gardner—a writer who may now be more famous for being a great creative writing teacher than for his own novels, which include *Grendel* and *The Sunlight Dialogues*—taught in the department for a number of years. In fact, Gardner was Charles Johnson's professor and mentor (Johnson would go on to win a National Book Award in fiction for his novel *Middle Passage*). In a book of John Gardner's uncollected writings, Charles Johnson remembers their fortuitous meeting:

> That circumstances should have brought me, six book-length manuscripts under my arm, to the Gardners' home on a rainy September night is one of those formative, fork-in-the-road events in my life that I have never been able to unkey. A few editors who'd rejected my fiction remarked that I could stand improvement on such matters as "voice" and "prose rhythm." Gardner's reply was, "Oh, I can help you with *that*." And it was true: he prided himself, as a trailblazer of the New Fiction that arose in the early 1970s, on his prodigious understanding of technique, his gift for voice and narrative ventriloquism, his magisterial, musical prose . . .

Granted, Johnson was a master's degree student at Southern Illinois University with six unpublished novels under his belt, but John Gardner was also teaching undergraduates at the time. I'm telling you all of this because I want to emphasize that you're likely to find great teacher-writers in the unlikeliest of places. In fact, before he taught at SIU, John Gardner was a young professor at Chico State University (now California State University–Chico), where he was Raymond Carver's teacher. If you can't afford to attend an Ivy League university —I certainly couldn't have—don't rule out your local state universities or small liberal arts colleges, where hidden treasures on faculty can be found—good teachers and writers who, for one reason or another, are not teaching in high-profile MFA programs.

BA in Creative Writing

The obvious distinction between this degree and the degree above is that you'll be getting a degree specifically in creative writing with this one rather than a degree in English.

A student in a creative writing degree program would most likely take more creative writing courses than she would in a degree program in which creative writing is a subset, concentration, or track. My wife, Amy Knox Brown, teaches at Salem College in Winston-Salem, North Carolina, where she directs the Creative Writing major. There, the creative writing student must take seven creative writing courses and five courses from the English Department. (The BA in English at Salem College requires twelve courses in English, a certain number of which can be creative writing courses.) Amy believes it's important for the major to be intrinsically linked to the English Department and the Division of Liberal Arts—as opposed to, say, the Division of Fine Arts—in order to maintain creative writing's direct connection to literature.

What are the perks of a creative writing degree over an English degree? At Salem, some of the creative writing courses are not offered to regular English majors. One called a capstone course requires each student to give a teaching demonstration, write a book review, research (and give presentations on) graduate schools in creative writing, write a statement of purpose (which is then presented to the class as a whole for feedback), and assemble a portfolio of her best creative work (also presented to the class for feedback). Furthermore, only the creative writing majors can have one-on-one meetings with visiting writers of note, such as Jill McCorkle and Kim Addonizio, to discuss their work. There are also annual monetary awards specific to creative writing majors. At the end of the year, the program sponsors a public reading dedicated to the work of the creative writing students.

I should pause here to mention Columbia College Chicago's Fiction Writing Department, a department devoted entirely to the study of writing narrative prose. It's an enormous program that originated within an English Department before breaking away to form its own program. (Interestingly, poetry writing is still taught as part of the English Department at Columbia College Chicago.) The fiction-writing major, which offers more resources and opportunities than many master's programs, is a hugely successful program, having graduated such writers as Stephanie Kuehnert (who has recently published two YA books with MTV Books), Joe Meno (author of the wildly popular novel *Hairstyle of the Damned*, among others), and Sam Weller (Ray Bradbury's authorized biographer).

You may be wondering why degree programs in creative writing exist. Why can't they all just be part of their home English Departments? Sadly, the decision is often a political one—and by "political" I really mean "unfortunate and based on pettiness." While the creative writing major at Salem College enjoys a healthy partnership with the English Department, the fact is that creative writing is still marginalized within many English Departments. In such instances, creative writing isn't taken seriously by the literature faculty (the irony here is staggering); there aren't many offerings; courses don't count toward the English major; the class sizes are too large for conducting workshops; advisers talk students out of taking creative writing courses in favor of taking more "serious" literature courses; etc., etc. One solution to these problems is for the creative writing faculty members, who are often treated like parasites, to break away from their host (or, as I prefer to imagine it, burst from the chest of an English professor, like the famous scene in *Alien*) and form their own major with its own curriculum and standards.

Creative writers are certainly not immune to causing problems, and the resident poet or fiction writer who acts like a superstar may exacerbate tensions. In these cases, English Departments are probably happy for any official division that permanently separates the two camps.

What's the downside to having a degree specifically in creative writing? A degree that's *so* specific (and, most likely, misunderstood) may not be taken seriously. And so the dilemma for the student who already *knows* that creative writing is what he wants to pursue is this: be part of an English major which may marginalize the very thing he wants to study, or study the thing he wants to study while bracing himself to be (potentially) marginalized afterward? Frankly, I wouldn't worry too much about this. You really need to look at the requirements for each program, along with what each one has to offer, and then determine what's important to you, which is why, at the end of the day, I can't really recommend one degree program over the other.

BFA in Creative Writing

I honestly don't see much of a difference between the BFA in Creative Writing and the BA in Creative Writing. In some instances, the BFA program is housed in the College of Fine Arts as opposed to the College of Liberal Arts. What does that mean for the student? That's hard to say. Creative writing faculty will sometimes find a more sympathetic audience within fine arts, which could lead to more flexibility with the curriculum, possibly even more funding. In the College of Liberal Arts, creative writers are often fighting turf wars with English professors, who may think that the writers are sucking students away from their major, thereby putting their survival in peril. (Have I mentioned yet how high the level of melodrama can be within universities?)

As more and more liberal arts colleges drop humanities requirements—a disturbing trend, I should note, that appears to be gaining momentum—the BFA may be an appealing option. The University of Nebraska at Omaha offers a BFA in Creative Writing through their College of Communication, Fine Arts and Media. In addition to requiring nine hours of Humanities courses, the major requires the student to take nine hours of Fine Arts courses outside the major. With thirty-nine required hours of literature courses and eighteen required hours of writing courses, University of Nebraska at Omaha's program is far more rigorous and humanities-oriented than most regular BA programs housed within Liberal Arts departments.

In the end, it's difficult to assess what any of this means for the student, so let me repeat: research, research, research. Don't be afraid to ask what the advantages are for a program to be affiliated with fine arts as opposed to liberal arts or vice-versa, whatever the case may be.

Graduate Degrees
MA in English with a Creative Thesis

For all of the graduate degrees in English, I'll be discussing those that require a creative thesis or dissertation, thereby making it, in essence, a degree in creative writing.

The MA in English is often a stepping-stone degree for someone planning to get an MFA or a PhD. You don't, however, need an MA to get an MFA, or vice-versa.

Typically, the MA is a one- or two-year degree. The MA is traditionally a more academic degree program, requiring more literature courses and fewer creative writing courses, but in the past ten years even this has changed. Some MA programs are almost indistinguishable from MFA programs. Probably more than any other degree, MA programs are wildly inconsistent from university to university. I recommend going over the degree requirements with a fine-tooth comb. Does the program require a creative thesis, a scholarly thesis, or both? How many creative writing classes will you be allowed to take?

Perhaps the most important difference between the MA and the MFA is that the MA is *not* a terminal degree, whereas the MFA *is* a terminal degree. "Terminal" means that this is the highest degree for the field. Although the MFA is still considered a terminal degree, there are now PhD programs in creative writing, and more and more English Departments want to hire PhDs rather than MFAs, further complicating the issue. On the one hand, the Associated Writing Programs, which represents the interests of writers in academia, still acknowledges the MFA as the terminal degree in creative writing. On the other hand, a colleague of mine yelled out at a meeting that the MFA is no longer the terminal degree in creative writing, which isn't technically true but might as well become "the truth" if hiring committees begin thinking this way, and in a buyer's market the candidate with the PhD will almost always be favored over the candidate with only an MFA.

What this means is that the person who holds *only* an MA as her highest degree is unlikely to land a teaching position at most four-year universities. While community colleges and some four-year city colleges will often hire teachers with only MAs, be forewarned: The pay and benefits are usually dismal, the classrooms oversubscribed with students, and the teaching course load high. See my chapter "Landing a Teaching Position" for more uplifting details. An MFA, on the other hand, does qualify a person to teach at a four-year university.

There are many good reasons why a creative writer might enter an MA program. He may have applied simultaneously to both MFA and MA programs, but if he didn't get accepted into an MFA program (or the MFA program of his choice), he can buy himself more time in the MA program before reapplying to MFA programs in a year or two. In some cases, the student enters an MA program to fill in the gaps of his knowledge of a particular period of literature. Or, if he has decided to stay in a given geographic region, the universities near him may not offer an MFA, in which case an MA program that offers the option of a creative thesis makes good sense.

I don't hold an MA, but many of my friends who have MFAs do. I applied to both MA and MFA programs, but after lucking out and getting accepted into my school of choice, the MA seemed a moot point. It's less common, though not unheard of, for someone to pursue an MA after receiving an MFA. If you think of going to school as a way of buying time to work on your writing, the MA will buy you an additional year or two, and as long as you're not putting yourself deeper into debt, I don't see anything wrong with that.

MFA in English

I graduated from my two-year MFA program more than twenty years ago, but when I think back now on those two years, it seems as though I crammed ten years into two. I was young when I started—twenty-one, to be exact—so I was more frivolous with my time than I am now. My habits were bad. How so? I drank so much I was arrested one night for public intoxication. I didn't read as much as I should have. I wrote regularly but not nearly as much as I should have. I spent a good part of my day perfecting my pool playing. I lost too much money playing poker. With a rum-and-Coke in hand, I would stand on my coffee table wearing untied high-tops and sing along to old Motown songs.

Despite this, those two years are among the most important of my life. I was surrounded by writers, some of whom were screwing up worse than I was, some of whom were working so hard they landed book deals by the end of their two years. I stood next to Kurt Vonnegut outside the library after a reading and listened to him answer questions from his fans; I talked to John Edgar Wideman after he danced at a house party; I had a meeting with Ann Beattie, while she was in town to give a reading, to discuss one of my own short stories. What else? I saw one of Mary Gaitskill's very first readings from *Bad Behavior*; I saw one of Ethan Canin's first readings from *Emperor of the Air*; I saw a reading by the slightly cantankerous W. P. Kinsella, who had returned to Iowa to watch the filming of *Field of Dreams*, based on his novel *Shoeless Joe*. Even when I wasn't writing, my life during those two years was all *about* writing. Even when I was playing pool, I was usually playing pool with other writers, so our conversations would inevitably turn to books, other writers, things we'd written, or things we were going to write. Do I wish I had written more during those two years? Sure. Do I regret any of it? Nope. None of it. Those two years are long behind me now, and I rarely think of them anymore, but they were a gift, even if I didn't always see this at the time.

Most MFA programs are two years long, but there are now some three-year programs (Southern Illinois University at Carbondale, for instance), while others may take up to four years or longer (University of Arkansas at Fayetteville). Hollins College used to be a one-year program, but they have now (wisely) switched over to the two-year model. A one-year program strikes me as an exercise in futility. Sure, you get a degree in short order, but what good is a degree in creative writing if it doesn't buy you time to work on a significant book project?

The advantage to a program that's longer than two years is that you have more time to work on that first book. Let's say you spend a year working on a novel that simply drops dead. (It happens more often than one would like to think.) If you're in a two-year program, you may start to panic. A three-year program would afford you the cushion to fail with one project and start another.

Most MFA programs are designed so that the student has plenty of time to write. At Iowa, I took a workshop and two literature courses each semester of my first year. The literature courses were taught by writers (mine were led by Madison Smartt Bell, James Salter, and Joan Chase), and each week we discussed the assigned books from a writer's perspective as opposed to that of a scholar's. During my second year, I took only workshops and thesis hours, which provided me with even more time to write (or to play pool, as the case may be).

Unlike the MA, the MFA *is* a terminal degree, which means that you will be eligible to be hired into a tenure-track position at a university. The MFA is still the degree most associated with the academic pursuit of creative writing. That said, more and more universities advertise for a creative writing professor with a PhD in English (with a creative dissertation), and even those that don't explicitly state that they want a candidate to have a PhD may lean toward the one with it (or the candidate with both an MFA and a PhD) for reasons which I'll discuss in my PhD section.

MFA programs don't promise that you'll land a job after graduation or get your book published. For my money, what the MFA program provides is a sense of community unlike any other you're likely to encounter. For a finite stretch of time, a group of students works toward one common goal: to become better writers. In a best-case scenario, you'll read each other's work outside of the classroom, struggle over the same writing issues, trade notes on the publishing world, celebrate each other's victories, and hopefully forge lifelong friendships with people who will continue to read your rough drafts years down the road. The writer's life is more often than not a solitary one. Attending an MFA program is an opportunity to make it a little less solitary.

Low-Residency MFA

To further make Flannery O'Connor spin in her grave, there are low-residency MFA programs in which students meet their professors only twice a year (each time for an intensive week) and then complete the remainder of their work together via long-distance correspondence. Every year, brand-new low-residency MFA programs crop up, often affiliated with schools I've never heard of. (If a particular program succeeds, it could become profitable for a university that might otherwise be struggling.) The appeal of a low-residency program for the university is that it's a cheap way to add award-winning faculty to its staff. For the student, there is a low student-to-teacher ratio.

Consider Queen's University in Charlotte, North Carolina. I'm sure it's a fine university, but I don't know anything about Queen's except for its low-residency MFA program. On their website, the MFA program advertises a four-to-one student-teacher ratio. Would you get that in a traditional program? Probably not. And who's on their faculty? Pulitzer Prize winner Elizabeth Strout, for starters. *New York Times* bestseller Lauren Groff. Commonwealth Writers' Prize for the Best Book of Europe and South Asia winner Naeem Murr. The list of impressive writers on faculty goes on and on.

A low-residency MFA is an excellent option for someone whose life situation is such that it would be impossible for them to spend two or three years in residence in a traditional program. You get to a certain point in your life, and your options begin to narrow: you have a full-time job; you have a family; you have geographic restrictions for any number of reasons. In a completely unscientific observation, I have never heard anyone complain about their low-residency program, whereas I have heard plenty of complaints about specific traditional programs.

Unfortunately, there is still enough snobbery in academia that a candidate for a teaching position who holds a low-residency MFA is often ignored by search committees, even when the candidate has a published book. This may be a moot point, as most of the people I've met who've gone through low-residency programs did so because they already had jobs or because they were raising families — in short, they weren't interested in careers in academia. (If you *are* interested in becoming a professor, you may want to take into account the bias against low-residency programs.)

What are the other downsides? From my perspective, the biggest downside is that you can't recreate in a low-residency program the same sense of community that you're likely to encounter in a traditional MFA program. That's not to say that you won't leave the program with lifelong friends, but there's something to be said about the value of spending two intensive years with like-minded folks, where you go to the same restaurants and bars, run into each other on the street, patronize the same bookstore, get together on a whim, wind down together after workshop, celebrate publications together, and occasionally fight each other. (I'll leave the more salacious details of lovers' trysts to your imagination.) Even though a pathological shyness kept me somewhat out of the loop when I was a student at Iowa, those two years were unlike any other two years in my life. That said, the sense of community that a traditional MFA program offers isn't for everyone. Some people feel suffocated by it, or they get sucked into the wrong aspects of it, like the competitiveness, of which there is a lot at a place like Iowa, and they finally succumb to it. For those folks, a low-residency program might have been a better option.

What about the success rate for those who attend a low-residency MFA program? This will vary from program to program, but I firmly believe that success has more to do with the individual than the program. One of the most successful authors ever to emerge from a low-residency MFA program is David Wroblewski, whose novel *The Story of Edgar Sawtelle* has become an international phenomenon. His MFA is from Warren Wilson's low-residency program, and on his acknowledgments page, he thanks several of the writing professors with whom he studied. "[Richard] Russo was one of five teachers I worked closely with when I attended the creative writing program at Warren Wilson College," he told Jenny Shank of *New West*. "I also worked with Margot Livesey, Joan Silber, Ehud Havazelet, and Wilton Barnhardt [. . .] In other words, I was fantastically lucky. I studied with writers whose novels and stories I admired tremendously. Rick [Russo] has a special place in Edgar's history because he was so enthusiastically behind the project and the writing, and also because his novel *The Risk Pool* was a great inspiration to me."

Would Wroblewski have succeeded had he gone somewhere else? Probably. It's hard to say if he would have succeeded on the same scale since success of any kind is so serendipitous. I always think of the Ray Bradbury story "A Sound of Thunder," in which the killing of a butterfly in the era of dinosaurs changes the outcome of a modern-day election. One small ripple may alter your life. That said, my hunch is that David Wroblewski would have written a publishable novel no matter where he'd gone to study writing.

PhD in English
Really? you may be asking. *A PhD with a creative dissertation?*
Yes. And guess what? I have one.

It's not as crazy as it sounds. You have to believe me when I tell you that I never had any intention of getting a PhD. Remember the part in my "honest" biographical note where I mention that I spent seven months living in a fourteen-foot camping trailer after all the part-time teachers in my department were let go? The way I saw it, I had two choices: work on a trawler off the coast of Alaska, or apply to PhD programs. (I was dead serious about the trawler, but my father —a man who usually never interferes with my plans—wisely talked me out of it.) I applied to four PhD programs, got accepted to two, and was offered money from one, so my decision was easy: I followed the money.

In full disclosure, I blew off a lot of my courses when I was an undergraduate. I did well in most of my English courses, but I failed three courses my senior year of college (yes: three!), and one of the courses I *barely* passed was Shakespeare. What I did as an undergraduate was go to the library the day before the final. Back then, there was a room in the library with a few dozen record players, so I checked out albums for all of the plays that had been assigned. The speed for an album is 33 1/3 rpm. (If you're under thirty years old, "rpm" means revolutions per minute.) As time began running out, I flipped the speed to the faster 45 rpm. The actors' voices were suddenly pitched higher, but after a few moments I was able to compensate enough to tell Othello from Desdemona. For the final two plays, in an act of utter desperation, I turned the speed to 78 rpm. The characters now all sounded like the Chipmunks. I couldn't tell one from the other. The two plays were tragedies, but their endings played out in high-pitched shrieks and comic death-groans.

This story makes for a good anecdote in a bar after everyone's half in the bag, but in the daylight, when I spend my time either writing or teaching, it's an embarrassment. Shakespeare! Of all writers! Well, the PhD program gave me an opportunity to undo that damage. As a PhD student, I could take pretty much whatever I wanted, so I stocked up on Shakespeare courses and, as a result, have a greater, deeper appreciation of his work now.

But, of course, there are other reasons to pursue a PhD with a creative dissertation, and chief among them is *time*. A never-ending task for the professional writer is figuring out ways to carve out large chunks of time to write. The University of Nebraska–Lincoln offered me six years of guaranteed funding, and although I ended up not using all six years, I wrote almost all of what would eventually become my first published book, *Troublemakers*, during the years I spent in residence there. (In a concerted effort not to waste any more of my time, as I did in Iowa, I also put together and sold a proposal for my first anthology, *High Infidelity*, to William Morrow while working on my PhD.) I was able to transfer credits from my MFA, as well as some credits from my BA, which freed up even more time.

Without a doubt, the PhD has given me a leg up on the job market. I was told by a fiction writer who interviewed me for my first decent visiting appointment that it was the PhD that sold the scholars on my candidacy. This is a sad reflection of the great divide between creative writers and scholars—after all, I already had a terminal degree with my MFA, and my first book was set to come out that October—but old prejudices die hard, if at all.

Working on a PhD was, for me, a vastly different experience than working on an MFA. There wasn't the same sense of community, for starters. I also saw for the first time the uglier side of department politics. Still, I'm happy to have gone through it.

While all of these programs—low-residency, traditional, undergrad, graduate—help to facilitate your growth as a writer, the final verdict depends upon what you bring to the table. Do you have the discipline? The talent? The stamina? The passion? These are not small factors, which is why—and I sincerely believe this—where you study is ultimately of little consequence. If you find yourself in a piss-poor program, don't use that as an excuse to give up writing. I run into people all the time who tell me about a teacher who was so cruel that they gave up writing or of a workshop that was so awful they shut down altogether afterward. *Really?* I want to ask. *That's all it took to make you give up?*

To those who end up in a bad program, I offer this advice. Buck up. And keep writing. In fact, write harder. College is a cakewalk compared to the world of publishing, where no one owes you anything. What Bette Davis famously says in *All about Eve*, "Fasten your seatbelts. It's going to be a bumpy ride," applies to every aspect of the writer's life.

The MFA Controversy

Before moving ahead to chapters about choosing the right graduate program and the application process, I need to weigh in on a subject that gets endless attention in the blogosphere. All you need to do is Google "against MFA programs" or "anti-MFA" to realize how contentious this subject is. I don't go out of my way to promote MFA programs, nor do I think everyone should go to one, but I'm quick to defend them against the anti-MFA contingent. If you read the arguments against getting an MFA—that they're Ponzi schemes in which only a few people at the very top benefit while the vast majority suffer; that MFA programs produce middle-of-the-road writers who are conventional, if not predictable; that thousands of MFA students graduate each year without the prospect of earning a living—you start to see a pattern in which the person complaining is positioning himself as a victim.

It had never occurred to me that my MFA program was supposed to land me a job upon graduating; that's not why I decided to get an MFA. Nor did it ever occur to me that all students graduating with an MFA would rise to the top of the pyramid. (Remember what I said about luck, chance, and serendipity being strong forces? Only the most naive would assume that two years in an MFA program would guarantee him *anything*.) As for the middle-of-the-road, bourgeois subject matter that MFA programs are supposedly mass-producing, does anyone really believe that once students enter an MFA program, they're given a set of guidelines about what they should write about, or that they're pressured by their professors to write a certain kind of story? (Flannery O'Connor, John Irving, George Saunders, Gail Godwin, and David Foster Wallace are all products of creative writing programs. Is their work so similar that you could rubberstamp it all as "workshop fiction"?) Furthermore, does anyone really believe that everyone outside of academia is writing startlingly original and radical fiction that's not getting recognized?

The person who is applying to an MFA program because he thinks it's the golden ticket to landing a *New Yorker* publication and a job at an Ivy League college has a misperception of what an MFA program is all about. The person who's afraid that an MFA program will indoctrinate him so that all he'll be able to write afterward is the dreaded "workshop" story should go to a psychiatrist; he clearly needs someone, other than me, to tell him that he has the free will to make choices about the things he does. Or, if he believes that going to an MFA program will stunt his growth as a writer because it's replacing all the wild adventures he could be having, like shooting wolves from helicopters, he shouldn't apply to an MFA program.

Many of the arguments against MFA programs ignore one basic point: No one is forcing anyone to apply! Go write your proletariat novel while working your forty-hour-a-week job. But don't assume that there's not someone in an MFA program who hasn't already spent many years working forty-hour-a-week jobs and is now in an MFA program to buy valuable time to work on that great proletariat novel and to be (perhaps for the first time in her life) around other people who care deeply about literature. Furthermore, no writing professor ever tried to force me—or anyone else in class—to write like him or her. Sure, each teacher had her own aesthetic, but who doesn't? And isn't that the point of studying with an established writer—to see the world of fiction writing through his or her eyes? At the end of the semester, you're more than welcome to dismiss everything that's been said.

Perhaps the most outlandish complaints against MFA programs come from famous personalities who don't know anything about them. Radio personality Garrison Keillor, offering advice to a would-be writer, says, "Skip the MFA in creative writing, Andy. It's a scam run by English departments to fatten their coffers and doesn't do you much good except as a social club (you can find better ones elsewhere). You're apt to find star faculty who never teach and a whole lot of semi-published writers doing the teaching and the prevailing culture is one of mutual flattery. You waste two years hearing people tell you how wonderful you are and then you graduate and find out that nobody wants to read your stuff."

Does Garrison Keillor have an MFA? No. Has he ever taught in an MFA program? Not to my knowledge. While I'm sure some MFA programs "fatten the coffers" of some English departments, I can assure Mr. Keillor that not all do. Some fine MFA programs struggle to get enough applicants each year. (What's wrong with fattening coffers? I suspect Keillor has fattened NPR's coffers plenty.) I've heard complaints about famous writers on faculty who do little or no work, but why should the exception be the rule? I know many fine "star" faculty who do teach regularly. One example is T. C. Boyle, who has been teaching at the University of Southern California for roughly thirty years now. I'm sure there are better social clubs than one comprised of graduate students in an MFA program, but there are worse ones, too, and many that are a lot less inspiring. Finally, it certainly wasn't my experience—nor is it the experience of anyone I know who's gone through an MFA program—to be told for two years how wonderful I was.

Nearly all the arguments against MFA programs are born of ignorance or logical fallacies. The exception becomes the rule, or truth is ignored (many of my classmates at Iowa were in their thirties, forties, and even fifties and had already lived rich lives before arriving on campus), or the entire enterprise of the MFA program is blamed for one's own personal disappointments or lack of due diligence. When my car breaks down, should I denounce the existence of cars?

I know an undergraduate who's almost sixty years old and wants to go to an MFA program. She had her first child when she was sixteen and has worked hard her entire life. This is the first time she's had the time to pursue what interests her, and, as it turns out, she's an incredible writer of both short stories and creative nonfiction. What she wants now, more than anything, is to go to an MFA program. She wants time away from the routine of her regular life to concentrate on writing; she wants more guidance, more instruction; she wants to surround herself with others who are also immersed in writing; she wants a change of scenery. It's only from a position of jealousy or privilege that someone can legitimately tell this woman that she shouldn't go to an MFA program or that she's wasting her time.

Why go to college to study *any* art? Why study dance, painting, or music? You go so that you can study with those who've had more experience than you. You go to study the sorts of things that might elude you if you studied on your own. You go to be exposed to different points-of-view. You go to be part of a community. You go to immerse yourself.

In addition to the MFA-as-pyramid-scheme theory, you're likely to hear conspiracy theories. Even though the arguments above are sometimes at odds with the ones below, they are often made by the same people. Here are four anonymous comments left on a blog dedicated to rejections in the literary world. The brackets are mine; the parentheticals are theirs:

Are all FIVE POINTS [literary journal] contributors really all connected to Academe? That is VERY revealing and I think a lot more research and work should be done in this area. The Internet can help us connect the dots . . . I am becoming convinced that there is a LOT of academic funny business going on right now and the ones who "make it" are the ones who play along and/or are part of it. Academia today is VERY stifling and politically loaded, and is it a coincidence that almost ALL literary outlets are academic? (And that no one else reads?) That is why we hear so much about "dumbed down" fiction, the lack of commercial outlets, mainstream becoming increasingly full of porn/violence, and is it probably why the publishing biz is just so lousy now.

Now, I'm not against the many writers who have MFAs, not at all; I just don't believe that literature and creative writing must be owned by academia, and that you must obtain a degree in creative writing in order to be allowed to publish your creative writing. I believe that it's a dangerous place for our culture to go in, and I think that something big has got to happen to get us out. Everybody remembers Eisenhower's warning about the military-industrial complex, and we all know how bad that is, but at the same time he also made another—lesser-known but equally dire—warning on the education-research complex. It applies to stuff like the drug companies today, but it also applies very much to literature, since the overwhelming majority of literary journals are tied into higher education programs. Since they have a vested interest in their own systems, it's only natural and expected for them to be hostile toward non-degreed writers or to moving literature away from academia and out to the vast, uneducated masses.

I responded to someone's comment about whether or not I had a MFA. I told why I didn't. Yes, I was sarcastic in regard to the prevalence of MFAers in the top journals. Before I started to read [Scott Snyder's short story "The 13th Egg," published in the *Virginia Quarterly Review*], I see Columbia [University] staring me in the face. I just couldn't resist being, as you call it, 'snide.' I do think there's a lack of life experience among many (not all) MFA-trained writers. They go from high school to 6 years of college. Then they get a teaching job. I mean, come on. Campuses are pretty, are pleasant, but they're not the real world. Maybe that's why we get so much writing like ["The 13th Egg"]. Juvenilia.

Academia and the MFA culture has been discussed quite thoroughly in here. We don't like the system, we don't like the product, we don't like the elitism and nepotism and the way that MFA culture squeezes everything else out. Pick up a copy of *Poetry* magazine and read the contributor notes. All MFA students and their teachers, every last one. That's bogus. Just like the great bulk of their poetry.

I'm not going to be generous; I'm not going to give the benefit of the doubt. These people simply have no idea what the hell they're talking about. They're fabricating conspiracies to justify their own rejections and failures.

Paranoia always lacks logic, and the gaps of logic in these arguments are staggering. Almost all of these claims are sweeping generalizations. While I'm sure elitism exists in some MFA programs (although, to be honest, I'm not entirely sure what these folks mean by "elitism" here), I would be hard-pressed to believe that elitism is the prevailing wind in the MFA programs of Columbia College Chicago, Western Michigan University, Wichita State University, or hundreds of other places where students, often of dismal financial means, gather to study writing. As I hope I've already made clear, I certainly didn't come from money, and the choices I made to become a writer led to many years in which I was barely able to scratch out a living.

I could spend the rest of this book refuting the various claims I've found on these blogs, but I'll tackle just a few. For starters, I know dozens of editors, and I don't know of a single one who's "hostile toward non-degreed writers." The bottom line for every editor I know is the work itself. If they like it, they'll champion it; if they don't, they'll reject it. As much as I'm sure the paranoid out there don't want to hear this (and won't believe it), it's as simple as that. In fact, I'm sure that most, if not all, of the editors I know would love to find someone out there writing brilliant stories who *isn't* connected to academia. My degrees are sometimes listed in the biographical note of my books (if it makes sense to make note of them, as it would for this book), but I never mention them when I send out query letters to agents or cover letters to magazines, and in all the years I've been sending work out, no agent or editor has ever asked me if I had gone to college and, if so, where my degrees were from. Why would they? It's absurd to think that this is par for the course.

There is also the sweeping generalization that *all* literary magazines are affiliated with universities. *Many* are affiliated with universities because universities have (or used to have) the funding, but many magazines *aren't*. *Glimmer Train* is one notable example. *Open City* isn't funded by a university, either. Neither is the *Sun*. The list goes on and on. But it's to the conspiracy theorists' advantage to claim that all are, yes? And who's stopping someone *not* affiliated with a university from starting his own magazine? No one I know.

You will often hear about friends publishing friends, these friends having gone to MFA programs together. First off, please name for me *any* vocation where friends don't do favors for friends. That's just how the world works. But there are two points I'd like to make. It's not how the world *always* works. I published short stories in literary magazines for over a dozen years before a friend of mine took over the helm of a journal. So, how in the world was it that I could get published without the help of a friend? The paranoid would keep chipping away at my answers until the "truth" was finally revealed—the truth, of course, never being that someone at the magazine actually *liked* my story and championed it.

Another missing piece of logic here is that writers—like lawyers, like doctors, like anyone in a profession who attends conferences or socializes in the same circles—come up together and, via these various venues, sometimes become friends. I'm not an active networker. By that, I mean that I don't go out of my way to meet people with the intent of getting any kind of gain from them. But I do meet people, and I happen to know hundreds of writers. Chances are that some of these writers are also magazine editors, and chances are that some of them have asked me to submit to their magazines. But I guarantee you that none of these editors would have asked me to submit if they didn't like my work, and I would hope that they wouldn't take a story of mine if they didn't like it, either.

If I were editing a magazine, would I say to my writer-friends that I wouldn't want them to send work to my magazine? Of course not. But the paranoid would claim that the reason friends with MFAs publish other friends with MFAs is because it's a self-perpetuating industry: You need publications to get a job, so you scratch the back of the MFAer next to you, who, in turn, scratches your back. I can't say that this never happens — it happens in every vocation — but I can say with certainty that this is not the way things typically work.

Most laughable are the claims that an MFA leads to a cushy teaching job. (Please read my chapter "Landing a Teaching Position" for a more complete picture of that grim scene.) If teaching 120 students while earning $1,000 a month (without benefits of any kind) is a cushy job, then I was living like a king a few short years after earning my MFA.

The implication here is that you need an MFA to get published, that the publishing world is made up of a series of gatekeepers who look first at your credentials before deciding whether or not you can move to the next stage. In other words, writers with MFAs are part of a cabal who know the secret handshake. If this is true, what about all the people out there with MFAs who don't ever get published? Did they miss the meeting about the secret handshake? And what about writers like Zadie Smith, Matthew Pearl, or Aleksandar Hemon — all writers who *don't* have MFAs? Granted, many contemporary writers of literary fiction have gone through MFA programs, but it's an apprenticeship like any other: woodworking, roofing, medicine. You study with those who have more experience than you. You work on your craft.

One thing I've noticed is that the would-be writers who sling rocks at MFA programs never offer up any self-critical evaluations of their own work. No, they all tend to be unsung geniuses who are held back because they don't have that silly but corrupt MFA. They are the wounded martyrs, and they play the role to perfection.

For all the controversy about whether or not to get an MFA, the final issue should be this: Do you want two or three years to work on your writing or not? If not, then don't go.

Choosing the Right Graduate Program

Some people go to a top-ranked writing program and love it; others go and hate it. Some people enter a program they *think* they'll hate and end up loving it. Some people think they can live anywhere for two or three years, only to discover that, no, they *can't* live anywhere, and those two or three years become a prison sentence. Some people go to a specific program to study with their favorite writer, realizing a week into the program that their favorite writer is a jerk, or their favorite writer, though still listed as faculty, never teaches, or both. Others go and find lifelong mentors.

These scenarios are endless, and I've seen them all play out at creative writing programs, good and bad, large and small, across the country. At the end of the day, picking a program, no matter how much preparation you do, is a crapshoot. Having said that, you should still make a list of what's important to you, if only to disqualify certain programs.

What should your list look like? That's really up to you, but I would take a good, hard look at your list of what's important to you to make sure that a degree in creative writing is what you really want. At Iowa, students were allowed to take electives in any other discipline that they wanted, as long as they took the required workshop and, in their second year, thesis hours. A few of my classmates decided that they would get a second degree with those electives. A second degree meant (most likely) even *more* course requirements, *more* course work, a *second* thesis, and so on. I don't know what's become of those classmates who got second degrees, but I hope they were able to get jobs in their secondary field, because none of them, to my knowledge, are working writers today. Either they didn't want to become writers badly enough, or they honestly thought they could handle getting two degrees at once. Personally, I fear they squandered valuable time.

When I was applying to programs, I didn't make a list. I was too naive to know what I wanted. I didn't even know the difference between an MA and an MFA, let alone what I *wanted* out of a program. But if I were applying today, I would most definitely make a list, and here are a few things that would be important to me.

1. Time to write: I would need a program that emphasizes creative writing, not academic requirements.
2. Variety of professors: I would want a program with a lot of writers on the faculty or with a rotation of visiting writers. That way, if I don't like one professor, I'm not stuck with him or her for two years.
3. Location: I have always thought it important to get away from one's comfort zone for a while. Shake it up a little. Distance can give perspective to the place where you grew up, thereby making it easier to write about.
4. Financial aid: Here is where I royally screwed up the first time. When I was told I didn't get funding, I didn't argue. I accepted it as a done deal. What I realize now is that everything is negotiable. For more on this subject, see my chapter "The Graduate School Application Process."

These are my personal top four issues. Yours may be different. You may want an urban campus. You may prefer a small program. You may not care about funding.

I urge my students, once they've put together their list of schools, to start thinking *beyond* it. I fear they sometimes get caught up in criteria that make no sense. For instance, my students at Wake Forest University and George Washington University have favored applying to graduate creative writing programs at private universities. I'm sure their line of thinking is that it would be a step down to go to a public school after spending so much money at a private school. What I hope to impart to them is that while, yes, there are some mighty fine creative writing programs at private universities, some of the best creative writing programs happen to be housed in public institutions. (Curiously, most of these students don't believe me or, believing me, still don't want to risk their academic pedigree.)

Once you've put together your list, show it to people. There's a good chance that your professor, or maybe even another classmate, will know someone who has gone through a program on your list and can give you the inside scoop. But don't believe everything you hear. Bear in mind that anecdotal evidence can be just as dubious as the university's own publicity machine. If, however, you begin hearing from several people that a particular program is poison, well, you may want to take it to heart . . . or, if you still really want to go there, dig a little deeper.

The Graduate School Application Process

How Many Schools Should You Apply To?

The difficulty with applying to graduate programs in creative writing is the same difficulty with trying to get your work accepted by a magazine insofar as the odds are stacked against you, even if you're talented. It's not uncommon for students with very strong writing samples to collect rejections from all the schools to which they've applied. The number of applications that some of these programs receive is simply overwhelming.

Another factor is the subjectivity of the people reading your samples. I applied to only four master's programs: the University of Iowa, University of Arizona, University of Southern Mississippi, and Stanford University (this was back in the 1980s when Stanford still offered an MA in creative writing). I assumed Iowa and Stanford, by far the most competitive schools, would reject me. I was banking on acceptances from Arizona and Southern Mississippi. As it turned out, I received acceptances only from Iowa and Southern Mississippi. Iowa's program was—and still is—the most competitive creative writing program in the country, so how was it that I could get into Iowa while receiving rejections from two schools that didn't receive nearly as many applications? Obviously, my writing sample didn't appeal as much to the faculty at Stanford and Arizona as did the writing samples of other applicants. There's nothing more mysterious to it than that, really. At the end of the day, after the pile of manuscripts has been winnowed down to the competent ones, the people judging the writing samples will go by their gut. This isn't a science, after all, and what readers are searching for in a story is sometimes rather elusive: an original voice, a vision, an organic structure.

I recommend applying to at least ten schools. Don't apply to just the ten most competitive creative writing programs in the country. Find some less competitive schools that appeal to you. Include a couple of safety schools as well, though let me warn you, there's really no such thing as a safety school in creative writing for the very reason of subjectivity. Even so, new programs are often eager for applicants, and some programs, such as those located in cities deemed less desirable, struggle to deepen their applicant pool, despite their excellent faculty.

Perhaps there are only five schools that interest you. Perhaps you don't want to attend a creative writing program unless you can get into one of the most competitive ones. That's all fine and good, and with any luck it'll all work out in your favor, but you should brace yourself for the possibility that you won't be going anywhere next year.

Applying to graduate schools is costly, and it may be that you can only afford to apply to three or four. If you really want to get into a program, I would urge you to apply to at least one school that's not as competitive as the others.

One last note. Rejection one year doesn't necessarily mean rejection the next year. Oftentimes, different readers will be winnowing the applications. You'll be competing against a new set of applicants. Your own work might be stronger the following year. As is often the case with submitting to a magazine, what doesn't appeal to a reader one day may appeal to her the next day.

Applying to graduate schools in creative writing is an arduous and whimsical process, and it's probably best to keep that in mind in order to maintain your sanity.

Letters of Recommendation

Autumn in academia. Sounds nice, doesn't it? The leaves on the trees are turning. Students are playing touch football on the quad. Professors are putting on their best tweed as the temperatures start to drop.

The fall semester has come to mean one thing to me: letter of recommendation time. If you're a professor, fall semester means writing letters of recommendation until your fingertips bleed.

A few years ago, I filled out forms for eighty letters of recommendations. Every year that I'm still breathing, the number of letters I write increases exponentially. And since Wake Forest University is the ninth school at which I've taught, I sometimes get e-mails from students I barely remember. A few years ago, I received an e-mail from someone who told me that he had been a student of mine in 1989 and wondered if I could write him a letter of recommendation. Back in 1989, which also happens to be the first year I taught, I was teaching anywhere between seventy-five and a hundred students each semester. I honestly remember very little about *any* of those classes, and I certainly didn't remember this particular student. I had to tell him no. I feel bad that I don't remember all of my students, even some of the really good ones, but I have been teaching for more than twenty years and have taught more than two thousand students. My brain just doesn't have that kind of memory capacity. I don't even remember what years I've lived in certain cities anymore.

For the student, hitting up professors for letters of recommendation can be a humiliating experience. When I was an undergrad, one of my creative writing professors told me no, she wouldn't write a letter for me. To this day, I'm still not entirely sure why. I received an A in her class, but maybe everyone earned an A in her class. Maybe she was just plain burned out.

It may seem obvious that you should ask for recommendations from professors who've taught your creative writing courses, but what if you haven't studied with three different creative writers? The next logical person to ask would be your English professor. Beyond that, any professor would do. I've written letters for students applying to graduate school in sociology, psychology, and film production, as well as law school and medical school. For my good students, I am always able to tailor the letter to show how what they did in my course would be transferable to their future as graduate students. Don't ask for letters of recommendation from your friends or family members, and you should probably avoid your bosses as well, unless you've tutored in a writing lab or interned at a university press, in which case the connection between your employment and your field of study is apparent and applicable.

How much weight do letters of recommendation hold? This will vary from school to school, but they're sometimes used to break ties or determine whether the applicant should receive a teaching assistantship. They are probably most often used as red flags. Let's say you have a great writing sample, the best writing sample anyone on the admission committee's ever seen, but your letters of recommendation clearly indicate that you're going to be a serious problem—argumentative, unmotivated, a prima donna. A strong writing sample will trump any number of factors—poor grades, poor GRE scores, a fifth-tier undergraduate university—but it is highly unlikely that it will trump testimonials that you're going to make the next two or three years a nightmare for everyone who comes in contact with you. The greatest short story in the world isn't worth the price for that particular brand of misery.

Bear in mind that professors have to be careful whom they write letters for. Their reputations are at stake. If they write a letter for someone who proves to be problematic, how much weight do you think their next recommendation will hold? Perhaps the most unfortunate letter of recommendation ever written in the history of recommendation letter writing was when the governor of Utah wrote a letter for Ted Bundy's law school admission. Ted Bundy, as you may know, turned out to be a notorious serial killer. It's hard to live that one down, even if it's just your friends ribbing you about it, never mind the electorate.

If you're a student in need of recommendations, here are a few helpful tips.

1. Don't piss off your professors. I know this is obvious advice, but you'd be surprised at the number of students who don't think beyond the present. I recently had a spate of students text-messaging in class or failing to turn in assignments on time, all the while making excuses and (sometimes) getting mad at me for telling them to put their BlackBerries away or reminding them that I don't take late papers. Should these students ever need a letter of recommendation from me—and, yes, they do sometimes ask—what do you think my answer will be? Foster good relationships, because you'll need at least three letters of recommendation. I may be too late with this advice, but you should know that you'll need letters of recommendation throughout your writing career, so it's never too late to change your ways.

2. Make the whole experience as easy for the professor as possible. If the forms aren't online, be sure to include self-addressed stamped envelopes along with your packet, and be sure to fill out as much information on the forms as possible, including the part that asks for the professor's name, rank, address, phone number, and e-mail. (My life is bliss if I don't have to fill this sort of information in eighty times.)

3. Give the professor enough time to write the letters. Don't spring forms on the professor at the last minute with the urgent request that they be mailed the next day or, worse, via overnight packaging. Your professors have lives, too. They have their own deadlines and obligations.

4. Give your professor a current résumé along with the recommendation forms.
5. If it's been a few years since you were in that professor's class,
   it might be useful to include copies of the work that you did
   for her. Don't presume that you can give the professor new
   material to read, unless the professor has asked to see it.
6. If it's been years since you were in the professor's class and
   you haven't maintained a relationship with her, you should
   probably work on making new contacts in the field, since it's
   likely that the professor won't remember you. Even if the professor agrees to write a recommendation letter, it may end up
   being a generic one.
7. Waive your right to read the letters. You want the letters to be
   honest. As illogical as this may sound, a great student may get
   a tepid letter of recommendation if he doesn't sign the waiver.

The Writing Sample

The writing sample is by far the most important part of your application. In fact, some MFA programs, usually the more prestigious
ones, place the bulk of their criteria for admitting a candidate on the
strength of the writing sample. When the committee is impressed
enough by the writing sample, the director of the program can over-
ride poor grades and GRE scores, even those that fall below the graduate school's minimum requirements. Thus, the importance of your
writing sample should not be underestimated.

The writing sample requirements for the application will vary
from program to program. If the program requests up to fifty pages of
prose and you have two great short stories totaling thirty-five pages
and a third story that you know isn't very strong but that would
nonetheless bring you closer to the fifty-page limit, don't feel compelled to submit the third story, unless the application requests at
least fifty pages of prose, which is highly unlikely. Better to submit
two strong stories than to muddy the waters with the third one. Rule
of thumb: Don't give the committee a reason to reject you. A weak
short story will almost always overshadow the good short stories. For
all the committee knows, the weak story may be your most recent
work, suggesting that those other two were anomalies.

Be sure to proofread. If the story is riddled with spelling and punctuation errors, you're going to give the impression that you don't

care about the application or, worse, you don't care about your own writing.

I can't begin to tell you how many students I've had who are good writers, capable of getting into a graduate writing program, if not for one issue: They refuse to learn how to punctuate dialogue. You may have written a couple of great short stories, but if you still don't know how to punctuate dialogue, you're going to lose all credibility. The same goes for any basic convention of prose writing. I teach at a supposed top-tier university, yet I frequently have students, some of whom are English majors, who don't know when to indent paragraphs.

Finally, neatness counts. Don't send off stories where the print is faint because you're running low on ink. Don't send stories without page numbers. What you don't want to do is give whoever's reading your stories an opportunity to turn down your application before she's read the first word. The more applications a program receives, the easier it will be to justify turning down an applicant for seemingly nitpicky reasons.

The Graduate Record Examination

The GRE is the annoying standardized test that (supposedly) gauges whether or not you're intellectually suited for graduate school.

For our purposes, there are two kinds of GRE exams: the general test and the subject test. The subject test, which is essentially a Trivial Pursuit test for literature, is required for some MA programs and many PhD programs.

Most of the multiple choice questions are designed to see if you can match a passage to its author or source, with passages ranging from the Bible to Joyce Carol Oates. In fact, there were *four* Joyce Carol Oates questions on the test I took. And, of course, Shakespeare. A *lot* of Shakespeare.

If you're asked to submit GRE scores for an MFA program, these will most likely be for the General Test, not the Subject Test. Some MFA programs have done away altogether with GRE requirements, but many still require them, oftentimes because of a Graduate College requirement. Before you decide to become cavalier and not take the tests seriously, listen to this. So convinced was I that no creative writing program would care what my GRE scores were, I stayed out drinking all night before taking the test. By the time the final section of the test rolled around—the logic section, no less—my head was pounding, and it was all I could do to keep from leaving the room, so I scribbled in the answer B for every question, then laid my aching head down on the desk. Fast-forward several months: I get a call from the dean of one of the universities to which I've applied, and he tells me that the head of the creative writing program really likes my writing and plans to admit me. "But I've got to be honest," the dean says. "Those are some of the worst GRE scores I've ever seen, and with scores like those, we honestly can't let you teach any of our classes." In other words, I wasn't going to receive any financial aid. Which brings me to my next subject . . .

Graduate School Funding

As I mentioned in the last chapter, I didn't get offered funding when I was accepted into Iowa's MFA program, and, foolishly, I kept my mouth shut. (Back then, I had a fear of authority, so I assumed that if I bluffed by saying I couldn't come without funding, the powers-that-be at Iowa would have said, "Okay. We'll give your place to someone else.")

If you don't get offered funding and you're brave enough, you should bluff. If you have an acceptance elsewhere, you can approach the department of the school where you really want to go and say, "I'd love to come here, but I can't without money. I've been accepted at University of Wazoo *with* funding, so I'll have to go there unless I can get some money here." Maybe you have no intention of going to the University of Wazoo. That's okay. That's why it's called bluffing. But whatever you do, don't lie. Bluffing is not the same thing as lying. Don't say, for instance, that they offered you funding when they didn't. If they didn't offer you funding but did accept you, find another justification for possibly attending the University of Wazoo. Maybe tuition is cheaper. Maybe it's closer to home. The fine line between bluffing and lying is this: bluffing is something that *is* possible whereas lying is something that's already been decided and is *not* possible. When all is said and done, you may decide to attend the University of Wazoo. The possibility exists. But to say that they offered something that they didn't isn't true from the get-go. I know hundreds of writers who are also professors. Many of them are good friends. All it would take is a phone call to discover the truth.

Funding comes in all shapes and sizes, with a variety of different responsibilities, or it doesn't come at all, and you're stuck with the bill. My feeling is that a program is more likely to respect you when they pay you something. (This is one of my guiding theories in life: The more money someone pays you, the less likely they are to crap on you—or, in some instances, the more someone pays you, the less you mind being crapped on.) Funding is the program's way of saying that they really want you.

A few programs give work-free fellowships to their top students. On the one hand, these are sweet deals. What could be better than getting paid for doing nothing? Don't we all aspire to that? If you don't have designs to teach, this fellowship would be pure heaven. On the other hand, if you're interested in eventually getting some kind of teaching position, a work-free fellowship denies you the invaluable hands-on experience of teaching, which a search committee will look for. Frankly, I'm not sure that I could have turned down one of these fellowships, even knowing what I know now, but if I were interested in teaching down the road, I'd certainly figure out a way to snag teaching experience of some kind before entering the job market in earnest.

Teaching fellowships are the most common form of graduate school funding. Should you be awarded one, you will probably teach composition courses or a basic multigenre creative writing course. Occasionally, you'll be given an introduction to literature course to teach or, even, a lower-level creative writing course in a single genre. Pay attention to how many courses you'll be asked to teach. Common teaching loads for graduate students are 1/1, which means you would be teaching one course each semester; 2/1, which means two courses one semester and one course the next semester; or 2/2, which means two courses each semester. There are all sorts of factors to consider here. If you're offered a 1/1 teaching load, will you be paid enough to live without having to find additional work? If you're offered a 2/2 teaching load, will you have time to write? Do the math, and figure out how much you'll be getting paid per class. Let's say one program is offering you $8,000 a year to teach a 1/1. Another program may be offering you $10,000, but the course load is 2/2. The first program, though offering less money overall, is paying you much better *per class* than the second school—$4,000 per course rather than $2,500. Don't be blinded by the final sum being offered to you. Always break it down.

Here's yet another factor: How many students will you be teaching? If the second program (the one that's paying you $2,500 per class) wants you teach four composition courses with twenty-five students per class whereas the first program (paying $4,000 per class) wants you to teach creative writing courses with no more than fifteen students per class, you're looking at the difference between dealing with fifty students (for two courses) per semester rather than just fifteen students (for one course), and believe me, that's a *huge* difference when it's time to grade papers. And if you *really* want to break it down, you can calculate how much you would be getting paid per head in the classroom. What you'll find is that the disparity is not an insignificant one. I offer these warnings because the decision you make will affect the amount of time you'll have to write and because most applicants don't think about these sorts of issues until they've been teaching for a few years and begin talking to friends in other programs. To compound matters, should you be so lucky as to receive more than one funding offer, you'll be making your decision under stress and with multiple deadlines.

As you can see, the final stipend figure is meaningless without looking at the fine print.

Finally, there are research assistantships. These tend to pay less than teaching assistantships, but there is also less work involved. Typically, the student is assigned to a professor, and the professor assigns an appropriate amount of work, which will range from photocopying and stapling to doing actual research. As I've already mentioned, I was T. Coraghessan Boyle's research assistant at Iowa. My primary task was to research the elusive pygmy sunfish of the Okefenokee Swamp for Boyle's novel *East Is East*. I benefited from this arrangement in several ways: I had a front-row seat to watch a prolific and important writer at work, I had an opportunity to contribute to a novel that was eventually published, I received an acknowledgment in the novel itself, and I developed a closer relationship with Boyle than I would have had if I had been simply a student in his course. Twelve years later, Boyle blurbed my first book, so my research assistantship, although monetarily paltry at the time, continued paying dividends long after the actual employment had ended. If you don't have any options—if the only school that admitted you is offering you a research assistantship—see if it comes with in-state tuition if it's a public university. The savings between out-of-state tuition and in-state tuition may make the research assistantship much more valuable than the actual stipend attached to it.

At most public universities, these assistantships (teaching *and* research) will come with in-state tuition as part of the bargain, but I have occasionally heard of universities that won't waive out-of-state tuition for a student's first year, so be sure to ask if that's the case. And whatever you negotiate, be sure to get it in writing. Oral agreements don't count for squat. Be polite—but firm—when asking for all amendments in ink.

Message Boards, Wikis, and Blogs

The Internet is great for disseminating information, but it can also be a nightmare for the same reason. There are message boards and wikis and blogs for just about everything these days, including discussions of creative writing programs where applicants share where they've been accepted and what they may do. On these sites, applicants also gossip about faculty, trade stories about programs, and complain about this or that. And here's the rub. Faculty at those universities also read those message boards, wikis, and blogs. I know this because they've told me. And if you don't think that the messages you leave will shape their opinion of you, guess again. Furthermore, some of these programs offer postgraduate fellowships, so even if you turn down their offer to attend their graduate program, you may end up applying there again in a few years for a fellowship. Or, if you publish a book, you may apply there for a job. What many people fail to realize in the impulsive moment of writing on any of these venues is that it's often not difficult to figure out who the author is, either by IP searches or old-fashioned deduction.

A word of advice: Don't shoot yourself in the foot before you've even begun the journey.

Student Loans

There are numerous kinds of student loans available to graduate students, and since the terms change from year to year, I won't go into each and every kind, but do know that they are available. The most common student loans for graduate students are the Perkins, which allows you to borrow up to eight thousand dollars annually, with a cap of sixty thousand dollars; the Subsidized Stafford, which allows you to borrow eight thousand and five hundred dollars each year with a cap of sixty-five thousand and five hundred; and the Unsubsidized Stafford, which allows you to borrow up to twelve thousand dollars (depending upon several factors), with a cap, for all Stafford loans, including subsidized and unsubsidized as well as undergraduate and graduate education, of one hundred and thirty-eight thousand and five hundred dollars. The money is there if you need it. However, you should carefully read over my section on employment before taking out a hundred and thirty-eight thousand dollars.

I couldn't have gone to college without student loans, but I probably could have gone to college with fewer student loans, and I certainly could have managed them better after I had graduated if I hadn't taken out so many.

I'm in my forties now, and I owe more on my student loans than I owe on my house. I took out my first loans during the Reagan presidency, which means that they came with usurious conditions. For instance, the interest on *all* of my student loans continued to be capitalized while in deferment. By the time I was earning enough to start making payments, I ended up owing *twice* what I had actually borrowed because of these terms. *Twice!* And that's not counting how much interest I'll be paying over the thirty years I'll be making payments. (Many of the more usurious rules were dropped during the Clinton years, but since the borrower is typically held to whatever rules were in place when he first took the loans out, these new conditions came too late to do me any good.)

I'm telling you all of this because it's important for you to know how much student loans—as wonderful as they can be—can rule your life after college. The sad reality is that I need a certain income —a sizable income—in order to make my minimum monthly student loan payments. Those monthly payments give me a hell of a lot less flexibility than I would like to have as a writer. Let's say I pay off my house and now make enough money with my writing each year to live modestly, and let's say that I want to dedicate more time to my writing and am willing to chuck my teaching position in favor of, say—oh, I don't know—a half-time job in a used bookstore. (Believe me, I've thought of it.) With my minimum monthly student loan payment, this isn't an option. The income from a half-time bookstore job simply isn't going to be enough for me to make my minimum monthly payments. A *full-time* job at a bookstore wouldn't be enough. I would have to use all of my bookstore earnings, plus some (or all) of my monthly writing earnings, in order to make the payments. If I decide to defer the payments, the monthly interest is added onto the principal, which means that when I *do* decide to pay them again, my student loans will be comparable to the national debt.

One of the best pieces of advice for writers I've ever heard was from Bruce Joel Rubin, the screenwriter of *Ghost* and *Jacob's Ladder*, who said, "Keep your overhead down." Once you start owing a lot of money, he went on to say, you end up taking writing jobs you don't want to take because you don't have a choice. If you want your freedom, not to mention your artistic integrity, then keep your debts low. Rubin was talking about buying a second house and expensive cars, but for fiction writers and poets that overhead may mean taking out loans for which you can't afford the minimum monthly payment, or it may mean taking out loans and frivolously spending the money on a new car, an expensive apartment, or too many nights out at the bar.

Rubin's advice came too late for me, but it may not be too late for you. Remember: You're borrowing money to become a writer, not a doctor. Borrow judiciously, if at all.

Feedback in the Workshop
Giving It and Taking It
....

The first thing to know is that there's a significant difference between feedback and criticism, as filmmaker Martin Scorsese notes in
regard to the first time he tried getting *The Last Temptation of Christ*
made:

> What I wanted was feedback from the studio, but what I started
> to get was criticism. There's a big difference. Feedback is, "I don't
> understand it." Yes, if you don't understand it, tell me, and I'll
> judge whether or not it is meant to be understood, and then I'll
> put it in the script or change it or whatever. But to criticize, to
> say, "This is no good," that stops the creative process.

A good workshop, in my opinion, is fueled by feedback and not criticism, and the more informed the feedback, the more successful the
workshop. By "informed" I mean that the students offering the feedback should become, over the course of the semester, well versed in
craft with the ability to articulate why some things work and why
other things don't.

In the workshops that I run, every student receives two or three
of their classmates' short stories to read the week before we discuss
them. I ask my students to write up a page of comments prior to the
discussion, beginning with "what's working" in the story followed by
"what's problematic." They need to be specific, sticking to the story
itself and avoiding discussing their own experiences, and to follow each assertion with a reason why. In other words, it's not good
enough to say, "I don't believe this character." They need to articulate
why they don't believe the character, my hope being that in doing so
they start thinking more complexly about the cause-and-effect nature of writing. *If a character does this, here's the consequence.* I ask
the student-reader to be concrete, to keep his criticism focused on
craft, to point to examples. Even though I ask the student-readers to
be objective, they sometimes can't help it, and a subjective comment
sneaks into their written feedback.

Each semester, before we actually begin workshopping each
other's stories, I give a speech to my class. What I tell them is that,

on any given day, the feedback that's offered up may be anywhere from five percent to ninety-five percent useful. More often than not, it falls somewhere in between. There are times, however, when I've seen startlingly original and sophisticated stories elude everyone in the classroom. The story may be too subtle, or it may not resemble what the students recognize as a short story. On the rare occasion when such a story is turned in and the readers are flummoxed, I advise the student-writer after class to ignore the other comments. The comments are from students who haven't yet had enough experience under their belts as readers, and they're responding negatively to those things in the story that they don't yet grasp. This, however, rarely happens.

More common is when the student-writers collectively champion a terrible story. (I never use words like "terrible" in a classroom, but since we're not in a classroom and I'm not your teacher, I'm going to say it: Some stories are terrible. But I will also add that I've written plenty of terrible stories, especially when I was first starting out. And here's something else to take to heart: My best students each semester are much better than I was when I was their age.) In general, the vast majority of my students' experience with narrative comes from watching TV, which is chock-full of melodrama and sentimentality. Very little, if any, of their understanding of narrative arises from an intimate knowledge of the contemporary short story. I sometimes spend entire semesters trying to differentiate for them "TV narrative" from "short story narrative." Students also like gimmicks, such as trick endings or wacky shifts in point-of-view at the story's end — the sorts of gimmicks that exhaust the patience of someone who's been reading student work for a couple of decades. And so the toughest part of my job is to persuade a student-writer who's written a clichéd, gimmicky story that creaks under the weight of melodrama and sentimentality that my opinion may just possibly hold more weight than the opinions of the other fourteen people in the room, all of whom love the story. (This battle, although hard fought, is not easily won.)

When it's time for the classroom discussion of a story, I ask everyone to follow the same pattern as the written feedback: positive comments first, constructive ones to follow. Furthermore, I ask that the student-writer not participate in the discussion. Not only can she not speak, she must also not sigh heavily, roll her eyes, or angrily wag her head. No Kabuki, I tell them. I can assure you that my students *hate* this rule, but I can also assure you that this rule is neither arbitrary nor capricious. I have suffered through workshops where the student-writer is allowed to talk, and what inevitably happens is that the student-writer wants to defend her story, sometimes going so far as to tell some of her classmates that their feedback is wrong. And what do you think happens after this? Everyone ends up hating the student-writer, and no one wants to offer up their feedback again. As soon as the student-writer begins to defend herself, she's pretty much closed herself off forever to the possibility that someone in the room may have a good point. But if she *didn't* talk, she would have to live with those voices in her head, and though she may, in the end, dismiss all of them, it's possible—likely, even—that a comment that initially seemed wrong would begin, after a few weeks, to seem right. Everyone needs time to digest and process feedback, but if you dismiss it outright, you'll never digest it, let alone come to see its value. Furthermore, what's the point of defending yourself when you have a choice to ignore everyone's comments anyway? After all, no one's holding a gun to your head and saying, "Dramatize this scene, or I'll shoot."

Dave King, author of the critically acclaimed novel *The Ha-Ha*, illuminates how a seemingly radical piece of advice proved to be an eye-opener that has stayed with him throughout his career:

> When I was first starting to write, I took a class with the marvelous Nahid Rachlin, who gave me the best piece of advice I've ever received. I'd turned in a chapter for the group to workshop, and Nahid began by saying, "Let's start on page 3, because the first two pages are not interesting." Whoa! And yet, blunt as it sounds, what's the point of debating a remark like that? I knew instantly what she meant, and I realized I'd forgotten a cardinal, self-evident rule: that one of the main reasons to even bother with all this is to interest the reader; and that if you don't do that, the penalty is skipped pages, naps, books left unfinished under trees and so on. I've tried never to forget it.

One thing to bear in mind is that your creative writing professor has probably read thousands upon thousands of pages of short stories written by students. I did the math once for my own self, and the page count was in the hundreds of thousands. I wouldn't be surprised if, by now, it's topped a million pages. What this means is that the professor has vastly more experience than the student at spotting clichés, plot contrivances, and overused structures, among other problems, and yet I will sometimes find myself having to defend the most basic points to a student who wants to champion the cliché, the plot contrivance, or the overused structure. My advice is to put the comment into context. If your teacher says something is a cliché, there's a pretty good chance that it's a cliché. The very reason I took courses in creative writing was because the professor had more experience than I did. My tuition money was paying for that experience, not for my right to argue with the person who had been writing longer than I had been breathing.

I realize that creative writing can be *personal*, and I also realize that putting your work out there for others to read makes the student-writer all *vulnerable* and what-not, but if your soul is crushed by a workshop (especially those as gentle as the ones I conduct), I've got some bad news for you. What awaits you beyond the classroom, where no one owes you anything, are years of cold rejection and harsher, sometimes cruel criticism (yes, *criticism*, not *feedback*). The critic becomes the published writer's constant companion. He's always there, looking over your shoulder and pointing, so you'd best shake hands with your classmates and make peace with their comments, because this part of the process never goes away.

Learn Punctuation and Grammar

Brace yourself: This is my "be sure to eat your peas" chapter. I wouldn't be including it if I hadn't noticed lately a pervasive problem: My students don't know how to punctuate dialogue. Dialogue punctuation isn't their only problem, however. They don't know how to use commas, semicolons, or colons. They leave off end punctuation. They don't indent. I'll point out these problems, write correct examples on the board, and explain why what they're doing is wrong. The one thing I can't do is learn it *for* them. Their excuses are lame at best. Sometimes they'll blame it on their computer, but more often than not they'll say, "I thought this was just a rough draft," to which I reply, "No one—*no one*—who knows how to punctuate correctly would punctuate incorrectly and consistently in a rough draft! If you know the correct punctuation, you would simply use the correct punctuation." What all of this suggests to me is that my students aren't reading, or, if they are reading, they're not paying attention to what they read. How can someone read novel after novel and not begin to see the difference between the possessive and the plural? (Remember what I wrote in an earlier chapter about liking sentences?)

While I was working toward my PhD, those of us who taught Comp 101 were trained to tell students not to worry about punctuation and grammar when they wrote. My wife, who was also working toward a PhD, brought up during a faculty meeting the crazy idea of using a grammar handbook in a composition classroom, and she was almost laughed out of the room by the composition theorists. One of them, unable to stop laughing, said, "Oh, my, I could just imagine spending the whole day discussing the *dash*." In our composition theory classes, the professors would say to us, "Grammar is patriarchal!"— whatever *that* meant. I still don't know. I'm guessing it means that grammar is *repressive*. The teaching assistants were also told by our composition professors that grammar *couldn't* be taught. To that, I say, "Bullshit!" Of course it can be taught; otherwise, no one would know how to punctuate or write a grammatically correct sentence.

Years later, I saw an essay in an academic journal co-written by one of my composition theory professors. It began (and I'm paraphrasing), "Staring out my office window, the city spread out before me." This was the essay's *first sentence*. Did the city really stare out her office window? Here was a professor who didn't want us teaching grammar to our students, yet she couldn't even catch her own dangling modifier. Her co-writer and editor couldn't either, for that matter. So, is it possible to write grammatically incorrect sentences and get published? Yes. Clearly, it is. But you should ask yourself what your goals are. If it's to write lazy sentences for an academic journal, be my guest. If you want to write fiction with the hope of getting published by a major commercial publisher or a good-quality small press, you should probably care where a comma goes, not because the editor will reject you on the basis of a misplaced comma but because the craft of your work should imply, on every level, from point-of-view to the perfectly used semicolon, a writer who cares enough about the written word to know where to put a comma. (Imagine Melville beginning *Moby-Dick*, "Call me, Ishmael." *Who's Ishmael,* you'd wonder, *and why does the narrator want Ishmael to call him?*)

Everyone makes mistakes. I'm always stunned whenever my copyedited manuscript is returned to me—a manuscript, I should note, that I've read over dozens of times—and the copyeditor has found grammar and spelling errors. I'm grateful to the copyeditor, of course. I'm also embarrassed that I hadn't caught the errors. Everyone I know who's published a book is guilty of letting errors slip by. Worse is when an error gets past everyone and ends up in the finished book. But here's the distinction I want to make. An editor can tell the difference, almost immediately, between the writer who cares about language and the writer who doesn't care. So, quit bellyaching, and eat your peas, dammit!

How Much Should You Bother Your Teacher after You're No Longer in Class?

If by "bother" you mean "ask her to read your work," the answer is, *As little as possible!*

Keep in mind: When you are taking a class with a professor, that professor is getting paid. Once you are no longer in that class, your professor is getting paid to teach *different* students. As cold as this may sound, she is no longer getting paid to read your work.

There are selfless creative writing teachers out there who will read everything by everyone, and there are tireless creative writing teachers who are incredibly fast readers, but, in all honesty, I don't know many of these teachers, and I'm certainly not one of them. I usually have a long list of things to do, and I'm always running behind. *Always.* In other words, there simply isn't enough time in my day to do the things that I am obligated to do. At the end of the day, I try to fit in a bit of leisure reading, although my leisure reading time gets shorter and shorter each year. What I don't want to do is sit down with yet another story that needs editing after an already long day of working on my own writing, teaching, reading my current students' work, and doing my daily chores. Some people will undoubtedly think that this is unkind, but I simply can't do it. My father was a roofer. The last thing he wanted to do, when he came home from a hard day of work, was climb a ladder and start hammering shingles onto a neighbor's house.

I've taught about two thousand students at this point in my career. Let's say that two percent of them want me to continue reading their work. Two percent of two thousand is forty. Forty students may not sound like a lot to someone who hasn't taught, but rest assured, forty is a *lot*, especially if those forty are sending you fifteen- and twenty-page short stories, along with the occasional novel, and expecting critiques. No one would ask a doctor to perform surgery for free, and yet few people blink twice before asking a professional writer to "look over" their work. Just remember: Time is a writer's most valuable commodity. If the writer's time is sucked up, the writer won't have time to write her next book. If you respect the writer, you won't take up her time.

One of the very best writing teachers I ever had was Allan Gurganus. His feedback was eye-opening, the sort of responses that, as John Irving noted of his own workshop experiences, saved me countless years had I been writing on my own. What a gift it was to study with him. At the end of the semester, Allan thanked us all for a wonderful class before adding that he unfortunately could not read any more of our work until our books came out. He explained that he now had to get to work on his own fiction but that he wished us well. And, really, what more could I possibly have wanted? He had already given us his time and energy. He had passed along to us advice his own mentor John Cheever had passed along to him. He had given us the best he had to offer. I was grateful for what I had learned. What better way to show my gratitude than to respect the man's wishes and allow him the time to do his own work?

The Professional Student

In the blue-collar neighborhood where I grew up, one of the worst insults you could hurl was to call someone a professional student. It meant that he was avoiding work; it meant that he was brainy but lacked common sense; it implied that he was too weak for manual labor; it also implied that he thought he was better than everyone else.

When I think back on it now, the people who were disparagingly called professional students had simply gone away to college. Yet there was a stigma attached to going to college, as if there was something wrong with the person who wanted *that* much education. The insult tended to come from my parents' generation, many of whom grew up during the Great Depression, and I suspect that going to college was akin to slacking off. The insult was also a class issue, one born of insecurities and, I'm sure, fear.

Because of my own intimate knowledge of the term "professional student," I hesitate to use it here, and yet there does come a time when you may ask yourself—or should ask yourself—how many workshops are too many workshops? When have you crossed over from "student" to *professional* student," when you should have crossed over from "student" to "*writer*"?

I don't know precisely where the line of demarcation is, but I have seen workshop junkies who are always in search of "the solution" that eludes their manuscript or who need the workshop for inspiration, just as alcoholics feel they need alcohol to loosen up before going to a party or a job interview. In other words, taking workshops becomes an addiction. Or it becomes an excuse, the excuse being that the person can't write unless they have a deadline.

At some point, you have to sit down and face the page alone. At some point, the final decisions need to be yours. At some point, you have to give yourself deadlines and stick to them.

Even though I continued on to get a PhD in creative writing, I took only one workshop while working toward that degree because I was already workshopped out. I also trusted my own judgments of my work by then. I went into that degree program to buy more time for myself. The *last* thing I wanted to do was sit through another workshop as a student.

I recommend taping to your wall James Joyce's famous quote from *A Portrait of the Artist as a Young Man*, with special emphasis on the final four words:

> I will not serve that in which I no longer believe whether it call itself my home, my fatherland or my church: and I will try to express myself in some mode of life or art as freely as I can and as wholly as I can, using for my defence the only arms I allow myself to use—silence, exile, and cunning.

Silence, exile, and cunning eventually become necessary for doing the work, day in, day out, and for calling yourself a writer.

Writing and publishing are two different sets of worries, and they should stay that way. As hard (and often disheartening) as it is to do, think of your writing as you would any other job you need to keep. Be professional. Be courteous. Be gracious. Be consistent and look for opportunities to challenge yourself. Keep in mind that no matter where your publishing career takes you, there'll always be those who have enjoyed more success by lesser means. Who have seemingly cut corners and glad-handed their way to the top. And for every one of them there are probably five of greater means who've enjoyed less success than you. So just worry about doing your own job in the best way you know how.
— Darren DeFrain, *Inside & Out*

3 Getting Published

The Secret to Getting Published

I'm going to let you in on the biggest secret to getting published. Ready? Here it is. There are no secrets. It's good old-fashioned hard work, combined with serendipity, luck, chance, or whatever else you want to call it. And perseverance. Keep working on improving your craft, and keep sending out your work. I've had stories rejected fifty times before they were accepted by a good magazine. I know a writer who collected sixty rejections on a short story before it was accepted by a superb magazine and then reprinted in the prestigious *Pushcart Prize* anthology. The story later appeared in his collection of linked stories, which was eventually made into a movie.

For me, the secret to getting published is to keep working on new stories or to forge ahead on a new novel while the older stories and novels are circulating. That way, I don't have to fixate. Remember those excruciating days in high school when you sat by the phone and waited for a call from a girl or boy you had a crush on—or, worse: the boy or girl who had broken up with you—and you were paralyzed to the point of being unable to do anything *but* wait by the phone? It was debilitating, wasn't it? Well, what you learn when you're an adult is that you need to stay busy to keep your mind off the thing that's plaguing you. And so if you find yourself checking your e-mail's in-box every few seconds, peering out the window all day for the mail truck, or clutching your cell phone like it's a grenade that will explode if you let go of it—you need to get back to work.

Publishing in Magazines

The market for publishing short stories has changed significantly even in the twenty-five years that I've been sending work out. When I first began writing, there were several commercial venues for short stories, places like *Redbook, Mademoiselle, GQ,* the *Atlantic,* and *Esquire.* Way back, in the glossy magazine's heyday, Kurt Vonnegut had even published a short story in *Ladies' Home Journal.* It seemed that nearly every glossy magazine used to publish *some* fiction. My wife's first publication was in the men's magazine *Gallery*—and, no, it wasn't a pornographic story. When she told me about this shortly after we had met, I was envious, especially since a section of John Irving's *The World According to Garp,* one of my favorite novels, had appeared in *Gallery* as well. (My wife would later publish a *second* story with them. The published story was accompanied by a wonderful full-page illustration. And, of course, she was paid for the story, too! On the day the issue was released, we went to a gas station in Lincoln, Nebraska, and, to the consternation of the cashier, asked for half a dozen copies, which were kept behind the counter.)

Most of these magazines have quit publishing fiction altogether, or if they still do, it's infrequent or insubstantial. Among the commercial magazines still publishing fiction are the *New Yorker, Harper's, Playboy,* and the *Atlantic* (which now publishes a special fiction issue that I always seem to forget about), and it's rare to find a newcomer in any of these pages. Even when the *New Yorker* publishes an issue devoted to "discoveries," most of those writers are already under contract for a book. In fact, an editor at the *New Yorker* had contacted my agent for a bound galley of *The Book of Ralph* to see if there was anything that might interest them for their "discovery" issue. It's hardly a discovery if the story is an excerpt from a book that's about to be published, but that's one way to guarantee that the editors appear prescient, I suppose.

I have all but quit sending to the big, commercial, glossy magazines—and not just because there are so few of them remaining. The last time I sent a round of submissions to these bad boys, I didn't hear back from half of them. The rules have clearly changed. When I first began sending work out in the 1980s, it wasn't uncommon to get an actual note from the main fiction editor. I have at least one handwritten note from Rust Hills at *Esquire*, and a personal note, typed on a manual typewriter, from Daniel Menaker at the *New Yorker*. At the very least, I *always* received a rejection of some kind, if only a standard one on nice paper. But these days are gone. You're lucky to hear anything anymore. A new editor at a major magazine wrote to inform me that they normally didn't read unsolicited fiction but that they had done me the favor this time of reading mine, and, sorry, but it wasn't right for them. The editor went on to tell me that I shouldn't expect a response the next time. (This, I should add, was after I had already published three books and won two writing awards from this very magazine. I had even become friends with the previous editor.) So, this is what it's come to: Editors are doing you a favor if they even *look* at your story.

That was pretty much when I decided *thanks, but no thanks.*

The good news is that there are hundreds of other places to publish—literary journals, like the *Iowa Review* or *Cutbank*, that are either affiliated with a university or, like *Gargoyle* and *One Story*, that are run independently. Some of these journals, like the *Virginia Quarterly Review*, are now competing against the big glossies for National Magazine Awards . . . and winning! (Not that the *Virginia Quarterly Review* is an easy magazine to break into; it's not.)

I still buy the annually published *Novel and Short Story Writer's Market*, which, for my money, is the most thorough of the reference books in terms of information it provides. Duotrope—www.duotrope .com—is probably the best online resource for finding magazines to submit to. There is a hierarchy of magazines—certain magazines tend to get more attention than others—and if you want to start learning which ones are at the top of the hierarchy, pick up the annual anthologies and see for yourself where the stories in them have been published. I suggest looking through *Best American Short Stories*, *Best American Poetry*, *Best American Mystery Stories*, the *Pushcart Prize*, and *Prize Stories: The O. Henry Awards*. In the back pages of *Best American Short Stories*, you'll find a list of a hundred notable stories. This is an excellent place to see which magazines are getting recognition. Certain magazines, such as the *Alaska Quarterly Review*, may never actually get a reprint in the anthology but often receive citations.

There used to be more specialty magazines that published fiction as well. *Punk Planet*—a magazine dedicated to punk culture—published a few very short stories of mine, but the magazine eventually folded. Fewer and fewer of these specialty magazines publish fiction, but it's worth looking into, since they aren't likely to attract submissions by Alice Munro or Salman Rushdie.

No one's going to get rich publishing short stories. If you're lucky enough to break into the glossy commercial magazines, you could walk away with a few thousand dollars. Literary magazines may pay, at the top end, a hundred dollars per printed page, as the *Virginia Quarterly Review* does, but most will pay you in copies of the magazine. The days of Fitzgerald, where one could earn a living from writing short stories, are over. I have never written short stories to make money. For years, I received only free copies of the magazines that published me (usually two copies), and that was enough moral support to keep me going. These days, I do try to get paid for the stories I write, but I definitely don't write them to make money. I write them because I love writing them. The conventional wisdom is that the rise of television in the fifties killed the short story market. You should be forewarned that the new conventional wisdom is that the Internet, which is rewiring our brains in such a way that our attention spans are getting shorter by the second, is killing such things as the novel, which requires sustained concentration. I hope this isn't true, but when I see students who can't sit through a fifty-minute class without peeking at their cell phones to check their text messages or without opening their computer for diversion, I can't help thinking that there's more than a bit of truth in it. In a rare interview, Cormac McCarthy had this to say on the subject:

> People apparently only read mystery stories of any length. With mysteries, the longer the better and people will read any damn thing. But the indulgent, 800-page books that were written a hundred years ago are just not going to be written anymore and people need to get used to that. If you think you're going to write something like *The Brothers Karamazov* or *Moby-Dick*, go ahead. Nobody will read it. I don't care how good it is, or how smart the readers are. Their intentions, their brains are different.

Which brings me to the next venue for publishing fiction: the Internet. Online venues are booming. It's free—or virtually free—to set up a site, and it's relatively easy to do a call for submissions. More and more anthologies are taking online publications seriously, and it's not infrequent now to find stories in *Best American Mystery Stories* that have originally been published in online magazines.

Despite everything I've just written, I have to admit I'm still skeptical about publishing stories online. I'm not a Luddite by any stretch of the imagination, and I've published a few stories online, mostly because friends have asked me to submit, but even then I'm disappointed when the website permanently goes down. Furthermore, it depresses the hell out of me to print my own story from a website so that I can have some record of it. (I should note that some online magazines, like *Freight Stories*, do an excellent job of posting stories so that readers can pull them up for printing as a high-quality pdf file.) I suspect that those reading short stories online prefer stories that aren't longer than four or five pages, but what about longer stories? Who's going to read 10,000 *continuous* words of text on a website? Nobody I know. I still love paper; I love the feel of magazines; I love their idiosyncrasies, their typeset, even the advertisements for other magazines. I like being able to put my publications on a shelf, not a flash-drive to be worn like a talisman around my neck. And I like long stories.

I'm sure that online publication is the wave of the future, given the outlandish costs of printing a magazine coupled with the abysmally low sales figures. My prejudices aside, there are now more opportunities than ever for getting your work published, thanks to online magazines. However, it should be noted that there are now even more mediocre and shoddily run magazines than ever as well, thanks to the Internet. In short, if you want to get published at any expense, a venue exists for you. Is this a bad thing? I don't know. Personally, from the first time I began sending work out, I have chosen magazines based primarily on whether or not I respect them. Are they publishing writers I admire? Do I like what they're doing? Is this a magazine that I would enjoy reading? I would answer a resounding yes to all of these questions for the online magazine *Freight Stories*. If I were to have started publishing just for the sake of publishing, regardless of where the story appeared, sooner or later I would have wondered what the point of it all was. I sometimes spend as long as six years working on a single short story. At the very least, I owe it to myself—for the sheer amount of the time I've spent working on it—to place it in the best possible venue I can, regardless of the format.

Why Publish in Magazines?

This is a good question, especially given that so few people read literary magazines and that the general public doesn't even know of their existence. Tell your mother that you just published a story in the *Chattahoochee Review*, and she's likely to think you're making it up. (The *Chattahoochee Review*, by the way, is a wonderful magazine.) Why write short stories or poems at all if so few people are going to read them?

First of all, people *will* read them. I occasionally get e-mails from people who've read stories of mine in literary journals. It doesn't happen often, but it does happen. Sometimes the person reading the journal isn't even a writer—an e-mail will come from that rarest of persons: a reader!—and sometimes the magazines are read by other editors. I published a story in *Chelsea* because the editor had read a story of mine in the *Colorado Review*. He tracked me down and asked me to submit a story to him.

Most importantly, literary journals are read by agents. Agents scour literary journals, looking for new talent. A famous example is agent Nat Sobel finding Richard Russo's work in the *Mid-American Review*. Sobel has since represented every one of Russo's novels. But Nat Sobel isn't the only agent flipping through literary journals. I've been contacted no fewer than half a dozen times by agents who've read my work in magazines like the *Sonora Review* and *Open City*. This is why it's important to publish in well-established magazines. The more established the magazine, the more likely that agents subscribe to it. Asking why one should publish in magazines is like asking a baseball player why he should play in the minors. Because he might get discovered! This isn't the only reason to publish in magazines, of course, but it's an important one, if you want a career publishing books.

Another reason to publish in journals is to build a list of credits that will instill confidence in an agent reading your query letter. The dilemma, however, is this: If you're publishing in literary journals, it's likely that you're writing short stories; agents don't want to see your short story collection, yet they like to see magazine publications listed in your query letter. If your letter states that you've published work in the *Georgia Review*, the *Sun*, and the *Gettysburg Review*, this tells the agent that your work has already been vetted by other editors, that it's already of a certain caliber, and that you already understand your market. I'm not suggesting that an agent won't consider a query by someone who doesn't have magazine publications, but I can assure you that a list of publications will make the agent more eager to read the manuscript.

Other reasons? For the writer who doesn't yet have a book, a certain number of magazine publications are required to apply for a National Endowment for the Arts fellowship or an Individual Artist grant given by the state the writer lives in. There are other fellowships, grants, and scholarships that favor writers who haven't yet published a book but have magazine publications under their belts, like the Wisconsin Institute for Creative Writing fellowships at the University of Wisconsin or the various scholarships offered by the Bread Loaf Writers' Conference.

Finally, it's good to have publications if you plan on applying for teaching positions. Teaching positions in creative writing are so difficult to get these days that even a book doesn't guarantee employment, and, in some instances, more than one book is required. But there are still those positions—mostly adjunct work—that will go to the candidates with notable or recognizable literary journal publications on their curriculum vitae, and I even know a few writers who have received good tenure-track positions with only magazine publications.

The Cover Letter

The cover letter, which is what you include with your short story or poetry submissions to a magazine, shouldn't be confused with the query letter, which is what you would send to an agent or (sometimes) a book editor, explaining your project and asking if she wants to see your book-length manuscript. (See my chapter "The Query Letter.")

While working toward my MFA, I studied with a fiction editor for one of the big glossy magazines. Early in the semester, he told us that he could tell by the cover letter alone whether or not a story was worth reading. This news scared the crap out of me. Had I been doing something wrong for all of these years? Was there some tell-tale sign of amateurism that I didn't know about?

A few years later, while interning for a literary journal, I saw with perfect clarity what he meant. A surprising number of cover letters were addressed to an editor who had been dead for several years. What did this tell me? For starters, the person sending the story hadn't looked at the magazine in a dozen years, if at all. Chances were good that the writer was using a seriously outdated copy of *Novel and Short Story Writer's Market* (probably back when it was still called *Fiction Writer's Market*) and hadn't bothered to check on the status of the editor. (Not only do editors leave magazines, they eventually keel over.)

Other cover letters were handwritten. "Here's another little ditty for you," one of them read on paper that looked like it was meant for writing a grocery list.

Some were overly personal, as though the authors knew the editor well, when, in fact, they didn't know the editor at all. Or the letters simply tried too hard to be funny. (A few years ago, after I gave a talk about publishing in which I stated that one shouldn't try to be funny in the cover letter, an older gentleman came up to me to show me his "funny cover letter," which was, essentially, a list of jokey rejections with boxes next to each one for the editor to check and mail it back to him. There was something simultaneously lame and unbearably sad about his cover letter, and seeing the man who had written it—the sort of guy who might squirt me with a fake carnation or palm a gag buzzer with the hope that I'd shake his hand and wet my pants—depressed me more than I can convey.)

A few of the cover letters were barely literate. (Could this person possibly write a publishable story? The answer was, quite simply, *no*.)

The infuriating cover letters came from academics who, having spent twenty or thirty years teaching literature and writing critical books on Emily Dickinson, had decide that it was time to do something fun, like writing fiction. (And, yes, they often wrote the phrase "do something fun.") Whether they meant to or not, their cover letters trivialized the hard work and many years that good writers put into their work. The subtext was that what these scholars had been doing—writing books for academics—had been serious and laborious, whereas writing fiction was something one could pick up at any point in one's life and effortlessly dash off for fun. Not surprisingly, the stories were almost always terrible.

Eventually, I began editing anthologies, and for a few of them, I put out calls for submission, and, again, I began seeing right away the tell-tale signs of amateur writers in their letters: writers who wanted to negotiate rights with me before I had even read the story, stories shrink-wrapped in Saran Wrap with cover letters warning that their anonymity had to be respected, cover letters that were weirdly passive-aggressive, or stories that looked twenty years old, printed on yellowing paper on a dot-matrix printer and with no cover letter whatsoever.

My rules for a good cover letter are these: Keep it short (don't go over a single-spaced page), keep it straightforward (don't try to be funny), be sure to identify the genre (these days, it's difficult to tell creative nonfiction from fiction), be polite (thank the editor for his or her time), and make sure that the editor you're thanking is still alive. Here's a sample cover letter:

October 17, 2010
343 Winsome Ave.
Losesome CO 23212

Jack Dunphey, Editor
Kangaroo Review
Department of English
Lower Kansas State University
Anywhere KS 45830

Dear Mr. Dunphey:

Please find enclosed my short story "Who Cares What You Think" for consideration in the *Kangaroo Review*.

My stories have appeared in *Esquire*, the *New Yorker*, and the *Big Zero*. I've won a Pulitzer Prize, a National Book Award, and a Timberlake Annual Fiction Prize. I'm a graduate of Snake Forest University, where I studied with fiction writer John Merving. At present, I teach writing at the College of East Kalamazoo.

Thanks in advance for your time.

Best,

Larry Czarnecki

Notice how the first paragraph after the salutation includes the genre, the name of the piece, and the name of the magazine. Why include the name of the magazine? I do so to show that my story is not out at four hundred other magazines. (I used to send to more than one magazine at a time, but I never blanketed the entire country with my story. If you do simultaneously submit, be sure to change the name of the magazine in that first paragraph, or the editor will know at least one of the other places that's considering the work.)

The second paragraph after the salutation includes a handful of previous credits, awards, and/or education. Personally, I list a few books along with a few awards. Before I published books, I would list three magazine publications and a few awards. What's important here is that you don't list everything you've ever published (if you've published a lot), that you don't list things that don't matter to the editor (no one cares if you collect stamps or have grandchildren), that you don't make a mountain out of a molehill (being *nominated* for the Pulitzer, which any publisher, large or small, can do, isn't the same thing as being a *finalist* for the Pulitzer, which *is* a big deal), and don't lie. Whatever you do, don't lie. You may be thinking, *But what if I don't have any publications?* While it's true that some magazines favor published writers, nearly every editor I know would love to discover the Next Big Thing. Imagine being the editor who could say, *I was the first to publish Flannery O'Connor*, or *I was the first to publish Raymond Carver.* I honestly don't believe that being unpublished is a detriment. I don't. You just need to make sure that the story you submit is good.

The third paragraph after the salutation is a simple courtesy. Even if you get rejected, the editor has spent time on the manuscript, and you should thank the editor for that. I know that some writers become resentful when they receive rejections from magazines, but bear in mind that magazines (especially the more competitive ones) receive 99.8 percent more stuff than they can use, and that, by reading your manuscript, the editor has already done more for you than you've done for her. Therefore, be respectful.

Always include a self-addressed stamped envelope with your submission. In the old days, you needed to include an envelope large enough for the entire manuscript to get returned, but these days an envelope big enough for your rejection slip (or, hopefully, an acceptance slip) will do.

Having said all of this, more and more magazines are accepting submissions online via their websites, which may make most of what I've written here a moot point, but if the online submission offers an opportunity to upload a cover letter, I would still follow this format.

Simultaneous Submissions

"Simultaneous submission" means submitting the same story to more than one magazine at a time, which shouldn't be confused with "multiple submission," which means submitting more than one work to a magazine in a single submission, which poets are usually allowed to do but fiction writers aren't. An editor at a big magazine once said to me, "Life's too short *not* to simultaneously submit," and I agree wholeheartedly. It may take a magazine editor anywhere from two to six months, on average, to respond (although I've heard back on submissions as early as a week after I mailed them and as long as two and a half years later). Let's do some math. My early stories were rejected by twenty magazines, on average, before finding a home. Now, let's assume that there are really only two good times to submit to magazines (spring and fall), which means that if you send your story to only two magazines each year (assuming most magazines will take about four months to respond to you), and your story is going to be rejected by twenty magazines before finding a home, you're looking at ten years of submissions on that one story before it's accepted.

Some magazines don't accept simultaneous submissions, and they state this in their guidelines. My advice? Don't submit to them, unless you plan on submitting only to them. Respect their guidelines. I have friends who've simultaneously submitted to magazines, including magazines that don't take simultaneous submissions, and they've been caught. What did the offended magazine do? In one case, they sent the story back ripped up. Another told the writer never to submit to them again. There are wonderful magazines I haven't sent my work to because they don't allow simultaneous submissions, but there are too many excellent magazines that do allow simultaneous submissions for me to waste time waiting to hear back from a magazine that, statistically speaking, is likely to reject me.

So, what are the rules for simultaneous submissions?

1. I rarely ever submit a story to more than ten magazines at once. How many places you submit to depends on what you think your likelihood is of a story getting accepted. If it's a long, complicated story that will probably take time to place,

send it to ten magazines. If it's a short story that you know will have more appeal than some other stories you've written—maybe it was lauded in workshop; maybe it already won an award; maybe it's a short, funny, linear story; maybe you just have a gut feeling about it—then submit it to fewer places.

2. As soon as you get an acceptance, immediately inform the other magazines that you need to withdraw your work. I tend to send both snail mail letters and e-mail notes to the managing editor. Even then, the story sometimes isn't pulled, and I'll get a note—an acceptance or a rejection—a few months after I've withdrawn it. If it's an acceptance, I then have to apologize and explain the situation. But at least I *tried* to tell them.

3. What if you get an acceptance at a *better* magazine after you've told the first magazine editor who accepted it that, yes, he can have the story? For one thing, when I put together a batch of submissions, I choose magazines that I would be *equally* happy to publish in. In other words, I don't simultaneously submit to the *New Yorker* and the *Woonsocket Quarterly*. I don't do this because I don't want to end up in the quagmire above. In the rare instance where two magazines accept the same story in close proximity, I always go with the magazine that accepted the story first. I think it's the honorable thing to do. If, however, it came down between reneging on my promise to the *Woonsocket Quarterly* to accept the *New Yorker*'s offer, I'd probably have to accept the *New Yorker*, knowing full well that I could never submit to the *Woonsocket Quarterly* ever again. But, again, I try not to put myself in those situations.

The Slush Pile

Anyone who wants to publish fiction should, if at all possible, intern at a magazine and read the slush pile. The slush pile refers to those stories/poems/essays sent to the magazine directly by the author and not through an agent; the author is usually unknown to the editors of the magazine, and the work itself hasn't been requested. Nearly all of the work that a magazine receives constitutes the slush pile.

It's impossible to read a dozen or more short stories a day from a slush pile and not begin noticing flaws in your own work. I see this same phenomenon in the undergraduate workshops I teach. At the beginning of the semester, before students have read very much of their peers' work, they will defend shoddy technique or express pleasure at heavy-handed plots, but by the end of the semester, after they've seen the shoddy techniques and heavy-handedness *ad nauseam,* they've grown both tired and suspicious of them. What happens, whenever you read fiction of varying quality in bulk, is that you begin to spot what I call default problems. By this, I mean that almost all writers utilize lazy language/techniques/structures at one point or another. The more experienced writers *know* it's the default mode they're writing in, and they'll fix it during a revision. The inexperienced writers, even those who are otherwise well read, often don't realize this because they haven't been exposed to enough writing by inexperienced writers to realize the difference between what's default mode and what's original. For instance, cutting to a flashback too soon after the start of a story is a default structure. Some semesters, I'll see this in 85 percent of the stories that are turned in. But how would you know this unless you've been reading hundreds of student stories or magazine submissions?

When you read stories in bulk, it becomes clear that 50 percent or more of the work received is unpublishable. When I interned for a magazine, I read the manuscripts blind, meaning that I wouldn't look at cover letters. Out of a hundred stories, half were either incompetent or entirely wrong for the magazine; the other half, with a few exceptions, were competent but dull, familiar, or not quite ready. And then there were two or three that stood out almost immediately. Those were the ones that made you sit up straight. Those were the ones that made you *forget* you were reading stories. Those were the one where you'd find yourself on page twenty-five when you thought you were on only page five or six. These are stories that *weren't* written in default mode.

However you slice it, interning for a magazine is useful. Sylvia Plath read the slush pile for *Mademoiselle*, as did Diane Johnson, who, in addition to her novels, co-wrote the screenplay for Stanley Kubrick's *The Shining*. As Sam Weller documents in *The Bradbury Chronicles*, an early Ray Bradbury story titled "Homecoming" was plucked out of the slush pile of *Mademoiselle* by a young office assistant. The magazine's editor, unable to work the curious story into a regular issue, decided to build an entire October issue around the story and its "Halloween vampire family" theme. The publication of "Homecoming" was a milestone for Ray Bradbury, giving him that much-needed acceptance into the world of New York publishing. And who was the office assistant who had discovered the story in the first place? A young man named Truman Capote. So, you could do far worse things for your own writing, like sitting in a bar all day and talking about writing the Great American Novel, than interning for a magazine.

The most common internships tend to be for college students. Graduate students frequently intern with literary journals housed by their English departments. Undergraduates are often eligible for magazine internships; information for these can usually be found on the magazine's website. More and more frequently, magazines and journals like *Zoetrope: All Story*, which aren't affiliated with a university, are using volunteer readers to sift through their slush piles. If you can't find an internship, start your own magazine. Reading dozens of unsolicited manuscripts daily may prove to be the best education you can give yourself.

Publishing a Book The Pros and Cons of Print-on-Demand, Vanity Presses, Small Presses, University Presses, and Commercial Presses

Print-On-Demand

The last few years have seen the rise of self-publication via print-on-demand publishers, making it possible for anyone to inexpensively publish his own novels, story collections, poetry, limericks, joke books, or what have you. And, I have to admit, many of the print-on-demand services produce books that look better than those published by some small and university presses. The cover stock is nice; the paper is high quality; the layout looks professional. Of course, much of this depends upon the author, whose aesthetics and wallet dictate the look of the book. If money is no object, there are book designers who can be hired to create professional-looking cover art and page layout.

Before going this route, you need to ask yourself what it is you want out of having a book published. If it's to get a teaching job, a self-published print-on-demand book isn't going to help you. If it's to get attention in national book reviews, like the *New York Times* or the *Washington Post*, it's most likely not going to happen with a print-on-demand book. Sometimes an author simply wants to get her work out there, perhaps to prove to those who previously rejected the work that there is, in fact, a market for her book, in which case a print-on-demand publisher provides an opportunity for the writer to do just that.

There is a wonderful blog called POD-dy Mouth (http://girlon demand.blogspot.com/) dedicated to POD books, which showcased well-done POD books, took to task the terrible ones, and analyzed various POD companies and services. (Unfortunately, the person running the website quit writing new posts a few years ago, but the site is still up and worth checking out.) The host of the website also interviewed authors with POD success stories, like fiction writer Will Clarke, whose two novels *Lord Vishnu's Love Handles* and *The Worthy* were both eventually published by Simon and Schuster after having been POD books. Both novels were roundly rejected by traditional publishers when his first agent sent them out, so he set up his own

POD publishing venture, MiddleFingerPress. The arc of Will Clarke's career went like this: Clarke sold his POD books on Amazon; a screenwriter in New Zealand read *Lord Vishnu's Love Handles* and wanted to option it for a dollar; the screenwriter then got the book attached to producer Michael London (*Sideways*); London, in turn, attached director David Gordon Green (*Pineapple Express*); together, London and Green were able to get the project set up at Paramount Pictures; Clarke called an editor-friend at Simon and Schuster to ask for an agent recommendation; the editor made an offer to buy *Lord Vishnu* while recommending an agent; the agent took Clarke on and landed him a two-book deal with Simon and Schuster; the second book, *The Worthy*, is now set up as a future project at Columbia Pictures.

In his interview with POD-dy Mouth, Will Clarke takes a philosophical view of his books' journeys:

> To me, my books are like people, like infants—baby kings riding on the backs of elephants. And I'm the guide who's been appointed to take them where they demand to go. If that means self-publishing, if that is where the book wants to go, then that is where I will take him. I have no shame in this. So long as what I am doing is in service to the work, then it's always worth it, and it's always valid. A book goes where it wants to go—it makes friends and creates its own enemies. It's an entity unto itself. As the writer I'm really just the Sherpa whose job it is to help the book on its way, be it traditional publishing or through POD.

Before getting too excited by the possibility of doing your own POD book, let me clarify that Will Clarke's story is exceptional. It's extraordinarily difficult to get attention for a print-on-demand book. If you don't have a platform, it's going to be difficult to *sell* copies of your book since bookstores won't stock them without a distributor. (A platform is an avenue by which you have a built-in audience, like writing a weekly newspaper column, hosting a talk show, or a lecturing to CEOs.) Short of a platform, you may find yourself selling books out of your car trunk.

Christine DeMaio, who published the children's book *Alex Meets Zorba* with a print-on-demand publisher, was pleased with the services the publisher provided but admits that marketing was the hard part. According to DeMaio, "We were listed on Amazon, our own website and the POD company's website. But there was a lot of work as far as the marketing and advertising and getting it all out there . . .

so my last word on it is, you have to be on top of it. You have to market the hell out of it and do all the stuff your publisher would do." It should be noted that some print-on-demand publishers, like Author House, now offer marketing services.

Will Clarke raises another excellent point, one that many writers may not want to face: "Because getting published through a print-on-demand publisher is so easy and getting published through a traditional publisher is so hard, will the more impulsive among us rush to publish things that maybe should have baked a little longer?"

In this DIY age, it's understandable why print-on-demand books are so popular, but I recommend anyone thinking of going this route to proceed carefully. There are always going to be POD success stories, like Will Clarke's, but those are anomalies.

Vanity Presses

With the rise of print-on-demand publishing, you don't hear much about vanity presses anymore. Vanity presses charge an exorbitant rate for a designated print-run of a book, promising marketing and distribution. These books typically aren't taken seriously, and the companies that offer vanity press services are always looked at askance by anyone who knows anything about publishing. I've heard horror stories of people who've signed up with vanity presses and ended up with a depleted life savings and five thousand unwanted copies of their book moldering in their garage. My advice? Don't do it. Get a hundred copies of your book published with a POD outfit, and give the rest of the money that you would have spent to a dog rescue group.

Small Presses

The range of small presses, in terms of quality and prestige, is vast. You'll find very small operations, run by only a few people with the help of several interns. Some of these, like Dzanc Books, are exceptional presses; others, not so much. You'll also find small presses that employ several people and have more than one editor, like Graywolf Press, which recently published a book that was a finalist for the National Book Award. In fact, a press like Graywolf may be just as difficult to break into as a commercial publisher. Graywolf began as a much smaller operation, as did Algonquin Books, which now has several national bestsellers to their credit, most notably *Water for Elephants* by Sara Gruen.

It's impossible to know if today's unknown publisher will become tomorrow's hot new small press, but there are a few questions you can ask yourself before signing a contract.

1. Does the small press have a distributor? Having an affiliation with a distributor is paramount in order for a publisher to get your book into bookstores, not only into such places as Barnes and Noble but also independent bookstores. Some distributors, however, are better than others, so it may be worthwhile to research that distributor by learning what other publishers they work with and whether you can find any books by these other publishers in your local bookstore. If the publisher doesn't have a distributor, you may find yourself selling your book door to door.

2. Does the publisher have an in-house publicist or, at the very least, a publicist-for-hire? Without a publicist, it's highly unlikely that your book will receive reviews. In fact, you can pretty much forget about any media coverage: feature stories in newspapers and magazines, radio interviews, TV appearances. A publicist is essential for constructing a media plan for your book, and while having a publicist doesn't guarantee that your book will receive any attention, it does exponentially increase your odds. You could always hire a publicist yourself, but before you do, read the chapter titled "Hiring an Independent Publicist."

3. Will the publisher supply advance review copies of your book? If the publisher has no plans to print advance review copies, which are typically sent to venues that may review your book, you can pretty much assume the publisher will rely on word of mouth to sell your book. No advance review copies probably means no marketing plan.

4. Will the publisher send you on a book tour? There are mixed opinions about the effectiveness of book tours (see my chapter "Bookstore Signings, University Lectures, and Other Humbling Experiences"). For starters, they're costly. I did a two-week book tour for my story collection *Ghosts of Chicago* that included stops in Chicago, Indianapolis, Iowa City, and Lincoln. The tour cost over four thousand dollars. It is probably unreasonable to expect a small press to send you on a book tour, but if they do, it may bode well for how much support they're

willing to put into your book. At the very least, you would want a publisher who would be willing to help set up readings for you, even if they won't be paying for an actual tour.

5. Do they have an efficient website? This question is a good one for any type of publisher, but it's especially important for a smaller publisher since their task is already a Sisyphean one and since this is one aspect of publicity that's in their control. Is the website never updated? Is it difficult to search books on it? Is it disorganized? Is it riddled with typos? Can a visitor purchase a book directly? It's possible that the publisher doesn't even have a website. Sadly, something seemingly minor, like having a navigable and aesthetically pleasing website, may suggest what the publisher will be like to work with. The website, after all, is the publisher's introduction of themselves to the world. It's like the person who shows up to an interview wearing a dirty T-shirt and flip-flops. Is this who you want to hire?

6. Do they have sales reps? Sales reps are the people who travel from bookstore to bookstore and talk booksellers into stocking publishers' books. While major publishers have their own sales force who scatter across the country and make the rounds to bookstores, smaller publishers often hire regional sales reps to do this job for them. Sometimes, the distributor provides this service for the publisher. If the publisher doesn't have any kind of sales rep working for them, they're probably relying on word of mouth or their website to do this work. Many publishers will list on their website who's repping their books, which is one way to find out if they do in fact use sales reps. Short of that, you can always go to the chain stores and independent bookstores to see if any of the publishers' books are stocked.

7. Are the publisher's other authors happy? Very few writers I've ever met would admit to being *happy* with their publisher. Ask most writers, and they'll tell you that their publisher could be doing more for them. "Happy" is a relative word here. Even so, there are definite red flags: the author didn't receive money owed to him in a timely manner; the publisher agreed to do certain things up front but never followed through; the author had difficulty reaching the publisher; the publisher

consistently did things that undermined the book's publication, like sending review copies to *Publishers Weekly* or *Book-
list*, which have long lead times, only a few weeks before the
book's publication date; and so forth.

You're likely to hear unreasonable complaints as well ("The
publisher didn't run a full-page ad in the *New York Times Book
Review*" or "The publisher didn't push hard enough to get me
on the *Today* show"). Differentiate between the reasonable
and the unreasonable. The more authors who have reasonable
complaints about their publisher, the more likely it is that this
is a publisher you will want to avoid.

A word of advice: Take a neutral position when e-mailing
an author to ask about his or her experience with the publisher. The author may be the publisher's friend. I would
write something to the effect of, "Hello. My name is John
McNally, and I have just been offered a contract by What the
Heck Press. I see that you've recently published a novel with
them. I'm writing to ask if you'd care to share any experiences
you've had working with them. They look like a very interesting press. Thanks in advance for your time, and all the best on
your own work. I look forward to reading your novel. All best,
John." Be courteous; be brief. And if you don't hear back, don't
badger. Also, don't take it as a sign that the author is unhappy.
I receive so many e-mails that, as hard as I try, I cannot possibly answer all of them. Hopefully, a few of the publisher's
authors will write back to you with useful comments, helping
you to make an informed choice.

University Presses

More and more university presses are publishing creative works
while publishing fewer scholarly monographs. In addition to the
various award series, such as those at the University of Iowa Press,
the University of Georgia Press, and Ohio State University Press, there
are now many general fiction series (series that aren't attached to
awards), such as the ones at the University of Nebraska Press and the
University of Wisconsin Press. As the larger commercial publishing
houses cut literary books from their lists, university presses seem to
be picking up the slack.

University presses, like small presses, will vary in terms of prestige, size, and publicity muscle, but you can almost always count on the books being distributed, and there's a good chance for decent library sales.

I have published a total of six books with four different university presses, and by and large, I've been allowed a hands-on approach, more so than I've had with any commercial publisher. Although a university press doesn't have a large publicity budget, it is more open to creative marketing ideas than the commercial houses, where creative ideas by the author are often nixed or, worse, accepted and then forgotten.

As a book collector, I can attest to the fact that thirty years ago some university press books were fairly ugly, with designers making use of some of the least palatable colors in the spectrum, like burnt orange and avocado, for their books' covers, but this isn't the case today. In fact, many university press books are indistinguishable from those published by the big commercial houses. (Why ugly books still exist is a mystery to me.)

As with a small press, the sales expectations at a university press are more realistic than what you're likely to find at a commercial press. A university press may be thrilled with sales of 5,000 copies for a fiction title, whereas a commercial house is likely to be disappointed by sales under 15,000. Yet, in reality, 5,000 copies of a literary title is a pretty good number. (It's the rare literary title that breaks out into five- and six-digit sales figures.) I'm convinced that commercial houses use what I call the "dart board theory," meaning that they acquire a handful of books (darts) and throw them all haphazardly at the board (the public) with the hope that *some* make the bull's eye (the bestseller list), full well knowing that many will hit the dart board's outer edges (modest sales), while others will fall to the floor (bomb)—all of this in lieu of coming up with an individual marketing plan for each book. Again, university presses don't have the marketing budget of a Random House or a Scribner—far from it—but they also don't have the leisure to throw out a handful of titles willy-nilly each season without at least *some* thought about how the market for Book A might differ from that for Book B.

University presses are committed to keeping their books in print. They can't keep all books in print in perpetuity, but they're not as quick to pull the plug on them as are commercial houses. My first book, *Troublemakers*, published by the University of Iowa Press in 2000, is still in print, whereas the paperback of my third book,

America's Report Card, published by Free Press (a division of Simon and Schuster) in 2006, was remaindered in 2009.

Another perk for the writer who is also a professor is that university press publications carry weight within university English Departments. Ironically, they sometimes carry *more* weight than a commercial house, if only because the culture of English Departments is steeped in research that appears in books published by university presses, and English professors' familiarity with commercial or small houses is sometimes limited. Over the years, I've received more grunts of affirmation from literature professors for my university press publishers than for any other press I've worked with.

My experiences with university presses have been, for the most part, extremely positive ones. So, where's the rub? Why not publish every book with a university press? For starters, it's likely that you won't get an advance of any kind—or, if you do, it will be a modest one. (On the one hand, I wouldn't mind a big, fat, six-figure paycheck signed over to me upon the publication of my book. The problem here is that if the book doesn't earn out the advance—and, let's face it, few literary books are going to earn out overblown advances—the publisher is likely to consider you a liability and cut you loose. With a university press, you'll earn money on every book you sell, so there's not the same pressure of *having* to sell an obscene number of books in order to justify your existence.)

The royalty rate is sometimes lower in contracts with university presses than you'd find in contracts with commercial publishers or even small presses. Occasionally, you can negotiate up a half- or whole percentage point, but most university presses don't have a lot of wriggle room. In fact, many university presses are operating in the red, which brings me to my next subject: budget cuts.

Part of a state university's annual budget is set by the state legislature, and every year my friends who work at university presses hold their breaths until the budget is announced, and often their response is, "It wasn't as bad as we'd feared," which means that it was still bad—often an across-the-board cut is expected for the press—but it's not as bad as it could have been, as in layoffs or, worst case scenario, shutting down the press altogether. This last scenario may seem unlikely to the uninitiated, but it happens. University presses—in fact, anything arts-related—tend to be first up on the university budget's chopping block. Presses that recently have been taken to the brink of extinction include Eastern Washington University Press, the University of Arkansas Press, and Louisiana State University Press. It would be disheartening, to say the least, to be signed by a press, only to find out that the press is dissolving before your book is scheduled to come out. More disheartening, of course, would be being an employee at a press that gets cut from the budget.

Another issue to consider: Some university presses that are new to publishing fiction and poetry still don't quite know how to market a creative work. They'll attempt to market it as they would a scholarly book—sending review copies to scholarly journals instead of literary journals; pushing the book at the Modern Language Association conference, which is where academics congregate, instead of at the Associated Writing Programs conference, which is for creative writers; and so on.

University presses don't carry the same clout as commercial houses when it comes to getting reviewed in certain venues, such as *Publishers Weekly* or the *New York Times Book Review*, which may ultimately limit sales. Publishing with a university press doesn't mean that a book won't get noticed, however. Occasionally, a university press will break through, as with John Kennedy Toole's *A Confederacy of Dunces* (Louisiana State University Press), Norman Maclean's *A River Runs Through It* (University of Chicago Press), and Tom Clancy's *The Hunt for Red October* (Naval Institute Press). More recently, Bonnie Jo Campbell's story collection *American Salvage*, published by Wayne State University Press, was a finalist for the National Book Award and the National Book Critics Circle Award. Campbell had previously published with a commercial house; the book published by the university press, however, has put her on the map.

Research the strengths of the university press you're querying. If they don't publish novels, don't send your novel to them. If they do well with regional work and you're writing about the same region, you may have found the perfect match—that is, as long as the publisher sees it that way, too. Arnie Bernstein's book *Bath Massacre: America's First School Bombing* was continually turned down by major publishers, who liked the book but felt it was too regional. Bernstein says, "I learned the hard way that with rare exceptions, major publishers consider a story 'regional' if it doesn't take place on the east or west coast. The elements of my book certainly were timely: it involves the deadliest act of school violence in American history. We think Columbine and Virginia Tech are some kind of modern phenomena; my story happened in 1927 and had many thematic links to today's tragedies." Fortunately, University of Michigan Press picked up *Bath Massacre*. The State Library of Michigan named *Bath Massacre* one of its Notable Books of 2010; Bernstein was one of twenty authors on the list, which also included three National Book Award finalists. Says Bernstein, "From start to finish I had a great experience with the University of Michigan Press. Because they are a smaller outfit, I had great communication with everyone who worked on the book: acquisition editor, book editor, designer, and marketing. They were open and eager to hear my ideas and be true to my vision. I didn't get lost in a corporate conglomerate."

Remember: One size doesn't fit all. One book might be a better fit for a university press than it would be for a commercial house; the opposite may be true for the next book.

Commercial Presses

Most writers dream of signing with a commercial house, a place like Knopf or Scribner or Little, Brown. These places are considered the crown jewels of publishing. For good reasons, too. Chances are you'll get a much larger advance than you would if you had published with a small press or a university press. The royalty rates with commercial presses are good. A certain prestige is attached to being able to tell someone that your publisher is Random House, whereas Soft Skull Press, a wonderful publisher, is likely to draw blank stares from your neighbors. It's possible that the publisher will send you on a book tour, during which you'll stay in nice hotels and be given a healthy per diem for food. Your book may get front-table display at the chain stores instead of being shelved, spine out, with all the thousands of other books. If you're lucky, an advertisement for your book might appear in the *New Yorker* or one of the major newspapers.

So, are there drawbacks? Is there ever a time to turn down a contract with a commercial press in favor of a contract with a small press?

I'm the first to admit that it would be difficult to forego a contract with Dutton or Simon and Schuster or Harper in favor of a contract with a lesser-known, smaller publisher . . . and yet there are some points to take into consideration.

For starters, will you be a little fish in a big pond? If so, is that bad? Consider this: My first book, *Troublemakers*, is a short story collection published by the University of Iowa Press as part of a series of award-winning story collections. As a result, it was one of that season's books that Iowa chose to push hard. In other words, it was a front-listed book. I was also able to participate in various stages of the publishing process, such as cover design and marketing. To promote the book, I attended BookExpo—the industry's huge annual conference for book publishing—where I signed advance review copies of *Troublemakers* for book reviewers, librarians, and managers of independent bookstores. Over a decade later, I'm still in communication with a handful of people I met that day. Do I think a commercial house would have allowed me the same level of involvement in the publication of my story collection? No, they would not have.

Unless you're Jhumpa Lahiri or Junot Díaz—writers who frequently publish in the *New Yorker* and *Best American Short Stories*—a commercial publisher is likely to dump your story collection while they wait for your novel. (By "dump," I mean that they're likely to ship it to stores but not invest any publicity energy into the book.)

My own experience with commercial houses is that I sometimes have a say in cover design but sometimes don't; I usually have little say in how the book is marketed (the University of Iowa Press printed postcards for *Troublemakers*, whereas postcard requests to commercial houses have always been denied); and I have never been invited to attend BookExpo by a commercial house. And why would they? My editor at Free Press was also Dr. Phil's editor. Which of the two of us—me or Dr. Phil—do you think got tapped to go to BookExpo?

Having noted all of this, I'll concede that it's entirely possible that the sheer name-power of publishing with a commercial house may garner attention for a short story collection, and that, when all is said and done, the book will sell as many copies or more than it would have with the university press. (This isn't always the case. I have friends who've published *novels* with commercial houses, only to sell fewer than a thousand copies because the publisher chose not to put any energy into publicity.) But let's say, for the sake of argument, that you do sell as many copies of the story collection with the commercial publisher as you might have with the university press. Which experience taught you more about publishing? Which experience fostered good relationships that you'll be able to use beyond this book? Which experience do you walk away from feeling good about rather than embittered? Furthermore, which of the two sales figures would be considered a success and which would be a failure?

My point is you should always carefully choose the right kind of publisher for the right book. A book that's good for a university press isn't necessarily good for a commercial house, and vice-versa. I would much rather be a front-listed author by a smaller press than an author whose book is going to be forgotten by a commercial press shortly after it's been acquired. How do you know if your book is going to be neglected? To begin with, I would ask you to be realistic. If you sign a two-book contract with a commercial house and the first book you turn in is a short story collection, chances are the publisher is waiting for your second book, which is probably a novel.

Publishing with a commercial house is a lot like gambling in Vegas. It's fun, it's sexy, and when you're hot, all eyes are on you . . . but once you start slipping, everyone moves over to the next table, where the Next Hot Thing is on a winning streak. I'll be the first to admit that it's hard not to be lured by the flashing lights and all that money, but you need to prepare yourself for the fact that fame is sometimes fleeting, and if it does all dry up, you need to remind yourself why you're doing all of this in the first place.

Agents

The relationship between the agent and the writer is often a curiously intimate one. *Emotionally* intimate, that is. You speak to your agent regularly; you e-mail daily during certain stages of the bookselling process; you call on your agent to defend you when a conflict arises with your editor; you want sympathy from (or get frustrated at) your agent when your book isn't selling; and you celebrate with your agent when good things happen in your career. And yet, since you are only one of many clients, there are times, especially when you feel you're not getting as much attention from the agent as you deserve, when you'll sulk like a spurned lover.

We forget sometimes that the agent-author relationship is a professional one. If the author always wants more than the agent can provide—round-the-clock emotional support, perhaps, or second-by-second updates on a book submission—the agent may feel the need to break things off with the author. On behalf of all agents, I would like to remind you that, should you sign on with an agent, you won't be her only client. Yes, getting a book deal is important, but your agent shouldn't be the person you depend upon to fulfill your emotional needs. For that, I recommend getting a dog or a cat instead.

Below are the most common questions I'm asked about agents.

What Does an Agent Do?

A lot of younger writers (and, again, "younger" here means less experienced) think that getting an agent is the golden ticket to book publication. Let me dispel that myth. Having an agent guarantees nothing. Even the best agents can't sell every book they agree to take on.

An agent attempts to sell your book. Before she starts shopping it around, the agent may make editorial suggestions on your manuscript and ask for a revision. The amount of revision an agent asks for will vary rather dramatically from agent to agent. Bear in mind that many agents are former editors. It's not uncommon for editors to become agents after they've lost their editorial jobs during corporate downsizing or mergers. And if you're a writer who wants an agent who'll take the time to comment on your work, you should try to find one who used to acquire books for a living.

Once your manuscript is ready to be sent off, the agent puts together a list of editors who might be interested in the book. How do they know who might be right? Agents get to know editors' likes and dislikes by familiarizing themselves with the other books the editors have acquired and by socializing with them. Oftentimes, an agent will get to know a few editors' preferences so well that she'll sell most of her books to those three or four editors. Friendships in this business sometimes go a long way. Of course, the editor still needs to get approval from an editorial board, so getting an editor excited about a book is only the first step toward publication, and as I can attest, hopes can get dashed pretty damned fast, especially when the editor is the *only* one who loves your book, or if no one else at the publishing house sees how the book can be marketed.

If, however, an editor gets the green light to make an offer, the agent tries to negotiate for more money. Even when there's no other offer on the table, my agents have usually been able to push the advance up some and, in one instance, by as much as fifty percent. It's always easier, of course, to get publishing houses to pony up more money when there are other offers on the table. The agent will also negotiate to retain certain rights, as well as various terms within the contract that would otherwise favor the publisher. (The publisher's contract *always* favors the publisher in every regard until the agent begins picking it apart, clause by clause.) Contracts are written in the foreign language of legalese, and as often as I've read over contracts, I still can't make heads or tails out of them. The contracts are especially tricky these days in regard to two issues: electronic rights (which are always evolving, especially now with handheld readers) and what constitutes a book being out of print (short-run digital printing, which is used much more frequently by publishers, has muddied these waters). The contracts are often a dozen or more pages long, with several more pages of riders, so you'll want an agent who is good with contracts, or an agent who's part of an agency with its own legal department, or an agent who used to be an editor (in other words, someone who knows the various ways the publishing house would like to exploit you).

Should you be lucky enough to have more than one publisher interested in your book, the agent may set up an auction. What usually happens is that the agent gives all of the editors who are still considering the book a specific day and time for making offers, as well as a closing time for any bidding. As soon as an editor calls to make an offer, the agent calls all of the other editors to say that there's an offer on the table, and though she can't tell them who bid, she can tell them what the offer is. From here, the other editors must decide whether or not they want to make an offer. In a best-case scenario, several editors volley back and forth with bids. During this process, the agent may arrange for the author to have conversations with the editors who are interested. The author, however, is under no obligation to take the highest bid. There may be any number of reasons for taking a bid that's not the highest: the author may have hit it off with one editor more than another; the author may want to be with a certain publishing house because of its esteemed list of authors; the author may not want to make the edits that the highest bidder is requiring. In a worst-case scenario, no one shows up for the bidding. The agent is waiting by the phone for calls that aren't coming in, and the author is biting his fist or eating everything in the house out of anxiety, all while calculating how to spend the small fortune that, unbeknownst to him, isn't coming his way.

Once the book has been sold, the agent acts as the buffer between you and your editor. You will, of course, have direct contact with your editor, your publicist, and various others at the publishing house, but if a problem arises, it's the agent whom you go to. This way, the agent can do the dirty work. Or, if you're overreacting, the agent can calm you down.

An agent also keeps tabs on royalty checks and other money you're earning. Typically, the publisher cuts a check to the agent; then the agent takes out her percentage and sends the rest to you. If a publisher isn't sending the check in a timely manner, the agent may turn into a pit-bull. After all, part of that money belongs to her.

Some agents help you map out a career path; others take more of a back-seat approach, letting you make your own decisions about what project you should work on next.

For all of this, the agent will collect a percentage of whatever you make on the book. Fifteen percent is the industry standard, although more famous writers can negotiate for a smaller percentage. This is money well spent. On the other hand, under no circumstance should you be paying money to an agent that isn't part of that commission. Occasionally, an agent will recoup certain expenses, such as postage and photocopies, after a sale has been made, but many agencies don't even attempt to recoup these. Agents who charge reading fees are scam artists, plain and simple. An agent—a good agent—should be earning her keep from the book deals she's landing for her clients.

Do I Need an Agent?

If you have a completed novel (not a partially written novel, not an outline, and not an idea for one, but a *completed* novel), and if you want to place it with a commercial publishing house, such as Random House, Simon and Schuster, Viking, etc., the answer is *yes, yes, yes*. These publishers will *not* look at your manuscript without an agent. Agents cultivate relationships with editors, and vice-versa. There are just too many people writing—and too many people writing unpublishable novels—for these publishing houses to accepted unagented manuscripts. Having an agent means, quite simply, that you've been vetted.

Agents often take on nonfiction projects based on their marketability—based on the idea itself—but generally agents take on novels because they love them. (They also have to believe that they can sell it, but since selling *any* first novel is going to be a tough row to hoe, the agent usually has to believe strongly in the book. It has to be the sort of book that they want to press into people's hands and say, *You must read this!* In other words, the agent wants to feel passionately about a novel before agreeing to represent it.) An agent isn't going to take on your zombie-vampire novel just because zombies and vampires are hot right now. An agent is going to have to *love* your zombie-vampire novel. At the end of the day, an agent's taste is going to play a significant role in whether or not she takes you. You may have written a brilliant novel, but if it's not that particular agent's cup of tea, it's unlikely that the agent will want to spend months trying to sell it, even if she recognizes its brilliance.

Agents are unlikely to take on clients whose books are probably going to earn minuscule advances, if any. Short story collections and poetry fall into this category. Remember: Fifteen percent of nothing is nothing.

How Do You Look for Agents?

Agent Query (www.agentquery.com) is a superb resource for finding an agent. Not only does it have a user-friendly search engine, the site also offers advice and information on all aspects of publishing, conferences, residencies, grants, and any number of other important topics for writers. To top it off, the service is free. If I were in the early stages of looking for an agent, I would start here.

I also advise writers looking for agents to subscribe to Publishers Marketplace (www.publishersmarketplace.com), which lists daily book sales, the names of acquiring editors, and the names of the agents who made the sales. The database is such that you can search by categories and genre (e.g., "fiction" and "literary"). You can also see what else a particular agent has sold recently. Not every sale makes it onto Publishers Marketplace, but most sales are listed, and it's an invaluable resource for finding basic information. Many agents have a special page on Publishers Marketplace with information on recent sales, along with how to contact them. Don't use the agent's e-mail that's attached to the listing of a sale until you know that this is the preferred way to contact the agent. Some agents prefer e-mail queries, but many would still rather receive a written query, so you don't want to misstep the first time you introduce yourself. This site charges a monthly fee.

Another way to find agents is to look on the acknowledgments pages of books that are similar to the novel you've written. Authors often thank their agents. If the agent isn't listed, you can call the publisher, ask for the rights department, and then ask whoever answers for the name of the agent who represented such-and-such book.

Occasionally, the author will have his agent's contact information on his website. If the author doesn't offer that information, don't contact the author directly and ask for it. It's not good form. Even as I write this, I can't help thinking, *Who would do such a thing?* and yet, at least once a year, I'll get an e-mail from someone, or I'll meet someone at a book signing, who wants me to put them in touch with my agent. One time, after giving a talk, I was approached by a person who said, "I'm going to contact your agent and use your name. Do you mind?" Hell, yeah, I mind! What would this person have said if I'd replied, okay, sure, but in return I was going to contact his employer and say that he had recommended me for a job in his company? There are *other* ways to find an agent than to ask strangers for a recommendation.

Agents frequently attend writers' conferences, and I do know a few authors who've found their agents at conferences, but it's a costly way to go about looking for representation. Know your strengths. If you're not good at selling yourself—if you're pathologically shy and awkward, as I most definitely was early on in my career—it may not be the best idea for your initial introduction to an agent to be a face-to-face encounter. (A word to the shy and awkward: There's hope! I have, out of necessity, outgrown my shyness, and I have become much less awkward around people simply by being in public almost continuously, either as a teacher or while out promoting my books.)

Finally, it's appropriate to ask other writers—writers you know personally—for recommendations, as in, "Do you know of any good agents I should contact?" It's not appropriate to ask, "Hey, would you recommend me to your agent?" If your writer-friend *wants* to recommend you to her agent, she'll do so—but asking her to do so puts the writer in an uncomfortable position. For starters, the writer may not like your work. Or, the writer may not have read your work. Or, the writer may not believe that your work is right for her agent. There are any number of reasons why your writer-friend may not want to recommend you to her agent, and if you push the issue, you're bound to put your friendship to a test.

If a writer goes out of her way to recommend your work to her agent, be gracious about it, regardless of the agent's decision. I have quit recommending my agent to people I know for one reason: I have had one too many experiences in which the person I've recommended, after getting rejected, wants to complain endlessly to me about the agent's decision. One time, the person I recommended sent me a several-page-long e-mail that detailed how unprofessional my agent was. Another time, the person I recommended told the agent that she was wrong about his project and that she was missing out by not taking him on. What all of these people failed to realize is that their behavior becomes a reflection of me. The agent may be thinking, *Why in the world did John recommend this jerk-off?* What these people also failed to realize was that complaining to me about my agent, who had done well by me, is not unlike complaining to a friend about that friend's spouse. What are you going to gain by that? If you complain to me about my agent—an agent I went out of my way to recommend to you—you're essentially testing my loyalty, and guess what? The agent is going to win. No, the best thing to do is be grateful to the person who did the recommending and treat the agent with respect, no matter the outcome. And should the agent take you on, don't use the author who recommended you to her as a sounding board for every complaint you have against the agent. The author has his own problems; he doesn't need yours on top of them.

Big Agency or Small Agency?

The answer to this question is a toss-up. The risk of signing with a huge agency is that you might get lost in the shuffle. If the agency is representing half the people on the *New York Times* bestseller list and you're writing modestly selling literary novels or, God forbid, short story collections, you may find yourself on the low-priority list. That said, large agencies consist of several individual agents who have their own client lists. The president of the company may be looking out for the interests of those bestselling authors, while another agent may have a very literary list of writers, a list distinguished not so much by its sales figures as for awards the books have won, which brings prestige to the agency as a whole. So, it's very difficult to generalize. The perks of the big agency include a diligent contracts department, a kind of power-in-numbers (agents within the same agency will help one another out by recommending editors), name recognition (tell someone you're with William Morris, and everyone will be impressed), possibly a foreign and subsidiary rights team (which means that all the burdens of selling additional rights for your book don't fall squarely on your agent's shoulders), and so on.

An agent at a smaller agency may give your book more attention. It may be easier to get hold of the agent. The agent at the smaller agency, especially a junior agent within the agency, may be hungrier. Furthermore, the smaller agency may specialize in a particular niche, like literary fiction, which might work to your advantage.

Having said all of this, I'm not sure if any of the above is actually true. I've been with two mega-agencies and several smaller ones, and one of my agents moved from a smaller agency to a mega-agency before, eventually, breaking off to start her own agency. I've had good experiences with mega-agencies as well as smaller agencies, and I've had terrible experiences with both. At the end of the day, how you're treated really depends upon the agent, regardless of the agency's size.

Will You Be My Agent?

There are a lot of desperate people out there, and there are times when I start thinking I've met all of them.

After one of my readings, an older gentleman, accompanied by his wife, rushed up to the table where I was to sign books. He told me he was a reporter, handed me his card, and said he'd love to do a story on me . . . would I have a few minutes after the reading to talk?

Turns out he didn't want to do a story on me. He'd read an article about me in the local paper and wanted me to be his agent. The idea was so preposterous, I didn't know what to say at first. It was clear, however, that he wasn't going to take no for an answer. (Am I imagining this, or did he actually say "I'm not going to take no for an answer"? I'm pretty sure he did, in fact, say this to me.) I tried explaining to him that I had my own agent and that my spare time was spent writing, not selling my own stuff. But nothing I said dissuaded him.

"No, no, you'd be perfect. You know what it's like. And you know how the business works."

"Yes, I do, sort of, but . . ." I paused. Was he putting me on? "I live right here, in Winston-Salem, same as you. You really need an agent in New York."

"But you *know* people," he said.

Meanwhile, the events coordinator was giving me a holy-crap-I'm-sorry look as she folded chairs.

All of this is by way of saying that only an agent can do what an agent does. Your mother can't do it, your neighbor can't do it, and your personal injury attorney can't do it. If you need an agent, get an agent. Oh, and don't ask your local author. He can't do it, either.

Can I Leave My Agent If I'm Not Happy?

Some agents ask their clients to sign author-agent agreements. Usually, these agreements specify the amount of time a writer must wait, after breaking off with an agent, before a manuscript can be sent to an editor by the author or a new agent. What this does is gives the old agent a window of time to close any pending deals. This applies only to those manuscripts presently being circulated by the agent. A reasonable amount of time is two months. Except in extraordinary circumstances, it would be unfair to dump an agent when the agent is on the brink of closing a deal. Hence, the author-agent agreement.

Read the author-agent agreement carefully before signing. I made the mistake of signing an agreement that kept me from doing anything with a particular manuscript for *two years*. When I foolishly signed this agreement, I had already worked with my agent at another agency, so I couldn't foresee any reason for leaving her when she moved on to the new agency in a seemingly more powerful position. What I hadn't anticipated was that the president of the agency would interfere with the submission of my manuscript, eventually putting me in the unenviable position of reconsidering my relationship with my agent. I finally broke away from her and signed with another agent, and when my new agent landed me a two-book deal, I received a congratulations from the head of the previous agency, along with a warning: "I hope neither of those books is the one we were representing. You're still contractually bound to us for that one." Fortunately, neither book was the novel they had been sending around.

So, while the short answer is, yes, you can leave your agent if you're unhappy, you should be careful what you sign when you first team up with an agent in case the day to leave ever materializes.

Over the past twenty years, I've had several agents. A few were people I genuinely liked but who were unable to sell any of my books. Do I think it was their fault? In all instances except for one, no, it wasn't. Most of them gave it their best shot, but for whatever reason—the market, the book itself—the book didn't sell. If it wasn't their fault, why did I leave them? Because I'm of the belief that stasis in the face of repeated failure is the kiss of death. Shake things up, I say. Stir the pot. Agents tend to work with the same editors, so maybe I needed an agent who worked with a different set of editors. Most likely, my own work needed to mature. Even so, I felt it was necessary to change the variables.

One agent I had was truly horrible. At the time, she was with one of the mega-agencies—you know, one of the agencies that people who have nothing to do with writing or the arts recognize by name, so it was impressive to tell people, "Yeah, I'm represented by Big Honking Mega-Agency!" For the entire year that this agent repped me, she sent my novel to only one editor, which means that for ten months, she did absolutely nothing on my behalf since the editor who rejected the manuscript got back to her within the first two months. Regrettably, I didn't learn any of this until the first year with her was over. I had tried finding out what was going on—who was looking at the novel, who had rejected it—but she wouldn't take any of my calls, Afraid of angering the agent at Big Honking Mega-Agency, I didn't push. Her assistant assured me that my novel was circulating. At the end of the first year, I finally called the agent's home number, which she'd given to me during our one and only phone conversation, way back when she had agreed to take me on. *It's sometimes hard to catch me at the office,* she had told me, *so go ahead and call me at home if you need me.* And so I did.

"Hello?" I said, speaking in the form of tentative questions. "This is John McNally?" Silence. I wasn't sure what to say, so I added, "You represent me?"

"I know," she said coldly. The chill in her voice was such that I might as well have said, *I'm the one who murdered your entire family and was found innocent? Remember? You saw me every day at the trial?*

I said, "Oh, yes, well . . . I was just wondering if you've gotten any responses on my novel?"

She sighed and said, "It's still being circulated, but I don't have that information at home with me."

I waited for more, but nothing more was forthcoming. "Okay then?" I said. "Thanks? Good-bye?"

She hung up; I hung up but not before holding the receiver out to examine it. *What had just happened?*

Four days later, my manuscript appeared in my mailbox, along with a note from the agent: "I guess I'm not as excited by this as I thought I was," it read.

And that was that. She'd dumped me before I could dump her. It was a preemptive strike on her part. And a year of my life had been squandered.

A good agent will keep you in the loop about submissions and rejections. A good agent will take your calls, unless, of course, you begin calling every day just to shoot the breeze. A good agent will keep your work circulating.

Other times, agents' and authors' career paths simply diverge. At first, the two may be a good fit for each other, but as an agent's reputation for representing certain genres solidifies, the author may find himself now an anomaly on the agent's list. This doesn't mean that the agent doesn't know how to sell the author's book, but it does start to raise red flags. Is the agent missing opportunities by sending the manuscript to too many editors who aren't right for the novel? Does the agent's reputation as someone who specializes in a certain genre affect an editor's perception of the manuscript, and if so, is it to your advantage or not? The answers to these questions probably come in the form of a gut feeling rather than empirical evidence. The fear, of course, is that you dump an agent who's done well enough for you in favor of a new agent who can't sell your work, but if you're at the point where you already have some published books under your belt, you probably have a good idea which agents are, in fact, good fits for you and your work.

If you do leave your agent, make sure that you explicitly state that you are taking with you any unexploited sub-rights. For every book deal the agent made for you, there will be rights that the agent wasn't able to sell: foreign rights, film rights, audio rights, etc. If you are not explicit about taking those rights with you, the agent may feel that she can continue selling those rights since she's the one who made the initial book sale. What you don't want is a sticky situation in which your new agent and your old agent are both trying to sell the same rights to a book, unbeknownst to each other.

The decision to leave an agent is never an easy one, and breaking up with one you've been with for years isn't unlike breaking up with a long-term girlfriend or boyfriend. The language of the break-up may seem eerily familiar, too. *It's not you. You're a great agent. It's just not working out. I do hope we can still be friends. I treasure all that I've learned from you.* Etc., etc.

At least you get to keep the dog.

The Query Letter

A query letter is your introduction to an agent or an editor at a publishing house. If it's for an editor, it's most likely for an editor at a small or university press since large publishing houses don't accept unsolicited queries, but even some of these publishers (usually the more competitive and prestigious small presses) are difficult to reach without an agent.

Typically, if you're a fiction writer, you write query letters when you have a completed book that's ready to be shopped around. (Many nonfiction projects are sold on the basis of a proposal, in which case the purpose of your query letter is to ask an agent or editor if she's interested in reading your proposal.) More often than not, the query letter to the agent is for a novel. Most agents aren't interested in short story collections, unless the collection fits into one of these three categories:

1. The short stories are linked and can be marketed as a "novel-in-stories" or, simply, "fiction" (as was the case with Melissa Banks' *The Girls' Guide to Hunting and Fishing*).
2. You're a regular contributor to the *New Yorker* and have had your work reprinted in *Best American Short Stories*, which means you're what New York publishers are always looking for—The Next Hot Thing.
3. The collection has some irresistible hook, such as "short stories about Palestinian refugees," and you are a Palestinian whose parents were once refugees. Your short story collection then has a hook for the marketing department that makes the book more appealing than, say, a collection of stories featuring disparate guys who live in Utah, Florida, and Vermont. Your personal connection to the subject may lend itself more easily to media, such as radio and TV interviews. The political angle may get you booked on shows that don't normally interview fiction writers. Also, the book may have more of an international appeal, which means that it would be easier to sell foreign rights for such a book.

Most query letters are written in three parts: the introduction ("I'm writing with the hope that you would be interested in my novel, *Deep in the Woods of Summer*"); the pitch; and a mini-bio that highlights your writing and/or educational credits, or any credits that would be applicable to the book (e.g., a former astronaut writing a novel titled *The Last Good Man on the Moon*).

Parts one and three of the query letter are pretty straightforward, but how do you pitch your novel? Write the main body of the query letter so that it reads like a *condensed* version of your novel's jacket flap copy. ("Jacket flap copy" is the description of the novel that appears on the inside flap of a hardcover book.) Don't call yourself a genius or the novel you've written scintillating, as a jacket flap might, but *do* work on capturing the gist of the book, the character arcs, and the tone, all in a hundred or so words.

This is easier said than done. There's a unique skill required to write good jacket copy, and it's not necessarily the same skill that is required to be a good fiction writer. Nonetheless, read several dozen dust jackets to get a feel for how they're structured. The more you read, the better you'll be able to discern a pattern to them, or a formula, and the better your odds will become of being able to knock out a good one when you sit down to write your query letter.

One reason a well-written query letter using dust jacket copy language is appealing is because you're doing everyone's job for them. The agent can use your query to pitch the novel to editors; an editor who wants to make an offer on the novel can pitch it to the editorial board using your query; the folks in marketing, who may have a voice in whether the book gets published, can see exactly how the book should be pitched; and, finally, if the book gets picked up by a publisher, passages from your query letter can be pilfered for catalogs, for sales meetings, and for the book itself. It's not at all uncommon for my final jacket flap copy to have been pieced together from my initial query letter.

Bear in mind that good jacket copy is not merely a summary of the novel, which is often dull and lifeless. A bad summary reads as such: *This* happens, then *this* happens, then *this* happens, etc. Who cares? A bad summary could drain the blood right out of the best novel, which is precisely what you *don't* want to do.

I didn't have to write a query letter for my novel *The Book of Ralph* —I already had an agent—but if I did have to write one, here's what it might look like:

February 23, 2010

A. Gent
We Sell Books Agency
Emporium State Building, Top Floor
New York NY 10101

Dear Ms. A. Gent:

I'm writing with the hope that you would be interested in reading my novel, *The Book of Ralph*, for possible representation.

We all know Ralph. He was the kid who failed grade school not once but twice, the kid who was constantly, unwaveringly up to no good. He was the outsider you avoided at all costs. But who was he really? And whatever happened to him? *The Book of Ralph*, a comic novel about boys growing up together, is Ralph's story from the point-of-view of Hank—a good kid, a solid B+ student—who, against his better judgment, is drawn to Ralph and sucked into a world he otherwise would never have imagined existed. It's 1978 in Chicago. Hank wants eighth grade to be his big year to shine, but thanks to Ralph, Hank's special year spirals into an odyssey that is as frightening as it is hilarious when, among other things, Ralph becomes a thug-for-hire and starts stalking a fellow eighth-grader with plans to bite off his ear (rate: $15.00), or when Ralph shows solidarity with Hank's grandmother after she's hauled off for a series of shoe-store robberies, or when, on Halloween, Ralph's older cousin takes the boys, who are dressed as Gene Simmons from KISS and an Etruscan, on a car ride that proves to be a dark night of the soul for all involved. As the boys seek to survive eighth grade, a bad economy, and threadbare family lives, Hank and Ralph give us windows into the ties that bind us together, hold us back, and sometimes redeem us.

I'm the author of one previous book, a short story collection *Troublemakers*, which won the John Simmons Short Fiction Award and was published by the University of Iowa Press in 2000. My short stories have appeared in the *Sonora Review*, *Columbia*, *Open City*, and *Colorado Review*, among others. A native of Chicago's southwest side, where *The Book of Ralph* is set, I'm presently on faculty at Wake Forest University in Winston-Salem, North Carolina.

I admire your strong list of literary novels, especially *Origins* by K. B. Frederick and *The Last of the First Group* by Jaimy Robidoux, books that share a sensibility with what I'm trying to achieve in my own work. I'm hopeful that *The Book of Ralph* will appeal to you. I appreciate your time and look forward to hearing from you.

Sincerely,

John McNally

Unlike the cover letter, which is double-spaced, the query letter is single-spaced (it's only double-spaced *between* paragraphs) so as to fit more text onto the page. Note that the query letter is still only one page in length. If you can't keep the query to a page, you're going to run into trouble. Agents receive hundreds of query letters each week. If yours runs two pages long (or, God forbid, longer), you might as well have glued it to a boulder and rolled it in front of the agent's door. The trick here is to be thorough yet succinct—a contradiction, yes, but one you should perfect for your query letter.

Also pay attention to the fact that I've mentioned two other books represented by the agent. This shows that I've familiarized myself with the agent's clients, which, in turn, suggests that my book may be in the same league as the other books the agent has successfully represented. An agent will receive countless queries each week from writers who have no idea what the agent represents. They'll get queries for self-help books when they've never represented a self-help book; they'll get queries for science fiction novels when their list is made up primarily of literary writers (or vice-versa); they'll get queries for children's books when they've never repped a children's book author. By showing that you know what the agent represents and that your book may share similarities to those books, you're already way ahead of the game. But don't fake it. One would hope that you *are* familiar with the books you cite. Also, don't go for the obvious. If you approach John Grisham's agent, don't compare your work to John Grisham's. Can you imagine how many queries Grisham's agent gets each week from would-be novelists claiming to be the next John Grisham? The only thing you'd be showing is a lack of imagination, which is precisely *not* what you want to illuminate in your query letter.

More and more agents are accepting query letters via e-mail, but this fact shouldn't change the content of your query letter.

Rejection: Putting It in Perspective

On a blog titled The Outfit: A Collective of Chicago Crime Writers, Barbara D'Amato writes about persistence in the face of rejection, and she offers up several examples: English author John Creasy, who eventually published 564 books under various names, received 743 rejections before his first acceptance; Sara Paretsky garnered 37 rejections before her first novel sold; Hugh Holton wrote seven 700-page novels before he sold one, which happened to be the *fifth* of those seven. "Sure, these are people who went on to publish," D'Amato writes. "But suppose they'd given up at the first, or seventh rejection?"

Crime writer Sean Chercover, a contributor to The Outfit, added his own illuminating anecdote in the comments section:

> An agent responded to my query letter and asked for the first 100 pages of my [manuscript].
>
> A month later, she sent me a very polite e-mail, explaining, "the storyline and characters lacked suspense and intensity . . ." She concluded by suggesting that I read some books about how to write, and recommended a few titles.
>
> Flash forward to this year's Thrillerfest: The same agent and I are chatting, she looks down at my nametag and a lightbulb goes on over her head. "We corresponded some time ago," she says. "How's the writing coming along?"
>
> "Pretty good," I say, determined not to say "nah-nah-nah-nah-nah!"
>
> "It's a very tough business," she says, "so don't give up."
>
> "I signed a two-book deal with William Morrow and the first book just went into a second printing, so I won't give up," I say cheerfully, careful to keep any attitude out of my voice.
>
> Her face falls, then she puts a smile on it and hands me her card. "If you're ever looking to change agents . . ." she says.

Rejection is a writer's constant companion. If you want to write professionally, you'd better get used to rejection because it's part of the deal. And it's usually not personal. Only a handful of times have I received unnecessarily nasty rejections, but you have to realize that such unpleasantness is more often than not a reflection of the editor who wrote it and not a reflection of you or your work. It's *not* a good idea to respond to the editor. Your time is better spent working on a new story, novel, or poem.

I still get rejection slips. In fact, I got a standard rejection slip this past week from a magazine edited by someone I know professionally. (I'd like to think that a student on his staff plastered a rejection slip on the story before reading the cover letter, but who knows?)

I always explain to my students about the serendipity of the editing process, the whimsy of editors, and then I tell them about my experiences on the editor's side of the table, how I might be inclined to accept a story one day that I'd reject the next, or how when you read 120 book-length manuscripts for a contest, as I did for the Associated Writing Program's short fiction contest as one of their first readers, you may find five manuscripts that you think are publishable, but if you can pass on only two manuscripts to the final judge, you'll have to let another three really great ones go. One of the years that I was a first reader, my top pick was chosen by the final judge, but one of the top five that I *didn't* pass along ended up getting published by a commercial publisher and doing extraordinarily well. Why didn't I pick *that* book to move ahead? I could spot the author's talent a mile away. In the end, it wasn't my kind of book. This is the dichotomy of the decision-making process: The first part—the winnowing out of manuscripts that clearly weren't publishable or, if publishable, weren't in the same league with the final five—seemed fairly objective; the final decision—picking two of those five to send on to the final judge—was clearly subjective.

My theory of the objective/subjective dichotomy in the decision-making process was reinforced recently when I pulled from my bookshelf a copy of the late John Gardner's magazine *MSS*, the issue (Winter/Spring 1984) that included Gardner's final editorial choices (he died an untimely death in 1982). In their introduction to this issue, the editors of *MSS* write the following:

> We're proud and very pleased to include two stories by Charles Baxter, the winner of the 1983 [Associated Writing Programs] Award for Short Fiction, as well as work by a finalist in the AWP Short Fiction contest, M. L. Moore, and by Barbara Schoichet, whose fiction came to the notice of L. M. Rosenberg while she was a preliminary judge in the contest.

Curious as to who the finalists were, I turned to the contributors' notes:

> M. L. (Lorrie) Moore is a lecturer at Cornell University. Her reviews and short stories have appeared in *Story Quarterly*, *fiction international*, and elsewhere. A collection of her short fiction is forthcoming from Knopf.

Lorrie Moore! And when I turned to her story, I immediately recognized Moore's signature voice in the very first sentence: "There is no dignity in appetites." So: Lorrie loses the AWP contest, with what I'm presuming was *Self-Help* (or an earlier incarnation), but she lands a deal with Knopf and changes her pen name from M. L. to (wisely) Lorrie. Were the judges stupid for not picking Lorrie's collection? Of course not. Obviously, one of the preliminary readers was keen-eyed enough to search her out and ask for work for her magazine. Did all work out to Lorrie's advantage? I would say so. Hell yeah, in fact. *Self-Help* is still in print, and Lorrie is a staple on the literary scene. What's lost on the one hand is gained on the other.

Any number of factors, including the stability of the nation's economy, may play a role in fate of the submission of your manuscript. In the fall of 2008, my agent began sending to editors my most recent novel, *After the Workshop*. The first responses from editors were positive—at least three editors expressed interest in buying it—but each time the manuscript made it to the editorial director, it got rejected. What we didn't know at the time—what no one, not even my agent, knew—was that the publishing industry, much like the rest of the country, was starting to feel the first rumblings of the economic meltdown. During the last few months of 2008, following news that the country was officially in a recession, the New York publishing industry began to implode. Dozens of editors were fired, in many cases *veteran* editors; publishers began rolling some of their imprints together, which meant fewer acquisitions and significant changes in *what* would be acquired; one major house actually suspended acquisitions altogether for a short while. Day after day, the news was grim and getting grimmer.

In January of 2009, my agent put together a second round of submissions for the novel, even as more news of firings came trickling in. More rejections for the novel also came in, and almost all of them were the same: *We really like the novel, but we're having to make tough choices, and we're not sure how to market this one.* One smaller publisher actually wrote that I didn't have enough credentials, even though I had already published four books of my own (two with commercial houses) and edited six anthologies.

Normally, I might have fallen into a dark depression, but instead I became angry. This was the first time that I was truly happy with a book I'd written, and it was looking, more and more, as though it wasn't going to find a home. More than once, I thought, *Okay, this is it, my career as a fiction writer is over.* I began sending out query letters on my own, mostly to small and university presses, with the hope that someone somewhere would be interested in publishing the new novel. One of the first replies to my queries came from the editor of a university press with a strong fiction list, who wrote the following:

> Hello, John McNally—
> I've had a conversation with our Press's director about your query, and we came to the same conclusion: neither of us is excited about the idea of a novel with the subject matter you describe below. Since we're so small an enterprise, we need to be enthusiastic about our projects; we live with them for many years and promote them to our sales reps and market them to the larger audience of general readers. We have consistently stayed away from projects involving academe and/or the publishing industry. This is purely a subjective choice. We are not impugning the quality of your novel: it's just that the subject matter to us is a turn off. We both wish you the best as you continue to search for a publishing home for *After the Workshop.*
> Best regards,
> [Name of Editor Deleted]

The very next day, my agent wrote to inform me that an offer was forthcoming from Counterpoint, a publisher whose list I've long admired and whose books are among the best-looking of any publishing house.

A few points. I know many writers whose books have been rejected for *years* before publishers (often very good publishers; sometimes publishers who had previously rejected the manuscript) finally accepted them. Rejection is sometimes a blessing. In my case, Counterpoint is an infinitely better publisher than the one that rejected the novel based on my query. Rejection often doesn't mean much of anything, so there's no point in analyzing it at great length.

(Consistent rejection early on in one's career may suggest that the author needs to improve. I shudder at the thought of my early work, yet I sent it out because it was the best work I was doing at the time.) At a certain point in your professional career, you need to find editors who *get* your work, which, of course, is easier said than done.

There are blogs dedicated to rejections, but if you ask me, wallowing in one's rejections—whining about them or conjuring up conspiracy theories to explain them—eventually becomes a self-fulfilling prophecy. If you're spending all your time chiming in on blogs dedicated to rejection, spouting off about how the system is rigged, what happens to your *raison d'être* when you finally do get an acceptance? Is the system still rigged?

What, then, should you do in the face of rejection? For starters, you need to keep focused on your work. And keep the work circulating. Years ago, fiction writer Richard Bausch said this to me at a writers' conference after I had expressed disappointment to him that I had written two novels and a story collection but couldn't get any of them published: "You need to honor the book by getting it into the hands of every editor you can before giving up on it. You owe the book that much." Five months later, my first book was accepted.

Conferences and Book Festivals

Anywhere where a publisher sets up a booth is a place for you to potentially land a book deal. I'm not suggesting that it's an easy thing to do, but it does occasionally happen at conferences like the Associated Writing Programs and the Modern Language Association or at some book fairs, like the Miami Book Fair International or the Los Angeles Times Festival of Books.

At the Associated Writing Programs conference, for instance, hundreds of publishers set up tables and booths displaying their products. Many of these tables and booths are reserved by magazines, but a good number of them are for book publishers. You won't find many commercial publishers here—although Norton tends to be there—but you will find dozens of smaller presses, like Unbridled Books, featherproof, and Coffee House Press, as well as dozens of university presses, like Wayne State University Press, the University of Chicago Press, and the University of Nevada Press.

Most editors I know don't want to lug home heavy book-length manuscripts, but they do want to meet prospective authors with the hope of finding book projects that are good fits for their list. Even if you leave the conference without a book contract or an invitation to submit your manuscript, you should at the very least walk away with a better sense of what each publisher wants.

One year, I talked to a few editors at publishing houses that specialize in textbooks. I didn't have a proposal with me; I just wanted to get a sense of what their criteria were for taking on an author who had a textbook idea. The idea I had was for a textbook on a genre that was not my primary specialization, so even though I'd had success as a writer within the genre, I didn't bring any teaching experience in the genre to the table. The editor's advice was for me to teach some courses at my university and, if possible, at some conference so as to establish myself as an expert in the area. That conversation took place three years ago, and I took it to heart. I have since taught the subject several times, in both venues that she suggested, and while I haven't yet put together the proposal for the textbook, I at least now have the credibility should I choose to pursue the book project.

It's taken me years to feel confident enough to approach an editor, face-to-face, about a book project, but what I've learned is that most want to hear what you're working on, and as for those who aren't interested, there's always another booth, another editor.

Your Critics, and How to Deal with Them

So, now you're a published author! Your first book comes out, and you couldn't be happier—that is, until people begin burning your book and throwing rocks at you. Or so it will feel. How do you combat so much ill-will? *Should* you combat it?

Your Mainstream Press Critics

While it's frustrating to receive a negative book review, you should probably be thankful that the book was reviewed at all, especially given today's climate, where so many newspaper book review sections are being reduced or eliminated altogether.

What should you do when you receive a negative review? Probably nothing. It's poor taste to write the reviewer. (A writer friend of mine told me about an author who wrote a passive-aggressive e-mail to him after my friend had written a mixed review of the author's book. What the writer accomplished was short-term satisfaction. The long-term result, however, is that my friend has told other writers about this exchange, which makes the author who'd written the e-mail look petty, especially since the review wasn't, by any definition, all that bad.) It's also unwise to write a letter to the editor of the newspaper complaining about the review of your book. If the letter is published, you'll look like a whiner. In any case, your letter may cause the editor to reconsider assigning your next book to be reviewed, which might have received a positive assessment. No, it's better to swallow it and move ahead.

Bear in mind that the relationship between a reader of reviews and the reviewer is sometimes complicated. A negative review of someone else's book doesn't necessarily convince me not to buy the book. Oftentimes, I'm familiar with the reviewer's other reviews and the times I've disagreed with him or her, so I tend to put reviews into a larger context. Other times, I'm familiar with the reviewer's own books, and my opinion of those books may persuade me one way or the other to purchase the book that's been reviewed.

Remember the old maxim: Any press is good press. A bad review in the *New York Times Book Review* will still sell more copies of a book than no review in the *New York Times Book Review*.

Your Amazon Critics

I happen to believe that negative Amazon reviews (or any on-line bookstore that posts reviews)—reviews written by anyone who feels compelled to take the time to write one, whether they've actually read the book or not—have more of a detrimental effect on sales than a poor newspaper review. Why do I believe this? Because online stores such as Amazon thrive on the serendipitous nature of shopping. In other words, we are constantly being tempted by other, possibly more interesting books while we're looking for a specific title, and if, after clicking on the title we've been searching for, we find a gathering of one-star reviews, our eyes are likely to wander to all of the other books being offered in the "Customers Who've Bought This Book Have Also Bought This Book" section. Think about it. If we go into an actual bricks-and-mortar store and find the book we're looking for, there won't be eight people standing there holding up signs with proclamations like, "Skip this one!" or "This one sucks!"

But who are these people writing reviews on Amazon? What are their qualifications? A person who gave one of my books a one-star review gave a three-star review to an electric steam cleaner on the same day. To date, these are this person's only reviews on Amazon. What compelled this person on a mid-December morning to write these two reviews? This person's review of my book was, "This is a book of dark and twisted stories. I couldn't even finish it." I suspect, though I could be wrong, that this reviewer doesn't read much contemporary literary fiction. The review of the steam cleaner read, "Works good but, wish it held more water so I could clean larger areas without having to refill so often," which only strengthens my opinion that this is a person who buys things without much investigation and then blames the maker for its perceived shortcomings.

My point is that your book is at the mercy of anyone with a computer. After the person above logged on the one-star review of my book, I sent out e-mails via my mailing list, asking anyone who read the book to consider writing a review on Amazon. I didn't ask them to refrain from writing a negative review, but since these were people who had willingly signed up on my website, I was sending a mass e-mail to a targeted audience of people already disposed to liking the book.

Some writers write reviews of their own book on Amazon, and some writers will respond to the negative reviews. Again, I would be inclined to avoid doing either of these things, if only because it shifts the spotlight onto the writer in a potentially unflattering way. These tactics also open you as a potential target for bloggers, which leads me to my next topic.

Your Blog Critics

Not to worry—they're out there, waiting for your book to appear so that they can take it down. One of my favorite blog reviews was for one of my short story anthologies (a collection of short stories featuring original superheroes) in which the blogger began the review by stating how much she hates short stories and how her creative writing teacher, by imposing what sounded to me like standards, didn't endear her to so-called literary fiction. Then came the review of my anthology. To no one's surprise, she hated it. It was boring, of course. The endings were all downers. Etc., etc. And then came the people commenting on her review. They appeared like villagers at the end of a horror movie, all carrying torches and sniffing for blood. One by one, they wrote comments to the effect of "The book sounds awful" or "I haven't read the book, but I'm tired of these literary types looking down their noses at comics." One poor visitor to the website challenged the blogger, wondering why she had bothered reviewing an anthology full of short stories when she didn't even like short stories, but after a few exchanges, the commenter was informed by the host that he or she was going to be banned from leaving any more remarks. The host of the site was then cheered for the banishment by her clan of angry villagers. I was sorry I had stumbled upon this sad exchange, and if I could have sent the banished visitor a cake, I would have. (Remember: A blog is actually a small dictatorship.)

What does all of this say to me? Well, for starters, you should hope for the best but anticipate the worst. If possible, avoid reading blog entries about your book. But most of all, never, ever try to combat the negative blogger. Once you've done that, the game's over. I've witnessed too many occasions where a writer who's been viciously attacked decides to weigh in and make her case, especially when the critique seems particularly unfair—e.g., people making spurious assumptions about the writer, claiming that he's been published only because of connections or his MFA, or some other nonsense. What ensues is almost always ugly. The commenters gang up on the writer; the charges against the writer become more ludicrous; other bloggers pick up on the story and begin linking it to their blog. Before long, the attack becomes viral, and the writer has no choice, really, except to retreat. Worst of all, the attack is now part of the permanent record for anyone to Google.

To engage with the negative reviewer is to expend energy best spent elsewhere. The best strategy, as difficult as it may be, is to ignore those negative reviews and keep writing.

The Sales Figure Myth

A pet peeve of mine is the publishing industry's obsession with sales figures. Time and again, I hear stories about how a publishing house won't take on a book that an acquisitions editor likes because the author's previous book sales weren't up to snuff. Or, you'll read about an author who was dumped by her publishing house because of previous sales figures. Why are past sales figures important? Bookstore chains base orders for a new novel primarily on the author's previous sales figures. Let's say Author X sold 5,000 copies of her first novel but then sold only 2,000 copies of her second novel. The chain bookstores look at those numbers and decide that even fewer copies of the third novel are likely to sell, so the chain orders fewer copies than they'd ordered for the author's previous books, resulting in the publishing house doing a smaller print-run, which, in turn, pretty much guarantees even lower sales while possibly killing poor Author X's career in the process.

So, what's wrong with this scenario? Bookselling is a business, after all, right? And doesn't an author's track-record accurately suggest an author's trajectory?

It's a logical fallacy to assume that the author is the problem with sales while ignoring all of the other potential factors: publicity budgets; subject matter of book; size of publisher; even world events. I know a few writers who had novels released on September 11, 2001. What do you think their sales figures looked like?

I can name dozens of authors whose past sales did *not* reflect future sales. John Irving's first three novels sold miserably. In fact, his second and third novels sold fewer copies than his first. By today's standards, it's likely that Irving's career would have been over before he'd had a chance to publish his fourth book. What happened, however, was that Irving moved from Random House to Dutton for his fourth novel, *The World According to Garp*. *Garp* became not only a publishing phenomenon but the book that cemented John Irving's reputation as one of today's best-known writers.

More recently, Lee Smith published with a commercial house for many years. Some of her books, most notably *Oral History*, sold well; others sold modestly. When her long-time editor died, Smith was dropped from the publishing house. I can't say for sure, but I suspect that her more recent novels, which were not bestsellers, hadn't sold up to the publisher's expectations. After getting dumped by the big New York house, Smith sold her next novel, *The Last Girls*, to the much smaller publishing house Algonquin Books. *The Last Girls* became a *New York Times* bestseller that posted the sort of sales figures that I'm sure had her previous publisher gnashing their teeth with regret.

And then there's Kent Haruf. His first two novels sold modestly at best. Nine years passed between his second novel and his third, enough time for most publishers to officially declare an author dead. But Knopf took on his third novel, *Plainsong*, and launched a massive campaign for the book. I still remember booksellers at my local independent bookstore reading advance review copies of his book and talking about it long before it came out. The ARCs were as pretty as a new paperback, and from what I heard, the print-run for the ARCs alone would have made most authors drool. In other words, Knopf ignored Haruf's previous book sales, determined to make something of a book that they believed in — and it worked. *Plainsong* was one of those novels that everyone spent the year talking about. Kent Haruf was fifty-six years old when the book was published. His dormant career was miraculously revived.

And what about Cormac McCarthy? His career didn't really take off until the publication of his sixth novel, *All the Pretty Horses*.

More recently, there's the story of Joe Meno. Meno published his first two novels with commercial houses and posted terrible sales figures. No one wanted his third novel. Thinking his career in the world of commercial publishing was dead, Meno decided to publish his book with Punk Planet Books, a brand-new, untested imprint of the small publisher Akashic. The novel was *Hairstyles of the Damned*, and it went on to sell a staggering 100,000 copies.

It's absolutely ludicrous for anyone — bookstores, publishers — to predict future sales by looking at past sales. Each book should be bought on the basis of that individual book and marketed appropriately. I certainly wouldn't expect a short story collection of mine to garner the sort of advance I might get for a novel, and I wouldn't anticipate the sales for a collection of short stories to trump the sales for my novels. In the current sales-figure-obsessed environment, however, an author who publishes a collection of short stories after publishing several novels is seen as someone hell-bent on career suicide. A better strategy would be for the publisher to treat the book for what it is: another step in an author's (hopefully) long career. And who knows? In addition to enriching the culture, the short story collection might turn out to be another *Birds of America* (Lorrie Moore), *Emperor of the Air* (Ethan Canin), or *Interpreter of Maladies* (Jhumpa Lahiri)—all national bestsellers. A long shot, to be sure, but not necessarily an impossibility.

Until this obsession with sales figures ends, you have two choices: Be cognizant of the reality of sales figures, work hard to promote your book, and avoid disastrous decisions about what to write next, or accept that most of what happens is out of your hands, and write the book that you want to write. As for myself, I do both. I write the book I want to write, and then I worry about how to sell the most copies.

The Necessity of Failure

My teacher Frank Conroy used to say, "The good writing is connected to the bad writing." This was his mantra. And what he said was true. You have to write bad short stories and poems—sometimes dozens of them—before you start writing good short stories and poems, and even after you start writing good ones, you'll still occasionally, maybe even often, write some bad ones.

The same is true of novels. You'll write novels that won't work. This is inevitable. I'm sure there are those writers out there who have found publishers for their first novels, but they are the exception. Richard Russo wrote at least one unpublished novel before his "first" novel *Mohawk*. In an essay about his mentor John Gardner, Charles Johnson (whose novel *Middle Passage* won the National Book Award) writes, "Included in my baggage were six novels I'd written in the two years before I met Gardner, all heavily influenced by the Black Arts movement and authors I then admired (Richard Wright, James Baldwin, John A. Williams)." Even Truman Capote, who was a prodigy, wrote a novel titled *Summer Crossing* in 1943 when he was nineteen; the book wasn't published until 2005, many years after his death. Similarly, John Kennedy Toole's first novel wasn't *A Confederacy of Dunces*, which was posthumously published and awarded the Pulitzer Prize. His first was *The Neon Bible*, written when he was sixteen. *The Neon Bible* was published many years later and then made into a movie.

Those first books were *necessary* failures. I doubt John Kennedy Toole could have written the hilarious and brilliant *A Confederacy of Dunces* had he not written *The Neon Bible*. One's first book is intrinsically linked to the next book. I'm reminded of that grainy film footage of the first would-be aviators trying to fly their first airplanes. Some tipped over upon starting; some rose and then fell; some moved forward but never got off the ground. Writing a publishable first novel is like building that first airplane. In order to learn from your mistakes, you *have* to tip over, crash, and stay grounded when what you want to be is airborne.

But there's another reason why failure is essential. It toughens you. It builds character. The few writers I've known who have struck gold the first time out, publishing what was truly their first novels, haven't dealt well with subsequent rejections or bad reviews. The psychology here is fairly obvious. When success comes too fast and at too young of an age, you start believing that *everything* you touch will turn to gold. In a worst-case scenario, you start believing you're a genius, and that those editors who don't make offers to buy your next book or reviewers who criticize it are too dumb to recognize your brilliance.

As you can imagine, this isn't a pretty sight. In any profession, I'll always favor the person who's failed before achieving success over the person who's never known failure for the simple reason that I don't want to be around when the person who hasn't yet failed *does* fail—and sooner or later, they will fail. The laws of gravity apply to success as well. What goes up must come down.

Thinking outside Your Genre

I'm a fiction writer first and foremost, but I've also edited six anthologies, written screenplays, contributed to the book review sections of newspapers (back when such things existed), done the occasional nonfiction piece when I've been asked to write one, interviewed fellow writers for magazines, and written the quasi-self-help book you're reading right now.

Some fiction writers write only fiction and nothing else. I admire that. But maybe you're the sort of person who gets antsy working on just one project. Or maybe you're looking for ways to make a few extra dollars. Diversify, I say. The reasons why I've taken on so many disparate projects are as varied as the projects themselves. Sometimes I'll take on a project as a favor to a friend. Other times, I do it for the money. Some projects I do to beef up my credentials. There was a time, before I had a tenure-track teaching position, when I wouldn't say no to a project, because every publication was another line on my c.v., another step in the direction of landing that elusive university gig — or so I thought. (In truth, a published book trumps all the other smaller publications.)

I've always been a fan of Franz Kafka, and as someone who is frequently concocting (sometimes ridiculous) ideas for new nonfiction books simply to make a quick buck, I was absolutely thrilled to read in Max Brod's biography of Kafka that he did the same thing. As you'll see from this passage, Kafka and Brod (Kafka's longtime friend) were actually way ahead of their time:

> We hit upon the idea of creating a new type of guidebook. The series was to be called 'On the Cheap.' There were to be titles like 'On the Cheap through Switzerland,' 'On the Cheap in Paris,' etc. Franz was untiring and took a childish pleasure in compiling, down to the finest details, the principals of this type that was to make millionaires of us and above all take us out of the hideous routine of our office work.

Sounds like the bestselling "Let's Go!" series, doesn't it? Kafka wasn't just a visionary in the world of surrealist fiction; he was a visionary in the world of travel guides as well. As with most of his fiction, it's too bad he didn't see the project through to completion.

If you're lucky, you may find financial security and, possibly, a life of leisure thanks to another genre. Novelist Richard Russo's screenwriting allowed him to quit teaching and focus on his fiction writing. Novelist James McManus's interest in poker led him to writing the nonfiction book *Positively Fifth Street*, which became a monster of a bestseller. Poet Donald Hall made a pretty good living writing textbooks. Prolific writer Ray González, who publishes in many genres, sums it up best with this advice:

> A young writer needs to find ways to acknowledge what he or she does best. Becoming a better writer doesn't simply involve revising weak points of craft. It also has to do with gaining confidence by identifying the strong points and the best aspects of the writing. These days, with the vast literary experiment of erasing genre boundaries in contemporary writing, it is essential for young writers to try to write in different forms. This includes poetry, fiction, and non-fiction. Practicing and working in each one helps the writer identify which genre will be the one to specialize in. Chances are the writer will be successful with more than one form. Of course, it takes practice and commitment. Learn to work on more than one project at a time. Mix things up and the best work will emerge through exploration, patience, and self-granted permission to write well.

It's entirely possible that you'll move away from the genre you're currently working in to focus on another genre altogether, as happened to John Sayles when his screenwriting career usurped his fiction-writing career, or Jerry Stahl, who moved away from the short story form to write for TV. Worse things have been known to happen.

The Future of Publishing

What is the future of publishing? This is the million-dollar question, isn't it? Independent bookstore owners, CEOs of chain bookstores, and publishing houses all want to know. I hate writing about technological advances because, by the time this book is published, some devices will already be outmoded and this book will seem like something found in a time capsule: "Ah, well, so *this* is what the world looked like in December 2010!"

I love books. I collect books. I love the artwork on the dust-jacket; the typography; the quality of the paper. I like a book's flaws. I like when other people before me have signed their books or stuck fancy nameplates in them. I like finding cryptic notes in the pages of used books. I like the personal memories attached to buying certain books. I like to have them all out, in front of me, in all of my rooms, one library after the other, so that I can read their spines. I like the publisher's various colophons, like the Random House house or Knopf's borzoi. I like the smell of old books. I like getting my books signed by writers, and I like when readers ask me to sign their books.

What I fear is that the rise of the electronic book (or any technology that does away with the traditional book) will mean the death of the bookstore. (We've already witnessed bookstore giants crush independent bookstores. Has the time come for *all* bookstores to be snuffed out?) Once bookstores are gone, the average reader's options will suffer. Now, I know that those who champion e-readers will say, "Oh, but, no. Now, *anyone* can have their book published! It costs nothing, and you can set up an account, and you'll make more than you would with a traditional publisher!" But here's what's missing from an e-book world. When people write to me to tell me that they read and liked my book, do you know what most of them say? They say, "I picked up your book because the cover intrigued me." In other words, they *didn't* go into the bookstore looking for my book; they went there for some other reason, saw my book, and bought it. Browsing in the company of other browsers is fast becoming a lost pastime.

Who will benefit from e-books? All those writers whose names you already know—John Grisham, Stephen King, Danielle Steele.

And who will lose? All those writers who *aren't* John Grisham, Stephen King, or Danielle Steele, because how will anyone find those books? Oh, and you dear reader—you'll lose, too. You'll lose because there will be thousands of writers whose work you'll never know about. Those writers will be the lost souls in the digital wasteland of e-Purgatory.

If you think this won't happen, consider the music industry. In an interview with *Rolling Stone* in 2009, Tom Petty discusses the difficulty of finding good music: "I don't think it's ever a case of there's nothing good. It's just getting harder and harder to find it. It used to be that to make an album, you had to do something pretty well. To get to make a 12-inch record—that was an honor. Now everybody does it. You go to a restaurant, and the guy playing in the corner has an album."

Once a market gets saturated, the consumer becomes wary of the product. An editorial director of a major publishing house told me that this is precisely what happens with all publishing trends, whether it's chick lit or African American lit. Once a genre becomes popular, all the publishers jump into the mix and start publishing that genre regardless of quality, and since all the cover art within a genre looks more or less the same, consumers will pick up anything that *looks* like the book they loved—that is, until they realize that the quality is much worse, at which point they abandon the genre altogether. "Eventually," the editor said, "we kill the genre by saturating the market with books that *aren't* good." My fear is that technology—the ability for anyone to publish anything they've written and package it as though it's a professionally published book—will have the same effect on literature.

Finally, there's the fleeting technology itself—the upgraded machines, the incompatibilities. Anyone who bought a Betamax in the 1970s can tell you his own personal horror story. And if you've ever lost music on iTunes, you know just how unreliable technology is. No, I want a *book*, no matter how bulky it is. Will anyone ever say, "I just want to curl up on the couch with my e-reader?" I hope not.

The future of the book—the actual book—is in your hands, folks. If you want to get published one day, you should be buying them. More importantly, you should be supporting new writers, writers whose first books have just come out. You should buy new hardbacks, if you can afford them. You should take chances on books by authors you don't know. You should be supporting small presses, too. And independent bookstores. The more you support them, the more likely it is that you'll be saving the very thing you love, because—let's face it— once the book dies, so will your dreams of publishing one.

You're a writer, not a publicist, so have fun with it. Whatever publicity you do should be a creative act of some kind—not just a series of e-mails, press releases or blog posts. Make it another project for your imagination, so you can dive in and not feel dirty when you come back up for air.
— Jonathan Messinger, author of *Hiding Out* and publisher of featherproof books

Publicity

4

Websites

I'm not so sure that you need a website before you publish a book, although plenty of writers without books have them, but as soon as your first book has been accepted for publication, you should definitely start putting one together. There are templates and do-it-yourself websites that don't cost anything, but I recommend having a professional design your website for you. It doesn't have to include moving graphics or an interactive message board (check out T. C. Boyle's or Joe Hill's for websites with all the bells and whistles), but it should *look* good, and it should offer the person who arrives there something he can't get elsewhere.

My website—www.bookofralph.com—was designed by one of my former students, and I'm always getting complimented for how it looks, which, of course, I had nothing to do with. What I wanted, more than anything, was for the website to have my individual stamp on it so that it couldn't be interchangeable with any other author's website, so in addition to the various categories (which I'll discuss in a moment), I tried to punch up most of the pages with mini-introductions before providing the content, with the hope that those introductions would give the reader a sense of my voice. I also included old photos of myself, various relatives, my wife, and (some of) my animals, but I didn't want to turn the website into an ad hoc family album, so I included captions for most of them or chose photos that (I hope) appropriately suited the content of a given page.

Here's a page-by-page look at my website:

1. Home Page: Here, you'll find a photo of me, a photo of my latest book, and a newspaper blurb about me. It's pretty straightforward, but I should note that I try to keep it up-to-date, posting the cover of the new book several months before the book is released. There's nothing grimmer than finding an author website that hasn't been updated after a new book has come out. It's as if the author had said, "Oh, to hell with it."

2. Books (Fiction): This page shows a thumbnail photo of each book, along with a few blurbs for each. Click on the photo of

the most recent book, and you'll end up at an online book-store's page for that particular title.

3. Books (Other): Since I also edit anthologies, I wanted a page that separated my fiction titles from my other titles (antholo-gies, nonfiction, etc.). At book signings, I often find myself explaining what an anthology is—some people have bought one thinking that it's another collection of my writing—so I thought it was important to make the distinction with this page. Again, you'll find covers of each book, blurbs for each book, and links to an online bookstore when you click on the books' covers.

4. Book Tour: I have an option on some of the pages to plug in information myself without having to pay the webmaster to update it, and this page is one of them. As soon as I know that I'll be reading or doing a book signing at a bookstore, library, university, or conference, I add it to the book tour page, along with as much information as a person might need: the time; what I'll be doing there (since I don't always do readings); address; contact information; and a link to the venue. Obviously, there are long stretches when I'm not doing much of anything, but I try not to leave this page en-tirely blank. Even if an event is ten months away, I'll post it.

5. Buzz: Here is where I add any positive press for my books. I'll offer up a few sentences or a short paragraph excised from a review, along with the name of the paper or magazine re-viewing it and the date of the review. I used to include links to the articles, but since I have been leaving these excerpts up in perpetuity, many of the links have ceased to exist, and it's become a pain to go through and edit them—therefore, no more links.

6. What's New? This page has evolved and devolved since my website went live in 2004. When I first started updating this page, I would add anything that I thought was interesting, including lists of favorite movies, underappreciated albums, and ruminations on, well, just about any damned thing that entered my mind. What I was doing, of course, was blog-ging, so when I had my website updated, I added a link to an outside blog that I maintained for the next book. But once I finally had a blog of my own, I started realizing all the pit-falls of blogging, one of which was that it's time-consuming,

so I quit writing that particular blog. The next time I had my website updated, I had the "blog" button deleted. I probably don't update the "What's New?" page as often as I should, but I'm trying to keep the content limited to *what's new with my book projects*, as opposed to *what's new in the world today and here are my thoughts on it*.

7. Mailing List: This page is where people who want to be updated on my every move can sign up for periodical e-mails. I tend to think that if you overwhelm someone with e-mails, they eventually quit reading them, so I limit my e-mails only to the announcement of important occasions: the release of a new book and the book tour. Since I have access to the names of the people who've signed up, I know for a fact that a few editors who've reviewed my books in the past are on it so that they can be notified of upcoming releases as well as my appearance in town to do readings.

8. Writing Advice: After the first version of my website went live, I was inundated with questions about publishing, so when it was time to do a major overhaul of my website, I decided to add a page where I try to answer some of the most basic questions I'm asked. Ironically, this page has gotten more attention than I had intended. While I get a lot of e-mails thanking me for "good, straightforward advice," I also received the offer to write this book—the book you're holding—based on my "Writing Advice" page. This page has given the website my fingerprint, separating it from other author websites that simply provide basic author information to the visitor. Check out crime novelist Marcus Sakey's website for another example of one loaded down with good writing advice.

9. Contact Info: This page is a mixed blessing. On the one hand, I receive many e-mails from people who've read and liked my books and want to tell me so, and that's terrific. What more, as a writer, could I ask for? I've also been contacted, via this page, to give readings, contribute to magazines, and judge contests. Some of the offers come with dollar figures; other offers are freebies. I've turned down some paying offers and taken the freebies, and vice-versa. The downside to this page is that it also attracts the people who want me to read their manuscripts for free, who want me to recommend them to

my agent, who (sometimes) want me to be their friend. It's also where people from my past find me, which is sometimes good but sometimes not so good—not that I have some dark, mysterious past or anything like that. At some point, I may eliminate my contact info, but at this point in my career, the benefits still outweigh the disadvantages.

10. Press Kit: On this page, I provide an author photo and book cover for downloading, as well as a recent, extended bio for pilfering. I don't keep this page as up to date as I probably should, and there may come a point where I'll eighty-six it, since I'm not convinced that many people use it, anyway. They do use the bio—I know because one of my misspellings has been widely disseminated—but I would simply move this to another page or create a page that's for biographical information only.

It's good if you can figure out how to bring readers back to your site. Do you offer useful tips about writing? Do you have a good collection of useful links? If you want readers to bookmark your page and return to it, I don't think it's enough for the website to say, "Hey, here I am, here's my bio, and here are my books!" You need to lure them back somehow. You need to put candy down along the trail so that they keep returning to nibble on it.

A function I would strongly suggest adding to your website is a way to track visitors. I use Statcounter (www.statcounter.com), which has been invaluable for showing how many hits I receive in a single day, how the visitor ended up on my site, where they're from geographically, which pages they've visited, and how long they stayed on each page. When Mitch Albom generously mentioned *The Book of Ralph* on the *Today* show, Statcounter started showing hundreds of hits happening all at once. Since I didn't know that Albom was going to mention the book, and since I don't watch the *Today* show, this was my first indication that something extraordinary had just happened.

Statcounter becomes useful for gauging the effectiveness of certain media. Whenever I've appeared on NPR, the website gets dozens of hits, but when I do other radio shows, including some very popular ones, the results are mixed. In some cases, the media appearance resulted in no extra hits whatsoever, which is useful information to know.

You can also identify where your fan base is. Mine, not surprisingly, is in Chicago. I'm from Chicago; I write about Chicago; I do a lot of events in Chicago. It's no surprise that the vast majority of my hits are from Chicago and its surrounding suburbs.

Your website is a great information tool for your readers, but when you add a device that allows you to look at the statistics attached to your website, it becomes an invaluable well of information for you to evaluate and, if possible, act upon.

Building a Mailing List

A list of e-mail and home addresses should be composed of people who are predisposed to buying your book—family, friends, colleagues, and, if you have already published a book, fans of your work.

In addition to being a great tool for jumpstarting sales when you have a new book released, these lists are invaluable for notifying people about your readings and book signings via e-mail blasts and/or postcards, hopefully insuring that *someone* will be at the event. (After a book-signing event, you want the bookstore manager to feel as though the event had been worth the time and energy. Such events are always more time-consuming—and disruptive to the usual flow of foot traffic—than most authors realize.)

Here are three good ways to build a mailing list.

1. Include on your website a mailing list option for anyone who wants to add their name, home address, and e-mail for periodic updates.
2. When someone writes a fan e-mail to you, save the e-mail. It's not a bad idea, either, to make a notation regarding why this person contacted you. (Not everyone who contacts you is a fan, and you don't necessarily want to tell them about a new book or where you're going to be promoting it.)
3. When you give a reading, provide a sign-up sheet for those people who want to receive e-mails about you and your books.

When constructing your e-mail list, be careful whom you include on it. As I learned recently, some people will look for a reason to be offended when there is absolutely nothing to be offended by. An innocuous mass e-mail that I sent announcing the release of my new book prompted two angry replies—one from an author, who must have e-mailed me in the past few years in order for me to have had his e-mail address in the first place, who thought I was trying to get him to review the book (I didn't know he reviewed books) and one from a bookseller who thought I was simultaneously urging people to buy the book online while insulting independent bookstores. This last e-mail, from someone who had supported my work in the past, ranks up there as perhaps the most bizarre misreading of one of my e-mails I've ever encountered, especially since my e-mail announcement specifically stated, "Support your local bookstore!" The bookseller informed me, however, that my plea was disingenuous.

Therefore, my advice for mass e-mails is to stick to friends, family members, and people who have identified themselves as fans of your work. Venturing beyond those groups may prove to be an unnecessary headache.

Social Networking—Or:
Where Did Those Last Five Hours Go?

Social networking is a slippery slope. It's easy to spend hours building up thousands of "friends" on social networking websites with little, if any, reward at the end of it. Oftentimes, these sites are full of authors adding other authors, or self-published authors adding authors published by commercial houses, or unpublished authors looking for someone to read their work. Are any of these people buying each other's books? My suspicion is that they aren't.

So, are these sites worthless for marketing? No. But you have to figure out how best to target your market. Once upon a time, during MySpace's five-minute heyday, I had my own MySpace page for which I spent countless hours accumulating friends. Since my fiction is very place-specific, and since a healthy percentage of my readers are from where I grew up, I added people who either went to my high school or grew up in neighboring towns. Since they tended to have fewer friends than a fellow author who was trying to add ten thousand names to his friends list, it meant that they—the people I was targeting—were much more likely to read bulletins I would send out to announce a new book or an upcoming book tour. The only writers I would seek out to add as "friends" were actually friends of mine. I would also add writers I didn't personally know who requested friendship, and in at least one instance, I was invited to teach at a writer's conference as a result.

As of this writing, Facebook and Twitter are all the rage, and Goodreads just received a few million dollars to improve their site. MySpace now looks like Las Vegas after a massive evacuation: The lights are still flashing, the music's playing, but nobody's there. By the time you're reading this, it's possible that Facebook will have been usurped by another, cooler site, or that Goodreads will have been bought up by a big conglomerate, chewed up, and spit out. And, yes, I'm on both Facebook and Goodreads, but for how long? The popularity of these sites is often fleeting at best, and what do you have to show for all the time you've spent accumulating friends? It's hard to say. As it turns out, MySpace was mostly a wash for me. Precisely two people showed up to my readings as a result of my MySpace bulletins, and of those two, only one bought a book. Now, *how* many hours did I spend collecting friends when I could have been writing a new novel? A word of caution: If you start using social networking sites to air grievances, or if you have a public meltdown on one of these sites, you may soon learn the full import of the word "viral," as happened recently to a few prominent authors.

Writing for the *Huffington Post*, Jason Pinter posits a particularly interesting question in an essay titled "Does Social Networking Kill the Author Mystique?"

> I have no doubt that some people buy books based on their online connection or discovery of an author through those means. But I also believe that what helps can also hurt if not done in moderation. I have never seen a movie based on an interview with a star or director. As a matter of fact, the oversaturation of an artist might make me less apt to try out their work (unfair, perhaps, but it's the truth). If you are subjected to a person ad nauseum, you eventually lose the curiosity factor. It becomes redundant. Familiarity breeds contempt. So I wondered . . . does knowing too much about authors take away some of the magic of their books?

It can't possibly bode well for creating what John Gardner called "the vivid and continuous fiction dream" for the reader who picks up a new novel when she knows what the author has eaten for every meal in the past year, what music he's been listening to, and what ailments he's suffered.

I'm sure other writers have had better success using social networking sites than I've had, so I wouldn't necessarily rule them out. Fiction writer Kevin Canty recently suggested that I should accept all friend requests on Facebook before the release of my new novel. According to Canty, he saw a definite uptick in attendance at readings while touring for his book *Where the Money Went*, and he credited Facebook for it. I'm hopeful that a site will come along that successfully bridges what Facebook is doing for the audience of Goodreads. I haven't seen it yet, but I suspect there's a sophomore at MIT working hard on it right now.

The Blog

Sounds like the title of a horror movie, doesn't it? But what would its tag-line be? How about *"Creating it was easy; killing it was another story"*?

Your publisher may want you to start a blog, and any number of books about getting published may encourage you to start a blog. I may be in the minority here, but I'm going to suggest that you don't start a blog . . . *unless* it absolutely makes sense for you to have one, or *unless* you can bring something so fresh and compelling to the reader that it would be silly not to.

Can we all agree that the Internet is a time-suck? Even though we all admit this, no one will turn it off. One way that it becomes a massive time-suck is when you start blogging. I know; I've been there. Did I have readers? Yes. Was it fun? For a while. Did my blogging yield book sales? Maybe a few. Was the increase in book sales worth the time spent blogging? Absolutely not.

Obviously, there are bloggers who've gotten book deals because their blogs generated tremendous traffic, but these folks are lottery winners, essentially. A blog by a former student of mine, Matt Gallagher, a former lieutenant in the Iraq War, ultimately grew into his memoir, *Kaboom: Embracing the Suck in a Savage Little War*, published by Da Capo Press. Gallagher's blog was receiving tens of thousands of views and became national news when the Army ordered it shut down. There are far more bloggers, however, with a modest number of readers who can't seem to finish writing their books or get a book contract. The time and energy that goes into maintaining a blog rarely seems worth it to me. Instead of writing a two-page blog entry, write two pages on your novel. Or, spend that time revising what you've written. Or, read a book. Imagine how much better your odds of getting published would be if all writers, aspiring or otherwise, spent their spare time buying and reading new books rather than reading and writing blogs.

Another danger is that you might turn off your readers with your tone. There are fiction writers whose novels I enjoy, but when I read their blogs, I discover, for one reason or another, that I'm not crazy about the writer as a person. This isn't always true, of course, but it's true far more times than I would have guessed. Perhaps the writer's blog was pretentious or self-congratulatory or full of false modesty or contentious, or maybe the tone was off-putting in some other way that I couldn't quite put my finger on. It's hard, then, to go back to those authors' books with the same sense of anticipation, if you can go back to them at all.

You might eventually piss off someone of influence with your blog. I'm certainly not a person of much influence, but I've been insulted, both overtly and inadvertently, on blogs written by writers I had previously supported. No one is immune to doing this. The longer you maintain a blog, the better your odds are of rubbing someone the wrong way.

One of the reasons I eventually quit blogging about writing was because I made the mistake of writing an ironic blog about an episode concerning science-fiction writer Ursula K. Le Guin. She had been one of my childhood heroes. When my second book was released, I wrote a letter to her and sent her a copy of my book. I signed it, sentimentally, *"For Ursula K. Le Guin, Whose own books inspired me to become a writer. With gratitude, John McNally."* Le Guin, in turn, wrote a very nice letter to me. A few years later, I discovered that the book was for sale on a used book site. A bookstore in Portland, Oregon—Le Guin's hometown—was selling it. Where another person might have been offended, I actually thought it was hilarious— enough so to blog about it. (I was always short of things to blog about, and this seemed tailor-made for my blog.) Laying the irony on thick, I feigned outrage that Le Guin had sold my book. How dare she! I also pretended that my feelings were deeply hurt. The insincerity of my tone, I had thought, would have been obvious to any reader. (I made the mistake of thinking that the vast majority of people who read my blog were my friends. Remember: The blog is out there for *everyone* to see. Furthermore, irony doesn't translate well for the masses.) Anyway, I wrote the post quickly and promptly forgot about it. What happened next, I could never have anticipated.

A much more popular blogger, who apparently followed my own blog, summarized my post in a few sentences, linking her summation to my Le Guin story. Within a few days, many other blogs picked up the story, oftentimes not linking it back to my original post while making incorrect assumptions about my response. Some of the people leaving comments on those blogs took me to task, writing things like, "Why the hell does McNally think Le Guin would have wanted his stupid book in the first place?" By the end of the month, *New York* magazine ran a photo of Le Guin on their "Approval Matrix" page, which breaks down celebrity news stories into four categories: "Highbrow Despicable," "Highbrow Brilliant," "Lowbrow Despicable," "Lowbrow Brilliant." The photo of Le Guin, along with a caption about how she had sold a fan's inscribed book, appeared in the "Highbrow Despicable" category. Shortly thereafter, the *London Times* ran a few sentences about Le Guin and my book in their gossip column. As ludicrous as it may seem, my ridiculous post on my silly blog had gone international.

Creating it was easy; killing it was another story!

In no time, I had created a viral monster. And, no, the publicity wasn't generating book sales. What it *did* prompt was Le Guin writing an angry blog entry of her own, this time about *me*. Naturally, she had assumed that I contacted *New York* magazine with this story so as to generate publicity for myself. She also explained how my book came to end up in the hands of a used bookseller. Apparently, she usually donated such books to the library, while selling review copies to the local bookstore. My book had ended up in the wrong pile. Not that I cared. To my way of thinking, she could have done with my book whatever she wanted to do with it. I really and truly was not offended.

The upshot is, I wrote to Le Guin, explaining how this crazy story began in the first place and apologizing profusely. She graciously accepted my apology and wrote an addendum to her blog, clarifying what had happened and placing blame on *New York* magazine. (I wrote a letter to the editor of *New York* magazine, clarifying the story and asking them to apologize to Le Guin, but neither one of us received a reply.) So there you have it—my own cautionary blogging tale.

The world doesn't need another blog by a writer blogging about writing, is my general feeling. Not one by me, in any event. These days, I maintain a sporadically updated blog titled "Beautiful Downtown Burbank (Illinois)," a blog dedicated to all things having to do with where I grew up. This blog gets far more traffic than my last blog and was even cited on *Time Out Chicago*'s and the *Chicago Reader*'s blogs, but I don't maintain it for publicity. I rarely mention my writing on it, and the few times I have, no one leaves any comments. It's a much more satisfying blog for me to keep up, however. I have no agenda, and I feel no pressure to keep it up-to-date, but best of all is that I'm unlikely to piss off Ursula K. Le Guin or any other childhood hero with it.

Networking

Another writer recently said to me, "You know just about every writer out there, don't you?" This isn't the first time someone's said this to me, but it's always a surprise when someone does. As I noted previously, I'm not an active networker. By that, I mean that I don't strike up friendships or go out of my way to meet someone with the hope of gaining something in return. I'm more of what you might call an accidental networker or a networker by happenstance.

I have already mentioned my pathological shyness. I like to joke that I didn't say a word in class from kindergarten through getting my PhD. When I tell people this, I'm only partially joking; it's mostly true. There have been dozens of classes in which I said not a word, and when a teacher would finally called on me, I would put my hand over my mouth and mumble, only making matters worse. All of this is to say that networking—and by "networking" I mean *talking* to people—has never come easily for me. I've gotten better at it after years of teaching and years of promoting books, but I still find myself in situations where I would much rather be home, in my basement, watching the Three Stooges than socializing. A few years ago, I was at a fancy party for Salman Rushdie, and a window of opportunity presented itself for me to go over and talk to him. He was alone and standing nearby. What did I do? I got myself another sandwich.

And yet, when someone says to me, "You know just about every writer, don't you?" the answer is, no, I don't know *every* writer, but I do know a lot. Probably more than most other writers.

How has this happened? I've moved around a lot, taking one-year teaching positions all across the country, which has brought me into contact with circles of writers (the writers in D.C., for instance, tended to hang together, as do many writers in Chicago); I've edited six anthologies, which has brought me into personal contact with well over a hundred writers, some of whom were relatively unknown when I first began writing to them, like Dan Chaon or Michelle Richmond, but whose careers have since soared; for every writer's conference at which I teach, I'll meet another dozen writers; I've attended the Associated Writing Programs conference for many years in a row, where writer-friends will introduce me to new writer-friends; a number of my old classmates have gone on to have significant careers; and so on.

There are those who think that networking is the nefarious plan of insiders who get together and plot how to take over the publishing world by exchanging favors, but this isn't the kind of networking that I know. In the course of a year, I meet people. Some of those relationships stick; others don't. For me, it's as simple as that. It wasn't until I sat down to write this book that I even began to think of what I do as networking. It is, though. I've certainly benefited from meeting and working with so many people. At the AWP conference in Vancouver, for instance, I gave a talk on a panel. Afterward, at the hotel bar, I struck up a conversation with another writer. By the end of our time talking and drinking, I had been invited to give a reading in Hawaii, where he taught. (The drinking, I'm sure, didn't hurt.) As a result of various friendships, I've been invited to give readings; teach at conferences; and contribute to magazines, anthologies, and textbooks. I have even been offered semester-long visiting writer appointments.

I should note that these invitations are not all the result of back-slapping nights out at a bar in a strange city. Your writing—your *work*—needs to prop you up first, or the invitations won't be forthcoming. Even in the instance of the Hawaii invitation, the writer had seen me give a talk, and the first thing he said to me, when he approached me at the bar, was that he appreciated that my remarks were prepared ahead of time and that I wasn't just winging it. I can't name a single invitation I've received where the person offering it wasn't familiar with my writing.

I used to look down my nose at the idea of networking. The very word suggested selling oneself. But the longer I've been doing this, the more I see that there's a difference between networking and schmoozing, and that it's possible to do the former and keep your dignity, whereas the latter strikes me as calculated and, well, a tad bit sleazy.

Getting to Know Booksellers

You may be surprised to learn how powerful bookstore owners, managers, and book-buyers can be. Publishers usually send advance reading copies of forthcoming books to bookstores, whose book-buyers (the employees responsible for ordering books to stock in their store) will peruse. If any of the books are appealing, they actually read them. Independent bookstore book-buyers are often the best-read people in the country, far better read than any professor of contemporary literature I've ever known. This is only one of many reasons to mourn the demise of independent bookstores across the country. Instead of having a well-read independent bookstore employee, who gets to know your tastes over time, recommend books for you to read—books that might have been published by smaller presses or books that might not have gotten their due in mainstream media outlets—you're now going to be impersonally pushed, via paid placement, toward the bestselling books *du jour* that the publisher is investing its resources in or has paid too much of an advance for. But while there are still independent bookstores, there are still people of influence working in them.

Nancy Olson, owner of Quail Ridge Books in Raleigh, North Carolina, is credited with selling 6,000 copies of one of her customer's books. That customer was Charles Frazier, and the book was *Cold Mountain*. In fact, she sold 1,200 copies at his first reading at Quail Ridge, a reading to which Olson had invited such well-known southern writers as Lee Smith, Kaye Gibbons, Jill McCorkle, Fred Chappell, and Clyde Edgerton. I have absolutely no doubt that Olson's efforts on behalf of her friend and customer proved to be that all-important spark that every book needs in order to end up a bestseller.

Charles Frazier isn't the only writer Olson has helped. Angela Davis-Gardner—a creative writing professor emeritus at North Carolina State University—had a difficult time placing her third novel, *Plum Wine*, which she had spent ten years working on. Her two previous novels, *Felice* and *Forms of Shelter*, had been published by major publishers but had sold modestly, and her agent eventually dropped her. On her own, Davis-Gardner placed her third novel with the University of Wisconsin Press, for which she received no advance. She was happy enough to have found a publisher for the book, but she was beaten down by the entire experience. Enter Nancy Olson. Olson held a publication party for *Plum Wine* at her store. Somehow, Olson got the book in the hands of someone at *Publishers Weekly*, who then reviewed the book after publication, which they almost never do, given that *Publishers Weekly* is an industry magazine that reviews books two or three months *before* publication. The *PW* review prompted other newspapers to review *Plum Wine*. It also prompted a high-powered agent to contact Davis-Gardner about representation. The short of it is that Davis-Gardner's previous novels are now back in print in paperback with a major publisher, the paperback rights to *Plum Wine* were sold to a major publisher, and Angela Davis-Gardner is presently under contract with a major publisher for her fourth novel. If you were to ask her whom she credits for the good things that have happened to her, I suspect she would tell you Nancy Olson.

Often, the first rumblings of buzz surrounding a book will begin with booksellers, and if there's enough buzz, the book may start to gain momentum. It may become an Indie Next selection (formerly known as Book Sense 76), a group of twenty new books chosen each month by booksellers and promoted heavily throughout independent bookstores. Or, your book may become a staff pick. Have you ever seen those little hand-written endorsements by staff taped below the shelved book? Customers do read those! Paul Ingram, bookseller extraordinaire of Prairie Lights Books in Iowa City, will actually press his favorite books of the season into customers' hands. Inkwood Books in Tampa sends e-mail blasts to its customers with staff recommendations titled Unchained Choices. All of these constitute buzz.

It's sometimes more difficult to get to know the managers of big chain bookstores, but it's by no means impossible. I presently live in a city that has no independent bookstore, so when my second book came out, I introduced myself to the manager of one of the two chain bookstores in town, and when I received a box of my own books from the publisher, I sent him a copy of the novel along with a note. He promptly read the book and, apparently, liked it enough to break a laundry list of corporate rules. He put stacks of my book next to stacks of the current bestsellers. (It doesn't hurt to have thirty copies of your book next to thirty copies of the latest James Patterson or Stephen King novels.) He put a poster up for my book signing a full month before the event, generating significant sales in the meantime. This particular store wasn't deemed an "events store" by corporate headquarters, so he broke yet another rule to accommodate me. He left copies of my book on the front table long after they normally would have been there. (Remember: Publishers pay for that kind of placement. By giving me front display for a period longer than I was supposed to have had, he was giving me something of significant value for free.)

Having said all of this, I happen to believe that it's best if your relationships with bookstore employees, whoever they may be, evolve organically. I had been shopping at Prairie Lights Books for thirteen years before my first book came out. Most of the people working there didn't even know that I was a writer. They knew, however, that I was a book lover and a faithful store customer.

But of course it's impossible to develop organically evolving long-term relationships with more than just a few bookstores, so I would also recommend going to conferences and expositions, if at all possible. At BookExpo, while promoting *Troublemakers*, I met several bookstore owners and managers. What had drawn them to our booth in the first place? The University of Iowa Press's publicist had sent out a notice that we would be giving out, in addition to advance reading copies of my book, beer. Not wine. Not cheese. Just cheap, lukewarm beer. Several of the bookstore folks who stopped by invited me to give readings at their stores. Thank goodness for a smart publicist—and for Old Milwaukee and the bookstore employees who drink it!

Conferences

I've already written about the importance of conferences for the writer looking for a publisher. For the writer who's already published a book, conferences can significantly boost book sales, but certain kinds of conferences are better for sales than others.

The Associated Writing Program's conference is the largest writing conference in the country—probably the world—and yet it's difficult to parlay being on a panel (which is what most writers at the conference end up doing) or giving a reading at an off-site location at night into significant book sales. For one thing, books aren't available at most of the panel discussions. For another thing, your book might not be available in the book fair, unless your publisher attends. Some writers will do book signings at their publisher's booth, but the results for these are mixed as well. There are, simply, so many things going on at any given time, it's likely that even your friends won't come to the signing.

The only way that I've successfully sold books at AWP was by renting a table for myself at the book fair. (A table is a smaller, cheaper space, usually reserved by literary magazines or MFA programs, whereas booths tend to be reserved by larger university and commercial presses or by smaller presses like Coffee House Press, which has an enormous backlist of titles.) The year that I reserved a table, I was promoting my anthology, *When I Was a Loser*. Since the table cost several hundred dollars to reserve, I was hoping only to break even. I brought about sixty copies of the anthology, along with a few of my own titles, and by the end of the conference, I had sold out of all but three books. I gave those three books away later that night. Granted, I didn't walk away any richer, but sixty people now had copies of the book who probably hadn't heard about it before the conference. Some of those people told me that they might use it for a class they taught. Others probably told friends about it. A few wrote blog-reviews of the book. I'll gladly give out sixty copies of a book, if I can afford to. The more copies that are in circulation, the more likely it is that my readership will grow by word of mouth.

Having said of all of this, I don't think it's a bad idea to participate on a panel. I've been approached by editors afterward and have even placed one of the essays I presented for a panel in a textbook pub-

lished by a prominent publisher. The guidelines for submitting proposals can be found on AWP's website.

I've had much better success, however, at other, smaller conferences, primarily conferences sponsored by universities over a three-
day period, during which I'll teach a workshop, be on a panel, give a
reading, and socialize. The participants get to know you a little by the
end of the conference, and they're much more inclined to buy a book
by the conference's end, if they've enjoyed one or more of the events
in which you've participated. Occasionally, the conference directors
will offer a semester-long course that's tied directly into the conference, assigning books written by the conference faculty as required
reading. When this happens, it can boost sales by another thirty,
sixty, or eighty books. I've also done one- and two-day stints at summer workshops for high school students. Fortunately, a lot of what I
write taps into that audience, and I've been able to parlay a reading
into a few dozen book sales. The bonus is that you usually get paid—
sometimes extremely well—to be a featured guest at one of these
conferences. The rub here is that teaching appointments for these
sorts of conferences are invitation-only, which is another reason why
it's good to network.

Next up are regional conferences and festivals. I've participated in
a few of these in North Carolina and Nebraska, giving lectures, par-
ticipating on panels, reading from my books. The more traditional
of these conferences have never really yielded much by way of book
sales, but I'm really not a North Carolina or Nebraska writer, despite
my ties to both states. A writer of Great Plains fiction would stand
a greater chance of gaining more fans in Nebraska than I would,
and the southern states really embrace their own regional writers.
I would probably do better at a conference for Illinois writers—or,
better yet, Chicago writers—so I suggest playing to your regional
strengths, if any. Alternatively, there are regional conferences and
festivals that play against regionalism with the hope of bringing in
a younger or hipper crowd than the state-commissioned festivals,
whose gaze sometimes lingers too long on dead writers of its region.
Timothy Schaffert's (downtown) omaha lit fest is an example of a festival that invites writers from all across the country and offers panels
on subjects, like sex and horror (although not necessarily grouped
together), that you're not likely to hear at a conference offering a
tribute to Willa Cather. Oftentimes, in order to participate at these
conferences, you have to send a proposal to the conference director.

Guidelines are usually found on the conference's website. If they're not, contact the director. Some, however, are invitation-only.

Finally, there are niche conferences. Perhaps the largest (and best example) of these would be Comic-Con—the massive conference dedicated to all things comic book related. While the main Comic-Con is held in San Diego, there are several regional conferences held throughout the year. I, along with my co-editor Owen King and illustrator Chris Burnham, promoted our anthology *Who Can Save Us Now? Brand-New Superheroes and Their Amazing (Short) Stories* at Comic-Con in New York. The three of us did our own panel discussion about the "literary superhero," and, to my surprise, the room was packed. Afterward, we signed promotional chapbooks, since the conference preceded the actual publication date. As with regional conferences, you'll probably find guidelines for submitting a proposal on the conference's website.

Your first publicity efforts are bound to be trial-and-error, until you begin seeing what works for the kind of books you're writing as well as what doesn't work. Don't be discouraged if something fails. Like writing, failing is part of the process. You'll learn from it and, hopefully, make adjustments for your next book.

Book Festivals

I haven't participated in many book festivals. I've done a few, but every time I look at the long list of marquee writers who are appearing, I get a bit depressed just imagining trying to compete with the rock stars of literature. Also, the size of these festivals can be daunting, and I don't do well in crowds. (I was trampled at a U2 concert in Iowa City in the late eighties. Seriously. Ever since, I get a little panicky in huge crowds.) Nonetheless, I have been assured by other writers that book festivals are worth a writer's time.

A few of the largest and most well-known festivals are the Miami Book Fair International, the Los Angeles Times Festival of Books, and the Texas Book Festival. Fiction writer Lynne Barrett says of the Miami Book Fair International, "It's a great place for selling books, it's good for networking, and it is a lot of fun. It is also a way an attendee who is not yet a published author can get a look at a tremendous number of published writers and their ways of interacting with the public. Our MFA students at Florida International University go and envision themselves representing a book there—which many of them have gone on to do."

These festivals typically feature author readings, a variety of panels on writing and publishing, book signings, and a book fair. It's not easy to get booked into the larger festivals, however, even when your publicist is pulling the strings to get you in. And, as I suggested above, it's easy to get lost in the crowd if you're not a marquee name. I participated in the *Chicago Tribune*'s Printer's Row Book Festival one year, and the panel that I was on was scheduled at the same time as an appearance by Chuck Palahniuk, who read his short story "Guts," a story that's so disgusting it's become famous for making people in the audience sick whenever he reads it. Yes, *this* was our competition. The turnout for our panel was decent enough, but I signed probably only three books afterward. Bear in mind that, unless you are Chuck Palahniuk or Toni Morrison or another Big Gun, the book festival won't be paying for your transportation, accommodations, or food. Unless you live nearby or can talk your publisher into footing the bill, the cost-benefit analysis won't likely be in your favor. On the other hand, you may have a good time and meet some interesting people, so long as you're not getting sick at a Chuck Palahniuk reading or getting trampled when the doors open for a rock star like Joyce Carol Oates.

Bookstore Signings, University Lectures, and Other Humbling Experiences

The Academy Award-winning song for the movie *Hustle & Flow* was titled "It's Hard Out Here for a Pimp," and let me tell you, a truer lyric has not been written. Fiction writer Donald G. Evans shared with me this response when he spoke to a Barnes and Noble Events Coordinator about doing a reading at her store: "What's your name again? Donald G. Evans? I never heard of Donald G. Evans. I went down to the basement, and I asked, 'Anybody ever heard of Donald G. Evans?' Nobody in the basement ever heard of Donald G. Evans. Nobody's ever heard of you."

And even if poor Donald had been able to set up a reading for himself, his woes weren't likely to end there. Here's a story that's all too common: You travel across the country, paid for by your publisher or out of your own pocket, to give a reading. You've been looking forward to this event for months, but when you show up at the event, there are only two people in the audience waiting to hear you. If you're lucky, both people are fans of your work. If you're not so lucky, one is a friend of the organizer who was called in at the last minute to fill out the room, while the other person thought you were somebody else. Fiction writer Wilton Barnhardt told me of an event he did in which the only person who showed up thought he was William Bernhardt, author of political thrillers.

I'd like to lay blame for low attendance on the demands of the times we live in, but, sadly, that doesn't appear to be the case. The following is an account from Kenneth Silverman's biography of Edgar Allan Poe:

> Poe's lecture at the Norfolk Academy, on September 14, was a modest success, appreciated but not well attended. A local newspaper observed that his "recitations were exquisite, and elicited the warmest admiration," but regretted "there were so few to partake." Poe himself noted that Norfolk was a small town and that two other entertainments had been scheduled for the same evening.

Edgar Allan Poe's lecture in 1849 could just as well be the account of any author on the road today. Of course, some authors can always draw a crowd, but as someone who has worked as a media escort for authors on book tours and as someone who now runs a university reading series, I can assure you that a large audience is an anomaly. Whenever I give a reading, whether it's part of a book tour or by invitation, I'm always stunned when more than a smattering of people show up. But even when the auditorium is packed or every seat in the bookstore is occupied, there's no guarantee that anyone is going to buy a book.

I can't begin to document the ways in which public readings can go wrong. I remember the time a man, who showed up to every reading on campus for the free food, stood up mid-reading, burped loudly, and asked if anyone had an antacid. I remember when a bookstore event for a well-known writer failed to make the monthly flyer and yielded only three people in the audience, one of whom was me, her media escort. At a library event I was invited to do, no one showed up. Not a soul. This, I should add, was the library in the city where I live and teach. The events coordinator disappeared for a few minutes and returned with a man who was apparently homeless. He gave the man a plate of food and then asked me to read. In this instance, I wasn't sure whom to feel the most sorry for: the homeless man, the events coordinator, or myself.

Not every well-attended event goes well, either. There are times when the author doesn't do himself any favors. At one reading I attended, a fairly respected author answered a perfectly reasonable question with so much anger that he shook when he spoke. (This same author, busy talking to some friends, didn't so much as look up at me as he signed a book I had brought to the reading, let alone thank me for coming.) I know of at least one author who won't sign any of his books, and another one who won't sign any first editions of his first novel. (I was at a Richard Russo reading in Iowa City when the host explained that the next night's reader wouldn't be signing copies of his book. Russo laughed and said, "*I'll* sign them." And that, my friends, is the right spirit!)

Another night, after I had waited in a rather long line, the author started hemming and hawing as I approached with a sack of five of his books to get signed. I was a fan; I had been teaching his short stories for years; I had bought copies of his books for friends. I should have been home that night packing boxes since my wife and I had sold our house and needed to be out of there in two days, but there I was, standing in line with my books. There were a handful of people standing behind me. The author, more annoyed than pleased, asked if I could stand at the back of the line so as not to slow down the line. I swear, in the time it took him to moan and groan, to stand up (yes, he stood up) and look inside the sack, he could have signed the damned things. Instead of heading to the back of the line, I put the books back into my sack and left the store. Had there been a garbage can next to the autographing table, I probably would have tossed all of his books inside. For the record, I have never bought another book by him, and I have never taught any of his stories again.

In each instance above, the author exhibited a lack of gratitude. He failed to take into account that there are a thousand other things a person could have been doing instead of attending, of all things, a *literary event*. The writer is competing with alcohol, with sleep, with inertia, with sex, with HBO, with whatever else is happening in town that night, with a good meal, with indifference—mostly with indifference. And yet they responded with a stunning lack of graciousness, a lack of gratitude. What the writer exhibited was an inflated sense of self-importance, which is never pretty. Does anyone think that the person who was berated for asking an innocent question would ever buy another book by that author?

But then there are those writers who completely win you over. I brought a sack of five books to Michael Cunningham. *The Hours* had just come out, and the audience was rather large, so Cunningham could have asked me to wait at the end of the line, as the other author had. Instead, he acted genuinely thrilled to see that I owned a copy of each of his books, and when he saw the copy of *Golden States*—a novel that neither he nor his publisher acknowledges—he laughed and said, "Where did you find *this*?" He signed it, thanked me for being such a fan, and clapped me on the back. All in all, I took up no more than two minutes of Mr. Cunningham's time.

I was a media escort for Andre Dubus III when he was promoting the paperback edition of *House of Sand and Fog*. Dubus is a charmer—funny and smart—but what I saw that particularly impressed me was how he took the time to talk with each person who stood in line to get a book signed. He asked if they were writers; he asked where they were from. He listened to their answers. He was, in a word, *genuine.* When you're at one of Dubus's book signings, the delight of the people leaving the room with their signed books is palpable.

Another writer who taught me the benefits of being decent while on a book tour is David Sedaris, who shows up early to make sure that everyone who wants a signed book gets one signed, and who writes thank-you notes to booksellers after his visit. (I have more to say about Sedaris in my chapter titled "Dealing with Fame.")

Before heading to a reading or book signing, I remind myself of the ripple effect. If there are only two people in the audience, it's possible that each person will tell two people about my reading, who, in turn, will tell two more people, and so on. The question is, what do you want those people to say about your reading? Hopefully, they'll say that you were a decent person who read some kick-ass stuff. But if you're not a decent person—if you're disdainful of the audience or annoyed by the low turnout—they're going to tell those two people what a jerk you were.

The world doesn't need another writer. You may think it needs you, but it doesn't. If my career went up in flames tomorrow, nothing—and I mean *nothing*—in the world would change, and the people who mourn the end of my career would be few. This is the sad reality of being a writer in America today. The worst *American Idol* contestant will still draw a larger crowd than nearly any writer on a book tour. If someone takes the time to show up to a book signing after a long day at work, the least the writer can do is show that person some respect, even if she's the only person who's shown up. *Especially* if she's the only person.

Libraries

Don't underestimate the power of libraries. I've had some terrible events at libraries (events at which no one at all has shown up), but I've also had some great events—some of my best, in fact. The best library events I've done have been, not surprisingly, at my childhood library, and there are probably four good reasons for this.

1. The setting of some of my books has been my hometown, making my childhood library a natural fit.
2. This particular library does an excellent job mailing out newsletters to everyone in the city. Would your publisher ever mail a flyer about your book to everyone in your hometown? Of course not. Many public libraries, however, have the budget to send out flyers, which, for you, translates into free publicity that would otherwise have cost you thousands of dollars and countless hours.
3. This library runs a successful events program in general, so they already have a system down for promotion. Furthermore, the event is always smoothly run, from the giant sign situated at the entrance informing anyone walking in about my event to the already set up folding chairs, podium, and microphone. The library requires preregistration for events, which means that they know in advance approximately how many people might show up.
4. The library plays up the "local boy makes good" angle, which doesn't hurt. The one thing I've discovered is that the people where I grew up are, by and large, happy for me and wish me well. It's not infrequent that I'll get an e-mail from someone from the old neighborhood letting me know that they're proud of what I've accomplished. These are people who, if they know about it, will show up to a library event and often bring friends and family. Even if I don't know anyone in the audience, there's a familiarity that's comforting because we have at least one common denominator: our hometown. For this reason alone, I love going back to my old library to do events.

One last point is that, in many very small towns, libraries are in need of events. I haven't done this yet, but I've been tempted to line up a few weeks' worth of library events across the rural Midwest. I was in Deadwood, South Dakota, a few years ago, and the local paper featured on the front page the writer who was scheduled to appear at the library. You're not going to get that kind of coverage in New York or D.C., I can assure you.

Finding the Odd Venue to Promote Your Book

My most successful book-signing event was not at Borders or Barnes and Noble, nor was it at any independent bookstore. Where I sold the most books was a place called Duke's Italian Beef Drive-in in Bridgeview, Illinois.

Duke's is a small restaurant that specializes in Italian beef and Italian sausage sandwiches or a combo sandwich that includes both beef and sausage. (If you're not from Chicago, you may be appalled by the gluttony that this sandwich suggests, but if you are from Chicago, you know that this is pure Heaven . . . unless, of course, you're a vegetarian, of which Chicago, I'll concede, has a couple.) In short, Duke's is *not* a place where hipsters hang out. What you'll find is food, lots of it, and, occasionally, you'll find me standing by a stack of my books with hand-written signs to let the customers know how much the books cost.

The first time I set up a display at Duke's, I signed over a hundred books. Why did I do so well there? For one thing, Duke's is located where my novel, *The Book of Ralph*, is set. Furthermore, one of the book's chapters is set in Duke's. When I wrote the chapter, I hadn't planned on doing a signing there, but when the book came out, I sent a copy of the book to the owners. A few months later, one of the owners showed up at a book signing that I was doing in a mall and offered to hang up a poster of the book in his store's window. Five years later, the sign is still hanging there. It's the best advertisement for the book I could have asked for. Whenever I receive an e-mail from a fan living on the southwest side of Chicago, chances are they learned about the book from the sign in Duke's. When the paperback was about to be released, I contacted the owners and ran by them the idea of doing a signing. Fortunately for me, they were all for it.

Book signings at bookstores are dime-a-dozen, but a book event at a place that sells Italian beef sandwiches is odd enough to garner media attention. Feature stories appeared in both the *Chicago Reader* and the *Daily Southtown*, while short notices were listed in the *Chicago Sun-Times* and the *Chicago Tribune*. A radio interview I'd done a year earlier for the hardback re-aired with a new announcement tacked on about the signing at Duke's.

I can't stress enough the importance of finding unique venues to promote your work, but I don't necessarily think that a unique venue in and of itself will generate the attention that my Duke's signing did. The venue should somehow be intrinsically tied to the book's subject.

Keep in mind that not every book lends itself to this sort of promotion. I have returned to Duke's two more times to sign copies of new books. In addition to the new book, I always display my older books, and, without fail, the book I sell the most copies of is still the older book—*The Book of Ralph*. Often, people who buy the book have already read it and are now buying it for friends.

Take a good, long look at your own book. Are there potential venues lurking within? My friend Sherrie Flick promoted her novel *Reconsidering Happiness* at the bakery that inspired the bakery in her book. If such a venue doesn't exist within the pages of your book, are there any unusual venues where your target audience might be found? I was offered an opportunity to sign books at a class reunion sponsored by my high school's class of 1979 (I was class of 1983). The reunion organizers decided to turn the event into a fund-raising opportunity and open it up for any graduating class to attend. Even though I wish I had sold more books there, I suspect I'll benefit from word of mouth from the few dozen books that I did sell as well as from the books I donated for the raffles.

Don't disregard doing readings at bookstores, but look beyond the traditional venue. You may discover that the most fertile places for selling books are in the unlikeliest of places. And, if you're lucky, you'll get a free beef sandwich and an order of fries thrown in.

Buying Copies of Your Own Book

Your publisher will give you a certain number of free copies of your book upon publication, but those will disappear quickly. You'll probably give most of those copies to family, friends, and colleagues. Before you know it, you'll be out of copies when someone who might be able to help you asks for one.

Buy extra copies of your own book when it comes out—not to boost your Amazon ranking or to put yourself on a bestseller list but to have on hand in case there's someone you want to give one to. While you may be able to convince your publisher to send out additional free copies to people *not* on their media lists—a blogger, for instance, who may have e-mailed you asking for a book—there will always be people who fall between the cracks, people who aren't editors or writers but who nonetheless may be able to help you.

The fact is, I'm always giving away copies of my books. When I go on trips to L.A., where I sometimes meet with producers, I bring along copies of my most recent book. If I'm going to a conference, such as the annual AWP conference, I'll pack a few extra copies in my suitcase in case I meet someone who should have one. I even gave a copy of one of my books to a guy at an auto repair shop. I had overheard him talking about something that made me think he might like the book. I had an extra copy in my truck, so I gave it to him. I believe strongly in the power of word of mouth, and if you can find someone who might spread the word, why not give away a free copy?

If you apply for teaching positions, you'll need copies of your book. It's entirely possible that you'll be sending out a dozen copies the year that you're on the job market. Even though the books are supposed to be sent back to you once the search is over, you'll be lucky to see half of those again, and of those, half will probably be damaged.

The publisher will offer to sell you copies of your books with a discount ranging anywhere from 40 to 60 percent. I try to keep at least fifty copies of a title on hand at any given time. When the book is about to be remaindered, the publisher often offers the book at a significant discount, sometimes for as little as two dollars for a hardback copy. If you think you'll be able to use them in the future, buy a hundred copies. Once the book goes out of print, you'll find yourself scouring used bookstores for your own book, probably paying more than if you'd bought discounted copies from the publisher.

Gimmicks

Some gimmicks work. Most probably don't. But if the investment in time isn't so much that it cuts significantly into your writing, you may want to give the gimmick a try.

Perhaps the oldest gimmick is a raffle for your book, advertising it on whatever social networking site is hot. People love free stuff, and if it brings extra attention to your book while driving traffic to your website for the ten bucks it's going to cost you for the free book plus postage, it might be worth it.

Or, hold an in-store drawing for one of your books. I did this for my novel *America's Report Card*. Since the novel was a satire on the world of standardized testing, I conducted a fake standardized test at the beginning of the reading, going so far as to pass out pencils and Scan-tron sheets. (The Scan-tron sheets alone resulted in a collective shiver, dredging up bad test-taking memories.) My quiz alternated between serious questions and comic ones. At the end, I collected the quizzes, revealed the answers, and held a drawing. By and large, the audience enjoyed the quiz, but was it effective? At a few of my events, the only copies of *America's Report Card* that left the store were the ones I had given away.

As of this writing, the latest gimmick is the book trailer. It's like a movie trailer for your novel. I love the idea behind this, but I suspect it's a more effective sales tool for someone like Stephen King, whose book trailers would go viral and exponentially raise awareness about his latest book, whereas a new writer (or a writer whose previous book sales have been modest at best) may have a difficult time getting the trailer noticed to the degree that it will significantly increase sales. If you make the trailer yourself, it'll cost you time; if you hire it out, it'll cost you money. But if you live in a town where there are film students looking for interesting projects, it might be a win-win situation.

A gimmick that appeals to me is the in-home book tour, for which the author arranges a series of readings in strangers' homes. Maybe I like this idea because I was a child in the 1970s when my mother was always being invited to in-home parties where someone would show up to sell candles or tell fortunes. What doesn't particularly appeal to me is sleeping on a couch in a stranger's living room.

As with any gimmick, you need to weigh time and money spent versus what you're likely to get out of it. I'm all for trying a new marketing approach to see if it works, but I've also learned that it's easy to get sucked into a thousand and one time-consuming tasks that drain away your time. Write this on a Post-it note: "Time is a writer's most valuable commodity." If you honestly think that your marketing gimmick will work for you, by all means try it; but don't start doing them just for the sake of doing them. Get to work on your next book. There's no worse feeling than promoting one book while realizing that you haven't made much, or any, progress toward completing another book. Raymond Carver, who alternated between writing fiction and poetry, spoke about this very feeling in interviews: "It's important to me, though, to have this new book of poems in manuscript in the cupboard. When *Cathedral* came out, that cupboard was absolutely bare; I don't want something like that to happen again."

Don't lose sight of the big picture, is all I'm saying. Marketing has its place, but it shouldn't trump your own writing. Distraction is the writer's archenemy, the devil whispering in your ear, and it's always tempting, always more fun to commiserate with the devil than it is to sit down and write.

Blurbs

Eventually, if you stick with writing long enough to publish a book, you'll need blurbs. Blurbs are those quotes by other authors, usually printed on the back of your book, that explain what a genius the writer is and how her book is like the effervescent love child of *Frankenstein* and *The House of Mirth*. In other words, blurbs are generous, clever words of praise by writers better known (usually) than you, often filled with hype and hyperbole. The word "blurb," which sounds downright gastronomical, was coined by the American humorist Gelett Burgess. He attributed the cover copy for his book *Are You a Bromide?* to a fictional character named Miss Belinda Blurb. Burgess' own definition of a blurb is "a flamboyant advertisement; an inspired testimonial."

In almost every instance, I have known the writers who have blurbed my books, and I have known many of the writers whose books I've blurbed. You'll hear people talk about how blurbing is just another example of the industry's log-rolling—and maybe it is—but please tell me in what industry log-rolling *doesn't* happen. I don't read blurbs on books to see who's endorsing it; I read the blurb to get a sense of what the book is about, or what the tone is, or to get a general feel for the book. I honestly don't think the person blurbing a book is what gets the average consumer to buy the book. It's what the blurber *says* about the book that's likely to persuade the customer.

One purpose of the blurb is to get industry people excited by the book *before* the book is published. If my editor has a blurb by a Pulitzer Prize–winning novelist when he goes into a sales meeting to pitch my book (yes, the editor at a commercial house has to pitch my book even after the book has been purchased by the publishing house), it may inspire the sales force to sit up and take notice of the book. More importantly, the blurbs get book review editors and booksellers to pay closer attention to the book when the review copies are sent around, with the hope that the book review editor will assign the book for review and that the bookseller will order multiple copies for the store.

But even then, I'm not sure how much weight blurbs really carry. After all, nearly every book passing before a reviewer or a bookseller comes with glowing endorsements by award-winning authors. Unless the blurb is from Harper Lee or someone else unlikely to give a blurb, like Thomas Pynchon (although I can think of at least two writers Pynchon has blurbed), the blurb will be read and noted but probably won't have much impact.

Even so, you'd best start thinking about whom you know who can blurb your book, since all of my blurbs, with two exceptions, have been the result of connections I've made. My publishers have sometimes solicited blurbs from big-name writers with whom I have no connection, but these have rarely panned out. I've said it before, and I'll say it again: A writer's most valuable commodity is his time. Why should a writer who doesn't know me take time from his own busy schedule to read my book and blurb it? Don't be offended if the person you ask *can't* blurb your book. It's always best to ask several potential blurbers rather than putting your hopes in the hands of one or two. Blurbing is a writer's *pro bono* work—a way of giving back to the community—but sometimes potential blurbers are too busy with their own work, or you've asked them at a bad time in their lives.

One last piece of advice: Should you find yourself in a position to blurb a book but don't like the book that the author has sent to you, don't feel compelled to explain to the author why you don't like it. It's humiliating enough for an author to ask for a blurb. Why add insult to injury? For my second novel, I had asked a much younger writer to blurb my book. She eventually sent me an e-mail in which she espoused what she called her "honesty at all times" policy and then proceeded to tell me why she "couldn't get behind" the novel. Was this necessary? Nope. Why would someone feel compelled to behave like this? Ego? A sense of entitlement? Probably. (This same author, I realized later, responds to bloggers who diss *her* books. Why doesn't this surprise me?) No, it's better to tell the author who's asked for the blurb that you're too busy to read the book. The author will suffer the wrath of reviewers soon enough, so be a decent citizen and lie.

Writing Book Reviews, Op-Eds, and Other Miscellanea to Promote Your Own Book

I have no evidence to back up this theory, but I suspect that if you review books for a number of newspapers, you'll increase the odds of getting your own book reviewed in those same pages. Let's ignore for the moment that the newspaper's book review section is almost extinct. In fact, by the time you're reading this, it's quite possible that you'll be thinking, "Newspapers? What are those? The word *sounds* familiar." The larger point here is that when you write for a newspaper or for a website with a readership like Salon's, what you're doing is bringing your name to the attention of an editor. Have you ever seen a book review editor's office? It's cram-packed with new books, and every one is being touted as the Next Great American Novel. How is the editor to choose which ones to review and which ones to ignore? Obviously, Philip Roth, Louise Erdrich, and Jonathan Franzen will get reviewed. But what about that open slot for the writer who *isn't* a household name? I suppose my theory may be no more sound than the superstitious gambler who has to wear a certain shirt before heading to the casino, but I would wager that if you write for enough venues, some of those venues will eventually pay out in the form of the editor assigning *your* book to a reviewer.

There are other ways to get on an editor's radar. Write an op-ed that ties into the subject matter of your novel. Remember: Op-eds always run a byline, and that byline will mention your new book.

Pitch to magazine and newspaper editors article ideas that somehow relate to the broader subject matter of your book. After my novel *America's Report Card* came out, I received an e-mail from an editor at a top-notch magazine asking if I wanted to write an essay about education in America. I probably should have taken the editor up on her offer, but I was too busy at the time, and I really didn't have much to say beyond the obvious, but I at least now have the editor's e-mail, should I ever be inclined to pitch an article that ties into another book. My novel *After the Workshop* grew out of my experiences as a media escort. A short nonfiction piece about the inside world of shuttling writers around would be the perfect tie-in article.

The more ambitious among us would pitch the idea of writing a column for your local paper. If your local paper is the *New York Times*, you're probably out of luck. But if your local paper is the *Winston-Salem Journal*, or any number of suburban or local arts papers, there's a good chance an editor will give you a shot if you have a strong pitch and irresistible writing sample. And once you start writing a weekly column, you're creating a *platform* for yourself, and a good platform, though difficult to establish and getting more difficult by the day, is an invaluable promotional tool for a writer to have.

Selling Serial Rights

Serial rights are those rights connected to the publication of excerpts from your book, "first serial rights" referring to the publication of an excerpt *before* the publication of your book and "second serial rights" referring to an excerpt appearing in a newspaper or magazine *after* the publication of your book. If your book is under contract with a publisher, you'll want to read over the contract to see which rights, if any, you control. It's possible that the publisher is the only one who can sell these rights. In some instances, however, you may already have placed excerpts of the novel or story collection before the book was even under contract.

To get the most bang for your buck publicity-wise, you should try to time the publication of the excerpt as close to the book's publication as possible. That way, if the person reading your excerpt likes what she's read, she can drive to her nearest bookstore and pick up a copy. Sad to say, but most people have two-second attention spans. I certainly do. If I read a story in a magazine that prompts me to want to buy the book, I'll try to buy the book right then and there. However, if the book isn't available (if, for instance, its publication date is still six months away), there's a pretty good chance that I'll forget all about it unless serendipity intervenes, calling my attention to the book again after it's been released.

Finally, if you still own the serial rights, placing an excerpt could mean putting more money into your pocket. If your publisher owns those rights, it could help earn out the advance faster, since, typically, a percentage of the earnings will go toward the advance while the other percentage goes into the publisher's pocket.

Alumni Magazines

You don't necessarily have to belong to your alumni association to benefit from the existence of one. The University of Nebraska-Lincoln's alumni association, like many alumni associations, publishes a magazine, with a section featuring recently published books by alumni. A color cover of the book, along with the publishing information, is followed by the book's catalog copy. Each issue features about six to ten books. So far, I've been able to have each of my books featured.

Sometimes, you can get the alumni magazine to do a tiny in-brief story with a photo of you or the book, or they may do a feature story on you. I've been told that Nebraska's alumni magazine reaches 80,000 readers. That's not bad, especially when you consider that the alumni magazine is something that nearly everyone who receives it will look at, unlike the book review section of a newspaper, which, although invaluable for a book's publicity, isn't read by everyone who buys a paper.

If all else fails, there is usually a section at the back of the alumni magazine for you to submit what you're up to these days in a short sentence. I don't know of anyone who doesn't read these, so even though it's not a prominent feature about your book, it's not without some worth, publicity-wise.

Hiring an Independent Publicist

You should think long and hard before deciding to hire your own publicist. For one thing, independent publicists cost a lot of money. While it's possible to spend as little as a thousand dollars for a publicist to focus on publicity for a single city, it's also possible to spend as much as $20,000 or more for national publicity. At the end of the day, you may not have sold many more books than if you'd simply let your publisher's in-house publicist do her job.

There are, however, a number of good reasons for hiring your own publicist. The publicists who work for large commercial publishers handle publicity for many books at once—*too many* books at once. They are overworked and underpaid. I can't think of another position in publishing with as high a burn-out rate. For one of my novels, I worked with no fewer than five different publicists. It got so that I quit memorizing their names or programming their phone numbers into my cell. One of the publicists who assured me that she was there to stay was gone by the end of the week. Also, because these publicists work on so many projects at once, the bulk of their energy will go toward high-profile books or books where the author was paid a small fortune for her advance, while the rest of the books fall into their let's-see-what-sticks category. What this means is that the publicist will blanket the media with press releases and review copies with the hope that the book starts getting some traction. It's less likely, however, that the publicist will personalize letters if there's a connection to be made or make follow-up phone calls.

Sometimes, an author working with a smaller publisher will hire an independent publicist because the publisher may not yet have the clout to get the coverage the author thinks his book is capable of getting, or because the publisher may not have its own in-house publicist.

In all of the examples above, a good independent publicist can be particularly effective. These publicists often have personal relationships with newspaper and magazine editors, radio show producers, and feature newspaper writers, allowing them to make phone calls and pitch the book directly. They can also tweak individual cover letters to make the book more appealing for that particular venue. Frequently, they'll work with a newspaper writer to brainstorm ideas for feature stories. The independent publicist can make those follow-up calls to make sure that the materials arrived and to gently pressure the editor/producer/writer into doing something on the book's behalf. Oftentimes, they can set up book signings in off-beat venues that the publisher's publicist wouldn't know about, or they can pull strings to get the author into a competitive reading series or a hard-to-book bookstore. (Yes, getting a signing at a bookstore isn't always an easy thing to do, particularly in large cities.)

That said, hiring an independent publicist doesn't guarantee that any of these things will pan out. Therefore, you need to take an honest look at your own book and determine whether or not it's a good candidate for an independent publicist. Remember: The independent publicist doesn't get paid based on how much publicity the book receives. The publicist gets paid an agreed-upon fee *regardless* of whether or not the book gets publicity.

I hired an independent publicist for my first novel, *The Book of Ralph*. Because of the novel's setting, I hired a publicist who lives in Chicago and specializes in Chicago-based publicity. My gamble, in this case, paid off, as it did years later when I hired the same publicist for *Ghosts of Chicago*, a story collection that features a real-life dead Chicagoan in every other story. Both books received significant coverage in Chicago media—reviews; feature stories; radio interviews; and, in the case of *Ghosts of Chicago*, a live interview on WGN-TV's news.

Not all media is effective media, however. I decided not to hire my own publicist for the paperback release of my novel *America's Report Card* because the publisher had subcontracted the publicity to a company that specializes in book publicity. What they did was set up a couple of days of back-to-back radio interviews for me, all by phone, most of them short and live, although I also did a few longer taped interviews as well.

What I was doing—and what became clear almost immediately—was filling dead air. I would appear for thirty seconds on a "Morning Zoo" show to explain what my novel was about, or I would be grilled for ten minutes by a conservative talk show host. My novel is a satire of, among other things, the standardized testing industry, and although the book targets such policies as No Child Left Behind, it is still a novel and not a work of nonfiction. And yet when I was questioned about the book, it was almost always as though I were an expert on education, not a fiction writer, and the radio hosts who were asking the questions, in almost every instance, had read only the press releases. I found myself in the odd and uncomfortable position of debating policy, rather than telling comic anecdotes about my own time spent working in the absurd world of standardized testing. I did twenty or more interviews over a two-day period, with a few more interview requests trickling in over the next month.

Did these interviews sell books? No. How do I know? There were no additional hits on my website; there was no fluctuation on my Amazon sales ranking; and there was no flood of post-interview e-mails. I'm not suggesting that radio interviews are pointless. Far from it. I've done several interviews on Chicago Public Radio's WBEZ, an interview for NPR's *Talk of the Nation*, and a number of other shows where the audience is comprised of precisely the sort of people likely to buy my book, with the right nudge. But when audience and subject matter don't align—when you're on a show simply to fill space—it's unlikely that the time spent (and, more importantly, the *money* spent, if you're paying for own publicity) is worth it. If you could be working on another book instead of talking to Crazy Larry and Road Kill Mama on Pawtucket's *Big Show on the Radio*, you should probably be working on your novel, unless you're a stand-up comedian whose next show is in Pawtucket or you've written an unauthorized biography of Toby Keith.

If you're going to hire a publicist, you'll want to hire one who understands the market for your book and works hard putting your books in the right hands. Here's a checklist of things you should consider:

1. Before contacting the publicist, get in touch with a couple of the publicist's clients. A simple Google search of the publicist's name plus the word "publicist" should reveal a handful of clients. Send an e-mail to each author, explaining who you are, that you're looking for a publicist, and that you saw that she has worked with Publicist X. How was her experience been with X? Keep your e-mail short and simple.

2. Has the publicist worked with books similar to yours? If you've written a literary novel and the publicist has handled only nonfiction books in the past, this publicist probably isn't right for you.

3. Does the publicist maintain a blog? If so, read it carefully. Some publicists offer useful tips and information on their

blogs, while trumpeting their clients' achievements. If, however, the blog is a forum for the publicist to whine, complain about past clients, or call industry professionals names, you don't want to work with this person. Also, read the blog for the quality of the publicist's writing. Remember: This is the person who would be representing you, so if the blog is riddled with misspellings, comma problems, or vague language, you can probably expect the same on press releases written by this publicist or in e-mails he sends to media clients. Finally, what's the name of the blog? If it's "I'm a Big Fat Loser: Confessions of an Angry Publicist," you should probably stop walking and start running.

4. Talk to the publicist before hiring him. The publicist will most certainly want to talk to you as well to gauge if you're serious and to make sure that you don't have unrealistic expectations. A publicist probably won't want to work with you if you think hiring him is a shoe-in for an appearance on the *Today* show or any other almost-impossible-to-land media spots. But you should be paying attention to the publicist as well. Does he sound bored? How articulate is he? Is he talking disparagingly about other people? What's going on in the background? Is the phone call professional, or are there barking dogs and crying babies nearby? Don't easily disregard tell-tale signs of unprofessionalism.

I offer these warnings as someone who has worked with one excellent independent publicist and one nightmare of an independent publicist. The first sign that the nightmare one was, indeed, going to become a nightmare occurred when he left a profanity-laced message on my answering machine, yelling about my publisher's in-house publicist, who he was convinced wasn't going to send him a box of books. Who swears into a client's answering machine, anyway, especially when the client (me) wasn't at fault? Turns out, the in-house publicist wasn't at fault, either. The hired publicist had misunderstood a message the in-house publicist had left for him and blew up, creating way more problems (and stress) than necessary. (If your hired publicist is creating more stress than he's alleviating, you're in trouble.) As you can imagine, this relationship simply got worse and worse, and by the end, I couldn't *wait* to be done with him. The thing is, all the warning signs were there from the beginning, including the glaring red-flag name for his blog, but I ignored them all, trying to give him the benefit of the doubt, until it became obvious that nothing was going to work, at which point it was too late for me to do anything about it.

There are also publicists who work exclusively with Internet publicity. They'll set up "virtual" book tours, where you engage in live chats with readers. They'll try to land you interviews on various blogs. They'll also get your book into the hands of people who may review it on their website. After having done (as of this writing) publicity for ten books, I'm underwhelmed by most Internet publicity. Oh, sure, there are always the exceptions—a news story about an author that goes viral—but, by and large, Internet publicity makes me feel like I'm spitting in the ocean after the polar caps have melted. There was a time when the Internet could generate some buzz, but there are so many sites now, and a site that's hot one year is all-but-forgotten the next. That's not to say that I don't promote my work on the Internet. And it's not to say that I haven't seen any results. I do, and I have. But would I pay someone to focus exclusively on the Internet? No. That's not to say that you shouldn't. Perhaps your book is Internet-friendly. If so, contact a publicist who specializes in Internet-only publicity. Just keep in mind my rule of thumb: Don't pay someone good money for something that you can do yourself.

Always consult with your acquiring editor before hiring an independent publicist. (Your acquiring editor is the editor who actually made the offer to purchase your work, the editor who is your primary advocate, not to be confused with the copyeditor, who reads over your manuscript looking for a variety of errors and problems.) In my experience, acquiring editors are open to the hiring of an independent publicist. But they are also sometimes quick to advise you not to spend tens of thousands of dollars. I'm sure they've seen plenty of authors kiss their money good-bye for publicity that the in-house publicists could have done for them. In addition to getting the editor's blessings, you'll also want to make sure that the hired publicist and the in-house publicist work together cordially so as to avoid overlap or needless confusion.

Hiring a publicist is a gamble, and hiring an expensive publicist is a high-stakes gamble. A writer friend recently told me about a writer he knows who spent twenty thousand dollars on a publicist. His friend's book was reviewed on the front page of the *New York*

Times Book Review. I said, "Yeah, but twenty thousand bucks? Was it worth it?" His reply: "If it means she gets a six-figure advance on the next book, I'd say, yes." Of course, no publicist can guarantee you a review in the *New York Times Book Review*, let alone a front page review, which brings us back to the role of luck, serendipity, and chance.

Learn a skill for which you can get paid.
Pay close attention to the sentence. Meet writers,
ask them questions, deflate your ego. Embrace
rejection. Celebrate victory. Pick a good signature
cocktail and stick with it. Revise, revise, revise.
— Sherrie Flick, *Reconsidering Happiness*

5 Employment for Writers

Jobs for Writers

The trick is finding a job that permits you enough time to write and doesn't sap your mental energy. There are a number of jobs that you can get with a background in creative writing, but once you land the job, you may find that the job becomes your life while your writing career stalls or dies.

Some would-be writers go into advertising, but advertising is a high-pressure job that can run a person ragged. I've known a few people in advertising who are incredibly successful, at the top of their game, but they don't have time to sit down and work on a novel. The more successful you are in advertising, the busier you become.

Also, there's the money factor. If you find a job that pays *too* well, it's going to become harder for you to justify putting the job on hold while you pursue a career in writing, which may yield nothing or next to nothing. The writing life is a speculative life insofar as there are no guarantees, even for those who've published books, unless they consistently produce bestsellers.

Certainly, there are writers who've found jobs that have little or nothing to do with writing, and it seems to have served them well. Pulitzer Prize–winner and former U.S. Poet Laureate Ted Kooser spent most of his professional life as an insurance executive. Fiction writer Martin Clark is a circuit court judge. Poet Philip Larkin was a librarian for over thirty years. Perhaps the secret here is to find a career outside of writing so that *that* part of your brain isn't fried at the end of the day.

It's no surprise that most writers try to land teaching appointments, which offer flexible hours and summers off, but it's easy to get sucked into exploitative teaching appointments that pay unlivable wages and take up more time than a full-time job. While I'm all for someone getting an MFA, if that's what they want to do, I feel it's my duty to warn you that a good teaching position most likely isn't waiting for you afterward. It's simple mathematics.

For instance, an MFA program like the University of Wisconsin-Madison will receive over 650 applications in fiction alone this year. Bear in mind, that's *one* program and *one* genre. Many of those applicants will wind up *somewhere*. Meanwhile, fewer than a hundred jobs were available this year in *all* genres—fiction writing, poetry writing, or creative nonfiction—and those positions include not only tenure-track jobs but also one-year visiting appointments. While some years the job market is better than others, the ratio I've just provided you—prospective fiction writing majors to available jobs— remains pretty steady from year to year. Now, add to that mix the number of would-be poets and creative nonfiction writers or the students in creative writing PhD programs, not to mention those who have jobs but want different jobs, plus all the people from all the previous years who don't yet have a job and still want one.

I'm not trying to drive you off a bridge. Honest. I am, however, trying to be realistic. What these numbers say to me is that not everyone who wants a good (or even mediocre) teaching position will get one, and you should diversify your education so that you can find gainful employment of some kind while you pursue your writing. A lot of writers I know have gone to library school to earn a master's in library science. There are some one-year programs out there, so the time commitment isn't so terrible, and while there are still no guarantees, I suspect the prospects for landing a library job, if you're willing to relocate, aren't nearly as bad as those for a tenure-track teaching position.

Unless you're independently wealthy, the money side of the writing life may not be so easy. Before my first book was published, I had enormous difficulty finding work that paid enough to make ends meet. Between the ages of twenty-three and thirty-five, I did a lot of adjunct teaching (which sometimes paid as little as $1,000 per month with no benefits for teaching four classes per semester), temp jobs (I gutted buildings; I greeted people at the new mall in town; I did data entry), scored standardized tests for about eight bucks an hour, worked in the acquisitions department of a library (a glorified shipping-and-receiving job), and spent several months on unemployment.

Before my stint on unemployment, I was reading the biography of a writer who moved to a cabin and hammered out his first novel in a couple of months. In a flash of foolhardy confidence, I thought, *Hell, I could do that!* And so, in what would prove to be a grim comedy of errors, I moved to a camping trailer in southern Illinois that my father owned.

It snowed heavily for several days after I arrived, effectively shutting me in for a week. I tried driving to a store, but I got stuck in the snow and had to walk back to my trailer. The trailer had no running water, save for a garden hose sticking in through the window by the sink. To get electricity, I ran an extension cord to an outlet attached to a wooden pole outside, and to keep warm, I used a kerosene heater. I spent most of my time inside, wondering why I was so damned tired all the time—that is, until I cracked a window and realized that I was probably asphyxiating myself from the kerosene fumes. When the garden hose froze, as it did each morning in January and February, I plugged a hair dryer into the extension cord and stood outside, ankle-deep in snow, blowing the hose until the ice thawed.

Upon moving in, I took great pains to set up my computer (which, at the time, was one of those monstrous, cheap IBM clones) on the dining table, which looked like a miniature version of a booth you might find at Denny's. Instead of writing, however, I began watching a lot of TV, including morning shows, like *Oprah!* which I had never watched before, and by the end of the month, after being snowed-in and eating nothing but crappy food, I had gained so much weight that I could no longer fit inside the little booth where my behemoth of a computer sat.

To make matters worse, the local newspaper ran an article about someone finding a woman's head in nearby Rend Lake. Next to the article was a drawing of the unidentified woman's head. There was no attempt by the artist to recreate what she might have looked like *before* the grisly murder. The drawing was simply that of a head that had been under water for a while. Since my trailer door didn't have a lock—my only security was a bungee cord keeping the door shut—I kept beneath my pillow a 9 millimeter gun that my father had left in one of the cabinets. As the weeks wore on, I spent significant time at the bars in town, more desirable places than my trailer, which was smaller than most jail cells. Many of the women I met were the wives or girlfriends of men who were doing time in the nearby prison. As winter thawed and the temperatures rose, the vinyl ceiling of my trailer began to droop so that every time I stood up it rested on my head, further driving me insane. By the end of my seven-month stint in the trailer, I'd written a pathetic thirty pages, none of them usable.

Fortunately, I had applied to PhD programs in the meantime. Before receiving my acceptance from the University of Nebraska in the mail, I was starting to think that no one would ever hire me for a job, *any* job, and I wondered if I could somehow build a house for myself out of cement blocks. *Could I afford enough cement blocks?* I wondered. Acceptance into the PhD program was the blood transfusion that I needed. It was there, in Lincoln, Nebraska, that I wrote what turned out to be my first book, and it was that book's publication that turned my luck around, job-wise.

Publishing Jobs

Allow me to begin with a caveat. A lot of my students who are interested in becoming writers want to get jobs in publishing, but the people I know who work in publishing—and I know a lot—put in extraordinarily long hours, often taking their work home with them. Furthermore, if you land an entry-level position in New York publishing, it's likely that you won't have enough money to live on, unless your parents are helping out.

Caveats aside, a job in publishing makes the most sense, at least in theory, for a writer. Not only are you working with the very things you love—words and books—but you're learning how the business works from the inside. A number of famous writers began their careers in publishing. Toni Morrison started out as a textbook editor before becoming an editor at Random House. E. L. Doctorow worked as an editor at New American Library before moving to Dial Press, where he was editor-in-chief and publisher of such authors as James Baldwin and Norman Mailer. More recently, novelist James P. Othmer (*The Futurist*) worked as a publicist for Delacorte before beginning a career in advertising. Novelist Amy Scheibe (*What Do You Do All Day?*) was an editor at several different publishing houses, including Free Press and Counterpoint. Poet Ted Genoways (*Anna, Washing*) is editor of the *Virginia Quarterly Review*, prior to which he was an editor at the Minnesota Historical Society Press. Fiction writer Jeanne Leiby (*Downriver*) is editor of the *Southern Review*. Frances Kuffel worked as a literary agent while writing her memoir *Passing for Thin*. Fiction writer Jonathan Messinger (*Hiding Out*) is books editor for *Time Out Chicago* as well as co-publisher of featherproof books, a small press.

I suggest to any student thinking about a career in publishing to get as much hands-on experience as you possibly can before diving into the application pool. This experience may come in the form of being a reader for the university's literary journal, starting your own journal, interning with your university press, applying for summer internships with commercial presses and large-circulation magazines, along with any other opportunities available through your school or in your community.

I also recommend attending a summer publishing institute. The two most prominent of these are New York University's Summer

Publishing Institute: Book, Magazine, and Digital Publishing and the University of Denver's Publishing Institute. At these institutes, industry professionals lead workshops in editing, marketing, and production. These are excellent opportunities for networking, but I should warn you, these programs are not inexpensive, and because they are short-term, you probably won't be eligible for government student loans.

A good place to find jobs in publishing is on the Publishers Marketplace website (www.publishersmarketplace.com). Jobs ranging from the lowly agent's assistant to marketing director of a major publisher are posted daily.

Landing a Teaching Position

Despite my warning that there are very few teaching jobs out there for freshly minted creative writers, most will still pursue this elusive beast. Therefore, I have dedicated the next several chapters to the profession.

The World of Adjuncting

Though I have held only one tenure-track teaching position thus far—I'm now tenured—I've taught at a total of nine colleges and universities in a variety of positions: visiting assistant professor, visiting writer, adjunct lecturer, teaching assistant, and so on. Since the adjunct position is the one you're most likely to get if you haven't published a book, allow me to walk you through this murky jungle of exploitation. As defined by Merriam-Webster, an adjunct is "something joined or added to another thing but not essentially a part of it." Some colleges—community colleges, in particular—piece together the majority of their faculty out of adjuncts. Adjuncts are cheap and dispensable. Best of all for the community college, there is an endless supply of PhDs and MFAs ready to replace an adjunct who leaves.

There's a community college here where I live in Winston-Salem, North Carolina, that was paying $1,000 per class back in 2002, when I first moved here. (I can't imagine they're paying better these days.) A friend of mine agreed to teach six classes there one semester. The classes offered at these schools usually have outlandish enrollment caps. A beginning composition course, which shouldn't have more than twenty students, is often capped at thirty. These jobs don't offer any health or retirement benefits, and there's usually no guarantee of work beyond the semester you're teaching. Sometimes, they even make you pay for a parking sticker. My friend wisely quit after a few weeks, once he realized that the work-load was unreasonable. (Normally, I would advise against quitting a teaching position once the semester has begun, but since this particular school didn't mind taking full advantage of its faculty, why should the exploited teacher care about the difficult spot he's put them in?)

So, let's review this. If my friend had taught there for the entire year, he'd have raked in a whopping $12,000 and had no time whatsoever to write because of the course-load and class sizes. Each semester, he'd have had one hundred and eighty students; if he assigned each class to write four five-page essays, he'd have been grading three thousand and six hundred pages each semester or seven thousand and two hundred for the year. Oh, wait, but he'd have gotten his summers off, right? Not if you're making 12K a year, you wouldn't. Whenever I took on adjunct work, I always had to find a full-time job in the summer to make ends meet. Hell, I sometimes had to find a nighttime job *during* the semester to make ends meet. In fact, one year, while working as an adjunct at a community college in Cedar Rapids, Iowa, I took a nighttime job scoring standardized tests along with whatever weekend work the local temp agency found for me. To supplement that income, I sold plasma. I wish I was kidding, but I'm not.

Why would anyone in their right mind put themselves through this? Good question.

Many people do it for the experience. What better way to get hands-on teaching than to pick up some classes at the local community college? Most likely you'll be teaching introduction to composition, but it's possible you'll get thrown a literature course along with some writing center duties.

Some do it so as not to have a gap in their teaching experience. They see it as a temporary situation before landing that tenure-track job. The risk is that you may never land that tenure-track job because you never have time to finish the book you're working on.

Some people do it thinking that it will eventually lead to a permanent position. These are people who still believe that the world is fair and that good students will eventually get rewarded. I took one adjunct job for this reason. I was led to believe that my position might become permanent. In November of my first semester, however, all of the adjuncts were told that there was no work for them the following semester, even though many of us had driven across the country for our jobs. Rule #1: In the world of adjunct teaching, no one gets rewarded.

Some people do it to make ends meet. I often took adjunct work when I couldn't find anything else. After getting lured across the country for one adjunct job, only to get dumped by semester's end, I began treating adjunct work as a last resort. I would do it only if I had no other options—and sometimes I didn't.

Some people do it to supplement their income, and this reason probably makes the best sense. They already have a good-paying job, so they'll pick up a night-class to teach so they can buy a new big-screen TV at the end of the semester or pay off the balance on a credit card. They *know* it's a shitty job, but this fact doesn't bother them because they're not pinning any of their hopes on it, and they're not living off the peanuts that the job pays.

When I taught at a community college in Iowa, I knew too many people who hoped that their adjunct position would be converted to a full-time position. When I pull up the community college's website today, over fifteen years after I taught there, I see the same permanent faculty, along with some of the same adjuncts, but I don't see any former adjuncts in full-time positions, at least none of the ones I knew.

The environment wasn't a healthy one, either. The adjuncts didn't have their own offices. Over a dozen of us shared four tables. There was no place to have a private conference with a student. When I worked there, there was a fellow adjunct who exhibited odd territorial behavior. Let's call him Bob. I was usually the first to arrive in the morning. When Bob arrived, he always threw his briefcase down on the table I'd occupied, opened it up and tossed his stuff out of it so that some of it landed on top of my papers and books. This wasn't a one-time occurrence. He did it *every day.* When he took off his jacket, he tossed it over another table. When he used the phone, which was attached to a wall, he'd stretch the receiver's cord all the way across the room, making it difficult for anyone to get where they needed to go without having to limbo under the cord. We were like rats stuck together in a cage, and I knew if I stayed there too long, sooner or later I was going to bite Bob.

But then things changed. In January of 2000, I drove twenty-five miles back home for lunch. I needed to drive back to the community college later to work in the Writing Center, so I sat in my car, trying to decide what I should leave there and what I should take inside. I was so beat down, however, that I sat in my car and stared blankly at the piles of papers. I didn't see my wife, who had come up to the driver's side window and was waiting for me to get out of the car. Finally, she knocked on the window, and I jumped. When I rolled down the window, she told me that there was a message for me on the answering machine from the director of the University of Iowa Press.

I had submitted my short story collection, *Troublemakers*, to the Iowa Short Fiction Award. The collection had been a finalist in several other contests—the Associated Writing Program contest, the Flannery O'Connor Award contest—and though I was pleased every time it was a finalist, I was also starting to feel like the perennial bridesmaid. Why was Iowa calling? A more optimistic person would have assumed he'd won the contest, but I had been conditioned to keep my hopes in check and, therefore, assumed the caller would tell me that I had been a runner-up. I was connected to voicemail the first dozen times I called. When I finally reached Holly Carver, the press's director, she informed me that I had indeed won. I was standing in the foyer, trying to grasp the import of the moment. After having written two unpublished novels and numerous versions of a short story collection, I would finally be a writer with a book! Regarding news of his first story publication, Erskine Caldwell wrote, "The accumulated disappointment of many years was suddenly and completely erased from my memory." In truth, I felt more exhausted than relieved, which is how I feel after the sale of each book manuscript, as though I'd just finished boxing fifty bare-knuckled rounds without any headgear.

Although I didn't know it right then, I would never be a lowly-paid adjunct again. I would have to finish out the semester, of course, but I would have only visiting writer or tenure-track teaching appointments ahead of me.

Back at work, I knocked on my dean's door to tell him the exciting news. I had to tell *someone*. And so I blurted it all out, but his only response was, "You're late for the Writing Center."

I looked at my watch. "No, I'm supposed to start in five minutes."

"That's not what I was told," he said.

On and on it went, until, finally, there was documentation that showed that I was right and he was wrong. Once more, I had foolishly wanted more out of the job than I was going to get. I had wanted a slap on the back. I had wanted the dean to congratulate me, but clearly I had hoped for too much.

Remember this: An adjunct position should also be adjunct to your life. Remember Merriam-Webster's definition? *Something joined or added to another thing but not essentially a part of it.* The problems arise when we try making adjunct work essential to our lives. You need to keep one simple fact in mind: You're being exploited. Once you accept this fact, it's easier to put the job into its proper context.

The Tenure-Track

As the first person in my family to go away to college, I realized quickly that academia was a world that I knew nothing whatsoever about. When other students talked about the Greeks, I had thought they were talking about Greek people. You know: *people from Greece.* I knew a lot of immigrants when I was growing up on the southwest side of Chicago, and I was familiar with my parents' Greek friends giving our Italian friends a good ribbing every chance they could, and vice-versa. But why were the Greeks being singled out in college? Why was everyone so interested in them?

Another term that mystified me was "tenure," which I first misheard as "ten year." When a professor said something about a position being "tenure-track," I always wondered what was going to happen to the professor when his ten years were up.

Tenure means (in theory) that your job is secure. (I say "in theory" because there have been recent cases in which tenured professors have been let go when the university eliminated that professor's department.) Tenure-track usually means that you have a six-year trial period, during which you attempt to fulfill the terms of your tenure document, after which you will be reviewed by your colleagues and the administration, who will decide whether or not to grant you tenure, which typically begins in your seventh year, if all goes well. (Where I teach, tenure-track professors are reviewed every two years and can be let go after any of those reviews until they receive tenure.)

I had gone on the teaching job market several times over an eleven-year period before the publication of my first book, and almost always I ended up with two or three interviews at the annual Modern Language Association conference where the first round of job interviews is conducted. These two or three interviews were almost always for terrible teaching positions (large course loads, large numbers of students in each class) in cities where I had no desire to live—not that I would ever reveal my reservations to the interviewing committee. I was desperate; I would have taken *any* job offered. Even so, I rarely scored an on-campus interview, and even when I did, I was never offered a position. As for the schools that weren't interested at all, their rejection letters frequently stated how many applicants they'd had—two hundred, three hundred, as many as five hundred.

After my first book was published, I went back on the job market and scored eighteen interviews. I had to cram sixteen of those interviews into the three-day conference, conduct one by phone, and turn one down because I couldn't fit it into my schedule. For the most part, these were pretty good jobs, too. My fortunes had changed—but not as dramatically as you may think. Of those sixteen positions, I ended up with three on-campus visits, and of those three positions, I received one job offer.

Tenure-track jobs in creative writing are not easy to come by. I served on a search committee for a poetry position that received over two hundred applications. Almost all the applicants already had published books, and many more than I would have guessed had PhDs in addition to MFAs. Even though I wasn't the one on the job market, I found it all depressing.

In any given year, there are roughly a hundred creative writing positions advertised in the fall leading up to the MLA interviews. Though the numbers vary slightly from year to year, we can usually assume that most of the positions are divided equally between poetry and fiction, with some creative nonfiction positions thrown in. About half of all the jobs fall into the "not particularly desirable" position for one reason or another (geographic location, heavy course load, several preparations, excessive administrative duties), which means that if you're a fiction writer, there are twenty good jobs out there if you're lucky. I guarantee you that those positions will receive at least two hundred applications, most likely many more.

Is a tenure-track teaching position really the much ballyhooed Valhalla that so many writers hope it is? Well, yes and no. Obviously, it depends upon where you teach, what your course load is, and how much committee work you're assigned. A tenure-track teaching position, in and of itself, isn't necessarily the Holy Grail. In some instances, it may prove to be your own personal hell—classrooms crammed full of students who don't want to be there; five different preparations each semester; not enough money to meet your monthly student loan payment, let alone live on.

The good tenure-track position can be good for as many reasons as a bad one is bad. Take mine. I teach two classes each semester, and since each class meets only once a week, I teach only two days a week, usually Mondays and Tuesdays. What this means is that I have Wednesday through Sunday to write during the school year. (Depending on the workload of the courses I'm teaching in a given semester, I sometimes have all seven days of the week to write.) The pay is good; the benefits are okay (they're not great where I teach but reasonable); I'm eligible for internal grants; I've already received a junior faculty leave, which amounts to a semester off with pay, as well as a senior faculty leave, which pays me two-thirds of my salary while I'm on leave for the year; class sizes are small; and I have autonomy in the classroom. In short, it is indeed Valhalla, right?

Sort of.

I've watched only one episode of Donald Trump's *The Apprentice*, but in it Trump offered up what may be the best advice I've yet to hear: *Don't get bogged down by the little stuff. It's the little stuff that will kill you.*

One of the looming dangers of a tenure-track job in academia is that you'll let the little stuff kill you. By "little" stuff, I mean departmental politics, insidious administrators, petty colleagues—things that you should shrug off but that, against your better nature, begin to eat at you, cutting into the mental energy you need for your writing. The little stuff becomes a deadly distraction. I wish I was exaggerating when I use the word "deadly," but during one particularly stressful semester my blood pressure rose to the point where I had to begin taking medication. Furthermore, stress also encourages me to exercise less and eat more. The problem was that I was letting the little stuff get to me, and if I didn't address the problems, it was likely to prove fatal. My solution was to have my office relocated to another wing of the building. My office is now on the same floor as the Philosophy Department, and my life has markedly improved.

There is also the larger problem of burn-out. Nearly every professor of writing suffers this, whether they're teaching composition or fiction writing. You reach a point where you feel as though you've been telling the same student the same things for the past twenty-five years. You start thinking, "What is it that you're not getting here?" And there are always the same resistances, the same arguments: "Well, I like trick endings," or "What's wrong with clichés?" They test your patience, these arguments. You take a deep breath; you smile; you count to ten. And then, for the thousandth time in your career, you patiently explain what the problem is with trick endings or clichés to a student who can't fathom that you've heard all of this before—many, many times before—and that her arguments and assertions are not as original as she thinks. But you have to keep that to yourself. You can't berate the student.

My solution is to keep what I'm doing in the classroom as fresh as possible. Most of the time, this strategy works. Some semesters,

I'll try new things in the classroom, such as conference calls to the authors whose books we've been reading, and these new additions to the course will prove to be a success well beyond my expectations. Other times, such as the semester I decided to teach screenwriting for a complete change of pace, the results were disastrous. The class may have failed, but at least I came out of it having learned a few things about screenwriting. I took *something* valuable away from what ended up being one of my most miserable semesters ever.

I am sure all of this sounds like a lot of belly-aching to those who don't have a tenure-track job, and I agree wholeheartedly. It *is*. And when I'm done belly-aching, I always remind myself that I have more time now for writing than I've ever had, more time legitimately off during the summers (since I make enough money now that I don't have to teach summer school or find another job), and more internal grants to fund research. I try to put it all into perspective. The problem is, we're still human, which means that most of us have a fault-finding device embedded in us, especially professors of creative writing, who, by our very nature, are always breaking down the very thing in front of us to see why it's not working.

Richard Russo drew a useful distinction between "work" and "job" in a commencement speech he delivered at Colby College, where he once taught:

> Search out the kind of work that you would gladly do for free and then get somebody to pay you for it. Don't expect this to happen overnight. It took me nearly twenty years to get people to pay me a living wage for my writing, which makes me, even at this juncture, one of the fortunate few. Your work should be something that satisfies, excites and rewards you, something that gives your life meaning and direction, that stays fresh and new and challenging, a task you'll never quite master, that will never be completed. It should be the kind of work that constantly humbles you, that never allows you to become smug—in short, work that sustains you instead of just paying your bills. While you search for this work, you'll need a job. For me that job was teaching, and it's a fine thing to be good at your job, as long as you don't confuse it with your work, which it's hard not to do.

Your work is your writing; your job is your teaching. I'm sure some professors—and many administrators—would wag their fingers at me for agreeing with Russo, but you have to decide what it is you primarily are: Are you a professor who writes, or are you a writer who teaches? I try to do a good job as a professor, but I am most definitely the latter. Whenever my priorities shift—whenever I become too invested in the squabbles on campus or the minutiae of departmental scuttlebutt—my writing begins to suffer, and I double my efforts to put the emphasis back where it should be.

Let's face it: All jobs, even the best of them, come with trap-doors through which you may fall if you're not careful. As for those few people who say to me, "But no, I really like my job," their voices, I've noticed, tend to go higher on the words *like my job*, as if they're trying to convince themselves more than they're trying to convince me. Would I write full-time if I could afford to? Yes. Absolutely. But very few writers I know can afford to tell their employer to take a hike. Even if you're making enough to live on, there's still health insurance to worry about, and retirement (well, okay, I've probably lost more money these last seven years in my 401K than I've made, but the *illusion* that a job will provide a retirement pension is still a pretty damned strong pull).

A life in academia isn't necessarily a bad one. It can be a good life, in fact. When I start getting down on the profession or my current lot in life, I remind myself what I was doing ten or fifteen years ago, back when I was a student with no money and no published book to my name, or when I was working three jobs and selling plasma. It's easy to lose perspective, so it's healthy to look behind you every once a while to remind yourself what life was like in the not-too-distant past. Also, it doesn't hurt to keep within reach the wisdom of the inimitable Donald Trump: *Keep your eye on the big picture; don't let the little stuff kill you.* Trump's insight may just save you from getting sucked into the black hole of triviality, where far too many bitter professors reside.

Seven Types of MLA Interview Committees

Should you be so lucky as to score interviews for a teaching position, you'll most likely have to fly to some far-flung city for the Modern Language Association conference, where the first rounds of interviews typically take place.

My sympathies go out to victims of natural disasters, abused animals, and first-time MLA interviewees. My first MLA was in December of 1988. I was twenty-three and, oblivious to what I was getting myself into, bought a suit off-the-rack at J. C. Penney with my last valid credit card and then took the train from Chicago to New Orleans, where the MLA conference was held that year. In the many years since that awful week, I have been to five or so MLA conferences for interviews. I wish that I could tell the fresh-faced interviewee not to worry, that the more interviews you do, the easier it gets, but I would be lying. What I've come to realize, however, is that you're likely to be interviewed by several different types of groups. The list below is a guide for the uninitiated, with the hope that it eases the pain.

The Partiers

Without question, these interviewers are the most enjoyable. Here we have a committee that looks like it just returned from happy hour. Everything you say is either hilarious or profound. Even though the college isn't what you had in mind—the course load is frightening, the class limits are exploitative, and the location is in a state you fear driving through—you begin imagining yourself working with these people. You like them, and it appears that they, unlike every other place you've ever worked, like each other. They're unpretentious. They tell good stories. This one, you conclude, is in the bag. On your way out, they slap your back and squeeze your arm. But don't be fooled: You'll probably never hear from them again. As with real happy hours, everyone is a friend or buddy until they step out of the room, at which point they are quickly forgotten. In this interview scenario, it's good to remember that you have only temporarily stumbled into the fold; you are not *in* the fold.

The Sad Sacks

This interview takes place off the beaten path, at a Days Inn far from the main conference hotel or at a table in the main hotel's commons area. Usually, someone is vacuuming nearby. These are all bad signs. Their department either can't afford to put the committee up at the main hotel, or they were too disorganized to register on time. The interviewers themselves look as though they arrived at MLA via a time machine, their hair and clothes from another era. When the interviewer says, "Everyone in this department wears two hats," you take it literally. This is the only interview scenario in which you'll feel bad for the interviewer, but your sympathy will quickly be snuffed out by the fear of a job offer. Brace yourself for that on-campus interview invitation.

The Clueless

In these interviews, no one seems to have looked at your c.v. Oh, sure, it's right there in front of them, but they'll start flipping through it, squinting as though someone, having played a joke on them, has slipped your file into the batch of legitimate candidates. For my very first MLA, I had traveled hundreds of miles only to experience such an interview. The department chair glanced at my c.v. and asked, "Do you plan on getting a PhD?" I had only an MFA. Mind you, the position was tenure-track. When would I have time to get a PhD? "Well, no," I said, and I began explaining how the MFA was a terminal degree, blah-blah-blah. While I was talking, the department chair broke the stem off his watch and spent the remainder of the interview on his hands and knees, crawling on the carpet, looking for the lost part. Another professor carried on with the questions. On my way out, the chair finally stood and wished me luck on my remaining interviews. "Good luck with your watch," I offered in return. Rule One: Don't expect the committee to have familiarized themselves with your materials. In fact, you may want to bring a copy of the job description with you to remind them why you're there.

The Obsessives

The lights in the hotel suite are too dim. At some point, something will distract these interviewers. A bird tapping at the window. A jackhammer miles away. While you're answering their question, they'll get up to investigate: "What is that? Do you think it will last long? Should we wait until it stops?" They may even apologize to you. "We're sorry about this. This is so awkward, really." You've just entered a scene from a David Lynch movie, where a bearded woman sings behind a radiator, or where you can hear millions of insects tilling the earth. Even as you are leaving the room, the professors will begin talking about the noise again, wondering where it's coming from and how they can stop it.

The Interrogators

Here is the stuff of academic parody. The first thing to understand is that you're the enemy. Therefore, expect a hostile reception. The committee has already formed a thesis about you. For one of my interviews, the committee had already decided that there was no consistency to my accomplishments and, therefore, I lacked a larger purpose—in short, a reason for being. The interview was merely a means of proving their thesis. They cut me off, dismissed my answers, laughed at my expense. When I had mentioned that it took a long time before I could write more autobiographical fiction without it being sentimental, one of the esteemed professors asked, "You remove sentimentality and replace it with *what?*" "Honesty, I suppose," I answered. "No, no," he said, "what do you *replace* it with?" "Honesty?" I said again, giving it another try. This went on, in one form or another, for twenty minutes. Remember the scene in *Marathon Man* where Dustin Hoffman is asked repeatedly "Is it safe?" by the Nazi played by Laurence Olivier? The answer didn't matter; Olivier kept drilling holes through Hoffman's teeth. Pretentious, self-satisfied, arrogant, these professors are the bottom-feeders of the academy. This interview isn't about you; it's about *them*. They're playing to an audience of their colleagues, and the not-so-subtle subtext is, "We understand your work better than you do; we have all the right credentials; we've gone to all the right schools; we have the larger purpose your life lacks; we are geniuses; you're not." Remember: Past behavior is the best indicator of future behavior. Be thankful that you're seeing their true colors now rather than later. My advice? Do what Dustin Hoffman did. Run like hell.

The Conversationalists

This committee has its priorities straight. They've asked for the interview because they're impressed with your c.v., or because they think you'll be a good fit. The questions, therefore, are designed to get to know you better *as a person* and *as a teacher.* "What are you working on next? How would you teach this class? Which authors have influenced your work? What are some examples of successes you've had in the classroom? How would you teach *this* course as opposed to *that* class?" Reasonable questions, all of them. This is not a dissertation defense, after all. And why would it be? You've already done that. It's not unheard of for such a committee to compliment you—a good sign that speaks to their egos, which may not be so fragile. The rapport is civil. The committee is engaged by what you say. All of this bodes well for the job, so keep your fingers crossed. The campus interview, if you're lucky, is where you'll see how they behave on home turf.

The Conference Callers

The conference call is its own beast. It may be comprised of any of the above—the Partiers, the Sad Sacks, the Clueless, the Obsessives, the Interrogators, or the Conversationalists—but it is complicated by technology. For starters, it's difficult to assess at a glance which group you're dealing with. (Partiers and Interrogators exhibit radically different body language, for instance.) The interviewers' voices are tinny and hard to hear, and there is usually a time delay. It's like talking to people in outer space. There are times when I've said something funny, waited, heard nothing, and then began talking again, only to be interrupted by laughter. The introductions are awkward—should you say hello after each person announces his or her name?—and there are often too many people involved for it ever to lapse into a comfortable conversation. One time, the chair of the committee called me a full hour before he was supposed to. I was taking a shower. When I reached the phone, I was naked and dripping wet. To my horror, I was already on speaker phone. I composed myself. I thought, *Okay, what the hell*, and sat down. It's a common recurring nightmare, showing up to an interview only to realize that you forgot to put on your clothes, but once it became clear that I was dealing with a committee of Interrogators and that this wasn't a job I wanted, I took great satisfaction that I was answering their questions in the buff. In fact, I highly recommend it, should the opportunity ever present itself to you. You'll be surprised just how liberating it can be.

The Effects of Academia on Your Writing

You write what you know, right? Even if you're writing a historical novel, you tap into some deep unconscious reservoir of personal material and then reconfigure it for the story you're telling, whether it's set in nineteenth century Boston or the battlefields of World War II.

The perceived danger of spending too much time in academia is that your subject matter will be limited to, well, novels about writers and/or academia. I've already addressed this issue to some extent in the chapter titled "What Have You Ever Done That's Worth Writing About?" but in this chapter I want to take a different approach and say, "So what? What's wrong with a writer writing about writers or academia?"

Let's pause for a moment and consider some writers who've written novels about writers or the academic life. Richard Russo's *Straight Man*, Donna Tartt's *The Secret History*, Mary McCarthy's *The Groves of Academe*, John Irving's *The World According to Garp*, Jane Smiley's *Moo*, James Hynes' *Publish and Perish*, Philip Roth's *The Human Stain* (to name but one), Stephen King's *Misery* (also, to name but one), Tim O'Brien's *Tomcat in Love*, Francine Prose's *Blue Angel*, Don DeLillo's *White Noise*, and on and on. Other writers who've dipped their toes into the genre of the academic novel include Jonathan Lethem, Michael Chabon, Jon Hassler, Richard Powers, J. M. Coetzee, and Saul Bellow — or, to put it another way, Nobel Prize winners, Pulitzer Prize winners, National Book Critics Circle Award winners, National Book Award winners, and mega-bestselling authors.

Though Bellow and Roth have written their fair share of novels about writers and academia and though Stephen King's characters are often writers themselves, the vast majority of the writers mentioned above haven't made a career out of writing novels about academia. When you think of Tim O'Brien, you think of fiction about Vietnam. When you think about Richard Russo, you think about novels set in blue-collar towns. When you think about Mary McCarthy, you think about novels that explore the world of Catholicism. David Lodge is one of the few writers who has made a career writing novels set in the academy, and he's damned good at what he does.

To *this* writer's way of thinking, I have no qualms with writers writing novels set in academia. In fact, one of my favorites is Edward

Allen's *Mustang Sally*, which nails the absurdity of this life. The nay-sayer may point out that of course I don't have any qualms. After all, I've written a novel about writers, edited an anthology of stories set in academia, and I've been associated with a university, either as a student or a teacher, for over twenty-five years now. To this naysayer, I would gladly point out all the other subjects I've tackled in my writing, all the stories and books that have nothing to do with academia or writing, but I would also point out the fact that *any* subject is a worthy subject for fiction, even the life of a naysayer, as Melville's Bartleby would tell you, should he so choose.

*You need to have the kind of patience
it takes to move the contents of a sandbox
from one place to another using a tweezers.
And then, more than likely, to move it back
again.*
— Geoffrey Becker, *Hot Springs*

6 The Writer's Life

Making Writing a Habit

Inspiration doesn't come when you sit around waiting for it. Inspiration comes after years of busting your hump. You know those writers who write a great short story or a great novel and say, "This one was a gift. It wrote itself"? The reason it was a gift—the reason it wrote itself—is because those writers had been writing every day, oftentimes for many years, working on stories and novels that *weren't* writing themselves.

The analogy I often use is playing pool. You go to a place where you can rent a table, and you work on a bank shot, over and over, or you practice putting English on the ball, or you spend the afternoon working on your break. What you're doing is very calculated; it's very *conscious*. You're internalizing all of these very mechanical moves; internalizing them eventually makes them second nature. One day, it all comes together: You're in a bar, playing competitively, and you win game after game. You hold the table all night long. And you're not even *thinking* about your shots. You look down at the table, and you instinctively know which shot is the best, where to leave the cue ball, what sort of spin to put on it. You're unstoppable. This night didn't happen because the muse visited you. It happened because it's the culmination of all those other days—those *years*—you spent practicing.

If you were lucky enough to watch the Chicago Bulls play the Portland Trail Blazers in the 1992 NBA finals, you'd have seen Michael Jordan shoot six three-point shots for the Bulls in the second half of the game. It's one of the all-time great moments in sports history. Michael Jordan was not only one of the greatest basketball players ever to play the game; he was one of the all-time great athletes. Even so, that night was not the result of some basketball muse descending upon Jordan. It was the end-result of *years* of practice. If Jordan hadn't spent those years practicing, it's unlikely that this night would ever have happened.

When students tell me that they wait for inspiration, I tell them that I don't believe in inspiration, that what I believe in is *work*. Most likely because they haven't done much writing in their lives, students in my beginning fiction writing course often mistake inspiration for simply "having an idea for a story," or they think of inspiration as the act of writing itself, as though it requires divine intervention to produce a short story, whether it's a good short story or a clichéd one. If they allow themselves to believe that their short story is the result of inspiration, then they can also allow themselves to believe that what they've created is precious and, therefore, beyond criticism.

To be honest, I do believe that inspired moments occur when you're writing; I just don't believe that they occur when you're sitting around waiting for them, and I think that "waiting for the muse" is more often than not an excuse not to work. And then it's easier to believe that such a thing as writer's block exists. Writing is like going to the gym. The less you go to the gym, the less you *want* to go to the gym. So, why doesn't anyone talk about exercise block?

Naturally, some people are more talented than others, whether they're playing baseball or writing, and those people are more likely to hit home runs with more frequency than the rest of us. That's not to say that we, who may be less talented, can't hit a home run, too, but I can assure you that it's never going to happen if we're not out there swinging the bat.

If you were your own employer, having to evaluate your performance as a writer, what would you say? Do you spend too much time on the Internet? Do you do other things when you should be sitting down and working? Are there days when you don't show up at all? If you were paying yourself an hourly wage for time spent writing, could you afford rent and food? Most importantly, would you the employer have fired you the writer by now?

I'm sure, early on in my career, I would have fired myself several years in a row. At a certain point, though, if you really want to make a go of this life, you have to accept a simple fact: *Writing is a job.* And you have to treat it as one. Oh, sure, you can work all day in your pajamas, or you can sleep in, or you can take long, contemplative walks — all of this, of course, if you're not otherwise employed. Sooner or later, though, you'll have to plant yourself in a chair and work — and work *hard.* That doesn't mean that you have to write fast or pound out a dozen pages a day. What I mean is that the time you spend writing shouldn't be treated like a hobby. I don't know of a single successful writer who doesn't treat writing with the same intensity of a job that they love and want desperately to keep.

The reason I would have fired myself early on in my career, if I were my own boss, is that I didn't have enough discipline. There were days I didn't write, and on those days when I did write, I was usually half-assed about it. There finally came a time when I had to say to myself, *Am I really going to do this thing or not, because if the answer is no, then I should quit pretending that this is what I do.* It took hitting rock-bottom a couple of times before I started taking writing more seriously. Getting accepted into a PhD program, which bought me several years' worth of valuable writing time, was the second chance I needed to hunker down and really make this career work.

I like to pile around my work area a variety of items to keep me inspired. I always keep books around me, but when I'm in the thick of a novel, trying to make it over the midway hump, I'll start piling several fat novels by a single writer around me—novels by John Irving or Joyce Carol Oates or Stephen King. The fatter the novels, the better. I try feeding off the sheer *bulk* of their writing. In other words, their thousands upon thousands of pages help to put the few pages I need to write each day into perspective.

I'm quick to point out, however, that it's not about writing quickly, and it's not about writing voluminously. Even so, I used to keep a sheet of quotes and facts taped next to my computer. On it: "John Irving published *The World According to Garp*—his FOURTH novel—when he was thirty-six." And: "Dennis Lehane wrote the draft of a novel in three weeks." I also quoted a letter by Thomas Wolfe: ". . . at present, I am writing about 3,000 words a day, which I hope to increase to 4,000. The novel will be Dickensian or Meredithian in length, but the work of cutting—which means, of course, adding an additional 50,000 words—must come later." I used all of these facts and quotes, along with several others, to fuel my daily writing, and to remind myself that I was not the first person in the history of the world to write a novel, even though it sometimes felt like it. I also kept a Post-it note next to my computer: "Don't waste time," it reads.

When I first began writing this book, I e-mailed a few dozen writers to ask for their best writing advice. Many of their quotes, scattered about these pages, you've already read. What I discovered, however, was that most of what they had to offer focused on discipline, on coming up with a schedule, on training yourself to sit down for hours at a stretch.

Mary Helen Stefaniak (*The Turk and My Mother*) offers up a "writing-as-a-job" model, which I couldn't agree with more:

Write regularly. Make a schedule that you can stick to [...] and stick to it the way you stick to the schedule at your place of (paid) work. Allow yourself a limited number of vacation days, but make them up when you can. If you've got a teaching job, re-make your schedule each semester so you'll NEVER have to forego writing to prepare for class. Don't wait for that sabbatical or fellowship, should you be so (sort of) lucky as to get one. Such unstructured—but finite—time to write has been known to make a writer "want to die like a dog," as Flaubert once said.

Lee Martin, a classmate of mine at the University of Nebraska–Lincoln, wrote for many years "in the cold," as Ted Solotaroff might have said, and didn't publish his first book, a short story collection, until he was in his early forties. His fifth book, the novel *The Bright Forever*, was a finalist for the Pulitzer Prize, but between his first and fifth books were the usual set-backs, namely in the form of rejections. His advice, not surprisingly, has much to do with remaining patient:

> The best advice I ever heard comes from something Isak Dinesen once said: "I write a little every day, without hope, without despair." I've been passing that advice along to students for over twenty-five years and doing my best to follow it myself. The longer I'm at this business of writing, the more I believe in patience, practice, and faith when it comes to being a writer, which is surely a life-long apprenticeship. I've learned to go about my business, letting words pile up day after day, not expecting too much, for fear that I'll never live up to the expectations, but also not giving up when things aren't going well, knowing that eventually, if I keep at it, something will click. The years have taught me that learning the craft requires dedication and discipline. When I hit a rough stretch and I begin to wonder whether I'll ever get things right, I remind myself that the reason I first put words on a page was that I was in love with language and expression. It helps to remember that and to get back to the business of a little of each every day, or as many days in a row as I can manage.

Michael Czyzniejewski (*Elephants in Our Bedroom*), who has served as an editor of the *Mid-American Review* for a number of years, also espouses the virtues of being patient:

Becoming a published writer is not an easy pursuit—not just a hobby. Becoming a writer is more of a commitment, involving a lot of rejection and necessitating a lot of patience. In the meantime, there's some good news: The time you spend being patient, waiting for publication, is also spent reading and writing. While you wait, you grow in your craft. In short, what you do to become a writer is just be a writer. If you can separate the actual writing from publication, if you can focus on the art, then the waiting isn't so hard. Plus, the harder you work, the quicker the spoils will follow.

Elizabeth Crane (*You Must Be This Happy to Enter*) begins each semester with this advice: "If you get nothing else out of this class, if you want to be a writer you need to do two things—you need to read, and you need to write." This may seem obvious, but I'm still stunned when students who want to be writers tell me that they don't read much, or when I have students in class who want to go on to MFA programs, but the only time they write is for their workshops' deadlines.

Notice how Lisa Gabriele (*The Almost Archer Sisters*) emphasizes *healthy* in her advice:

> The best advice I could possibly give a writer, any writer, aspiring or established, is to find a healthy way to sit still and be alone. Most of the frustrated writers I know (published and unpublished) have ideas, can string words together, and can find a half an hour a day before the kids get up, or six long hours on a Saturday afternoon to write. They've also found a voice and a great story to tell. Some even have agents and book deals. What they seem to lack is the ability to sit still and be alone for good stretches of time. I had no troubles with the alone part, but I had to teach myself how to sit still. Yoga and meditation help. Walking, too. Whatever it is that can keep you still, conscious and attuned, and also organizes the voices in your head, do it, do it, do it, until it's second nature. (Unless it's drugs and alcohol—writers aren't exempt from the law of diminishing returns.)

Writers *do* have problems sitting still for long stretches at a time. How many writers, after all, are battling demons of one kind or another, whether in the form of depression or addiction? We're an anxious, fidgety lot. To sit still for hours at a time, day after day, requires the sort of endurance needed to go to the gym regularly. Sitting still is simply another kind of discipline. Novelist Ayelet Waldman (*Love and Other Impossible Pursuits*) gives similar advice:

> Writing is a physical discipline, not just a mental one. If you make a time and a place for your work, and require of yourself the discipline to sit down in that chair every day (or five days a week), the muse will (generally) come when it's called. If you wait for her to arrive before sitting down, she'll visit someone else instead.

Are you seeing a pattern here? Sit, sit, sit. Write, write, write. "The writer is the person who stays in the room," is what Ron Carlson (*The Signal*) wrote to me, but why is staying in the room so damned hard? Janet Burroway (*Bridge of Sand*) broaches a subject that the other writers didn't—namely, *not* writing and its root cause:

> Procrastination, anomie, dread, laziness, disinclination, and their ilk are forms of fear. The fear is justified because you are proposing to take an internal nothingness and body it forth for anyone to judge and maul. Therefore, willy-nilly, anything you put willy-nilly on the page is an act of heroism. Junk will do; just do it. There. Now you have a something on which the work may now begin.

I would lie to you if I told you that I don't feel fear each time I begin writing a new novel, especially knowing that the writing of a novel will take years out of my life, and that there are no guarantees for publication when the novel is done. Fear is crippling, and sometimes you have to write your way out of it, until the joy you take in your project is the act of writing itself and not what it may or may not become, which is always out of your hands.

Here are two more philosophical issues to consider, the first by Holly Carver, director of the University of Iowa Press: "I often ask writers *why* publication is so essential to their validation (money and jobs aside)." She believes that the goal of publication sometimes unnecessarily hobbles the work of writing. Similarly, Tom Jenks, a former teacher of mine, posed this question to my workshop: "What's at stake for *you* in what you're writing?" Both of these are tough questions, but I think at some point you have to ask them of yourself.

Finally, Judith Claire Mitchell (*The Last Day of the War*) succinctly offers up advice that you may just want to tattoo to your arm so that you can read it every day: "Discipline is simply remembering what you want." And it is, isn't it? Because, really, if you *don't* want it, there's no reason to be disciplined about it, right?

Talking about Writing Isn't Writing

If you're spending more time talking about writing than actually writing, you may want to reassess your priorities. I've seen this happen in writers' groups, in coffeehouses, in MFA programs, in bars, on Facebook: writers who haven't yet published anything, or who haven't published much, talking or twittering about their "writing." Sometimes, these people are talking or twittering about their writer's block. Maybe it's therapeutic to spend so much time talking about it, but I suspect it's the opposite. I suspect it drives the supposed muse away. Take the time that you'd normally be talking about writing and *write*. Even if what you're writing is crap, it'll be more worth your while than talking about writing, because I believe you can write your way out of crappy writing, but it's unlikely you're going to talk your way into good writing.

I get paid to talk about writing. I teach for a living, and I'm occasionally invited to give lectures. If I find myself giving too many lectures, and if these lectures cut into my writing time, I start feeling like a fraud. *I should be writing*, I think. There are semesters when I feel as though I should be sending my students away for four months to write every day instead of having them sit in a classroom and listen to me. What better education about the writing life than to spend it writing every day, seven days a week? Instead, my students—many of them, anyway—wait until close to their deadline and then hammer out a draft of a story in a day. No matter how sincere their looks are as I prattle on about the importance of writing day in and day out, most of them ignore this advice.

The semester that I took a workshop from Allan Gurganus, he was in the galley stages of his behemoth novel *Oldest Living Confederate Widow Tells All*. Everyone will warn you that you're not supposed to revise at the galley stage. The text has already been typeset, and changes to that text become costly. And yet Allan was still revising. He had invited our class over to a party at the house he was renting that semester, and that's when what it meant to be a writer finally sunk in for me. Page proofs were taped everywhere, including around the bathtub so that Allan could revise as he bathed. I have stated over and over in this book that a writer's most valuable commodity is time, and Allan wasted none of it. He had thrown himself fully into this novel. He wasn't merely skimming the surface of the writing life; he had submerged himself in it, like a baptism. He *breathed* it. And I was a lucky person to have seen it.

Reading with Humility

It's easy to read a book and complain about it. I do it all the time these days. But I didn't do it when I began reading seriously. I was eighteen, and my first creative writing professor had given me a list of books to read. I was reading, for the very first time, the short stories of Raymond Carver, Flannery O'Connor, Tobias Wolff, Ann Beattie, John Barth, Mary Robison, and Robert Coover. I would sit in the hallway of my dorm and read, or I would read in the dorm's lounge, or on the second floor of Morris Library, or beside the escalators inside the student union. I remember reading Jerzy Kosinski's *Steps* and thinking, *How bizarre! What the hell IS this?* or reading about ice-nine for the first time in Vonnegut's *Cat's Cradle*, or reading all of John Irving's novels, one after the other, and experiencing the utterly compelling worlds of wrestling, bears, and Austria. I liked most of the books my professor had recommended. A few, like Irving's *The World According to Garp*, I loved. But I spent most of my day thinking about the ones I *didn't* understand or like.

I had assumed (correctly, I should note) that if I didn't understand something, or if a book bored me, that it was *my* fault. It was a reflection of my own deficiencies as a reader. To remedy these deficiencies, I would search out interviews with the authors, along with criticism of the books, to get a better handle on what exactly it was that I was reading and missing. (These were pre-Internet days when finding such things was a treasure hunt, and when you were likely to find other, more interesting things buried on library shelves during the search.) More often than not, I came away with a greater appreciation for the book in question. In some cases, I walked away with an understanding of an entire literary movement. In other words, to best understand the book, I needed a context; and in order to attain context, some extra work was involved.

We have since entered what I cynically call the Age of Opinion, and in this new era of public opinion polls, Amazon reviews, blogs, Goodreads, and Facebook, anyone can post an opinion about anything without having to have any expertise on the subject. I hate to sound like an old fogey—I'm only forty-four as I write this—but my fear is that having all of these outlets for expressing one's opinion is eroding thoughtful analysis. More and more, people believe that their opinions are as valid as anyone else's opinion by virtue of its appearance on a blog. Each year, my students seem more committed to their snap judgments of books I've assigned, and each year I find myself talking more and more about approaching the work with humility.

What I mean by "approaching the work with humility" is that, whether or not you like the book, the writer has created something that you yourself have yet to create: a published book, an *acclaimed* book, a substantial work of art. If you don't like it, don't automatically assume that it's the fault of the book or the writer. Instead, take a good, long look at yourself. What are *your* deficiencies as a reader? Where are *your* gaps of understanding? What is it about *you* that's not allowing you to appreciate the book more fully? Put your opinions aside. Read with an eye toward growing as a writer. Let curiosity fuel your reading. You have a lifetime of opinion-spouting ahead of you. Take the much more difficult path of trying to view the book from the author's perspective. What was she trying to do? What did the author's editor see in this book? And don't, in answering these questions, play the cynic's role: *The editor, clearly a fool, must be entertained by boring prose.* I'm not making a plea to throw critical acumen out the window, but this sort of response is too easy, letting you off the hook in terms of any kind of meaningful self-examination.

Raymond Carver, who was a student of John Gardner's, writes in the foreword to Gardner's *On Becoming a Novelist* about the time Gardner had assigned Robert Penn Warren's short story "Blackberry Winter." "For one reason or another," Carver writes, "I didn't care for it, and I said so to Gardner. 'You'd better read it again,' he said, and he was not joking." I recently tried out Gardner's approach in a fiction-writing class when a student announced to the class that the novel I had assigned could have been written by a fifth-grader. The other students didn't blink at their classmate's uninformed (and ludicrous) opinion, but when I said, "You better read it again," everyone looked nervously toward me, as though I had insulted the poor guy.

I stand by that advice: *Read it again.* I'm not suggesting that one should worship something published simply because it's been published, but if you're serious about becoming a writer, don't stand above the work and dismiss it out of hand without asking the tough questions first. The student should have thought, "Okay, my professor assigned this book, and this book has received universal acclaim, so maybe I should figure out why it was deemed important enough for us to read." But all opinions being equal in this day of Internet message boards, such a thought clearly didn't enter his head. He had read the book not as an aspiring writer; he read it like an impatient student who couldn't wait to write a 140-character Twitter comment about it.

I end many of my semesters with this passage, which can be found on the last page of Vladimir Nabokov's lectures on literature, with the hope that students will raise their own bar the next time they sit down with a book:

> I have tried to make of you good readers who read books not for the infantile purpose of identifying oneself with the characters, and not for the adolescent purpose of learning to live, and not for the academic purpose of indulging in generalizations. I have tried to teach you to read books for the sake of their form, their visions, their art. I have tried to teach you to feel a shiver of artistic satisfaction, to share not the emotions of the people in the book but the emotions of its author—the joys and difficulties of creation. We did not talk around books, about books; we went to the center of this or that masterpiece, to the live heart of the matter.

In the courses of mine where the students show the least growth, they either condescend to the work ("I could have written that," a student once said of a Raymond Carver story) or approach the reading as a chore. In those courses where the students have shown the most growth, they approach the readings with excitement and respect, even as they scrutinize and criticize.

The Writer's Vices

....

I'm no saint. I spent years drinking more than I should have. When I was a student at Iowa, I was arrested one night for public intoxication. I was photographed, fingerprinted, and thrown in jail. That was over twenty-two years ago. I continued drinking heavily for a number of years, until, eventually, I put a lid on it. I'll still drink a few times a year, mostly at writing conferences, but even there I'm scaling back.

The last thing I want to do is sound like the clichéd reformed alcoholic who's going to preach sobriety. But here's the deal. When I think back on all those years that I drank heavily, I wasn't writing a whole hell of a lot, and I wasn't getting much published. It's probably not a coincidence that my output as well as my publication rate increased exponentially when I cut back on drinking. Furthermore, I realized that many of my short stories and one failed novel were set in bars, and my characters were almost always in some altered state. This was fine for a story or two, but it grows stale pretty fast.

Occasionally, I'll get a student in my class who fancies him- or herself (usually himself) a writer but is actually drawn more toward the *image* of being a writer, and more often than not, that image resembles Charles Bukowski or some other writer who's more famous for his alcohol intake than his prose. This student sees this image of the writer as romantic, and isn't that what being a writer is all about, anyway? Hanging out in smoky bars? Chatting up the barkeep? Bourbon with a beer chaser next to a pack of cigarettes, matches, and a handful of loose change?

All you need to do is read the section "C.V." in Stephen King's book *On Writing* to see how distinctly *unglamorous* it is to be an alcoholic and drug addict. He writes of the day his wife, Tabitha, organized an intervention, with family members and friends present: "Tabby began by dumping a trashbag full of stuff from my office out on the rug: beercans, cigarette butts, cocaine in gram bottles and cocaine in plastic Baggies, coke spoons caked with snot and blood, Valium, Xanax, bottles of Robitussin cough syrup and NyQuil cold medicine, even a bottle of mouthwash." For further evidence of how ugly this sort of life can get, read Blake Bailey's biographies of Richard Yates and John Cheever to watch in excruciating detail how alcoholism wreaks havoc on everything and everyone within the alcoholic's orbit.

The rule of thumb is that you get better as a writer the older you become, but in nearly every instance that I can think of, the writer who's known for his legendary drinking wrote his or her best books early on. The later books are almost always pale comparisons, as in Richard Yates' case, or embarrassments, as in Frederick Exley's. Not long ago, I tried giving a reading after drinking on an empty stomach and taking medication. Not surprisingly, the reading was a disaster. Later, I jokingly compared my performance to Elvis's last few concerts, where he was drugged and bloated, sang only a few songs, and then read lyrics from a sheet of paper before calling it quits for the night . . . but we all know the end of Elvis's story, and it's not a pretty one.

Money and the Writer

If you've decided to become a writer for the big paycheck, let me make a suggestion: Play the lottery instead. The odds of winning are better. *Much* better. That's not to say that there isn't money to be made as a writer. There is. One problem is that you can't count on it. Another problem is that you probably can't live solely on your writing income.

I don't mean to be discouraging here, but the reality is that very few writers can afford to quit their day job. Let's do a little math. Let's say that a commercial publishing house has agreed to pay you $100,000 for your first novel. Not bad, right? By all accounts, this would be an exceptionally good advance. (Most first novels do *not* get $100,000 advances, but I'm feeling generous today.) First, let's take out the agent's 15 percent commission. That leaves you with $85,000. Next, let's take 25 percent out for taxes. That gives you $63,750. Now, let's assume that this novel took five years to write. Some novels take longer; some can be knocked out in a few years. For a literary novel that has a *chance* of earning 100K, you probably would have spent about five years on it. What this means is that you will have made $13,150 for each year of your hard work. In other words, you made less than what you would likely have made working at Wal-Mart.

I earned a pretty good advance for my two-book deal with Free Press. It wasn't the best advance in the world, but it was certainly more money than I was anticipating. You know what I did with that money? I paid off my VISA bills. I didn't even make enough to put toward my house or my student loans.

That said, a published writer can sometimes supplement his or her writing income in various ways: teaching at conferences; giving readings at colleges; writing book reviews; or receiving grants and fellowships. These offers could mean anywhere from a few hundred bucks (for writing a book review) to a few thousand (for teaching at a conference). There's no set figure for any of these opportunities. I've been paid anywhere from two hundred dollars to three thousand to give a reading. The same is true for conferences. I've agreed to teach at conferences for as low as five hundred and for as much as three grand. Unless you're famous, it's difficult to draw a line in the sand and say, "This is how much I work for, and I won't go any lower."

Everything is negotiable, however. What may lure me to a conference or a reading for significantly less money than I might otherwise want could be any number of factors, but one factor stands out above all the others: the opportunity for book sales. Occasionally, this means that I might be able to sell my own books at the venue, thereby opening up more money-making opportunities.

Earning extra money without sacrificing your writing time is a delicate balancing act, and if you're lucky enough to have published a book that's gotten some attention, it's easy to get lured by the fast cash, but as the cliché goes, moderation in all things.

Dating (or Marrying) a Writer

I'm not a matchmaker, nor am I a marriage counselor, so I'm not going to offer much by way of advice, but I will point out a few observations. Dating a writer can be tricky for a number of reasons. For one thing, you're likely to be reading each other's work. What if one writer is more sensitive to criticism than the other? Or, what if one is prone to offering harsh, uncensored criticism? You'll probably need to find some middle ground or set some ground rules.

What if you don't respect the work of the person you're dating? I don't know how one gets over this hump, but on those very few occasions when I've been around a writer who's disparaging the work of their significant other, I've walked away with a sense that the lack of respect goes deeper than the work itself. These couples probably shouldn't be together in the first place, but if they are, I don't want to be around when the truth, held like a weapon, is finally revealed.

In long-term relationships, you have to worry about finding two jobs for writers in the same place. If you're both shooting for jobs in academia, good luck! This may be the most pervasive stumbling block for two writers trying to make a life together. One gets a good job while the other does grunt work for a lousy wage. Is it possible to live this sort of life and, if you're the one with the miserable job, not feel resentment? Yeah, sure . . . but the gainfully employed partner should be attuned to the other's sacrifices and help remedy the situation, if at all possible.

And then there's the writing career itself. A career in writing is a movable feast. One day you're hot; the next, your book is in the remainder bin and no one remembers you. It's entirely possible for one spouse's career to be the hot one for a couple of years while the other spouse's career is hot thereafter. As one descends, the other ascends. The ego is a nasty fellow, and it's easy to become resentful and jealous. Resist, I say. Try to remind yourself why you're a writer in the first place. Take as much pleasure in your significant other's accomplishments as you would your own. It's not an easy life, two writers living under the same roof, but it can be a gratifying one if you can put all the ego and accompanying b.s. aside while staying attuned to each other's highs and lows.

Writing as a Competitive Sport

Once you start viewing writing as a competition—once you start keeping tallies for who won awards that you didn't win—it's time to pack it in. This is a losing game because there will *always* be people who are getting awards and book contracts and advances and jobs that you won't be getting, and you'll only end up driving yourself insane thinking about it. At the end of the day, what's the point? Is it that you're more deserving? Is it that the world isn't fair? And when you start complaining about it to other people, how do you think that looks?

In John Barth's essay "Doing the Numbers," he calculates how many writers you're likely to be competing against during your lifetime. He concludes, "Many are called and few are chosen, but those few *are* chosen, usually. Inasmuch as the few can never mean the many, you had as well relax and trust your muse, for there's little you can do towards that final election except read everything and practice your ass off."

The only person you should be competing with is yourself, and by that I mean that you should be constantly raising the bar for your own work and pushing yourself to become a better writer, because I guarantee you that the person you think you're in competition with isn't even thinking about you.

Manners

In 1946, Orson Welles was directing a play for which everything was going wrong. In anger, he threw his cane, which struck a stagehand. The stagehand picked up the cane, walked over to Welles, and struck him with it. Welles had the stagehand thrown out of the theater. Later that night, the stagehand, who was living in a boardinghouse, heard a knock at his door. Turns out it was Orson Welles. He had come to apologize. He hadn't realized that the cane had hit the stagehand, and he wanted the young man to return to work.

Fast-forward to 1967. After years of struggling to come up with financing for movies, Orson Welles was once again in need of money. He received an offer to appear on *The Dean Martin Show* and accepted, though it was a mystery as to why Dean Martin would have wanted him on his show. What he eventually learned was that one of TV's top producers, a man named Greg Garrison, was behind the invitation. Garrison, as Welles eventually learned, was the young stagehand who had been struck by Welles' cane twenty-one years earlier. This was Garrison's way of thanking Welles for his late-night apology and the invitation to return to work. In the coming years, Garrison offered Welles many more TV appearances, as well as a TV pilot that, unfortunately, didn't get picked up. It was, I'm sure, because of Garrison that Welles became a staple of late-night TV in the seventies.

There are many lessons to be taken from this anecdote, but two are applicable for this section: Don't look at apologizing as a weakness, especially if you're the one who's been an ass, and don't think that hierarchies won't ever shift. Of course, some people aren't gracious enough to accept an apology, and there's nothing you can do about that except cut your losses by moving on.

I am always stunned when someone is rude apropos of nothing, but I find it especially perplexing — and preposterous — when the person who's rude justifies it because they believe that they are somehow higher up the ladder than the person they're being rude to. The thing about literary hierarchies (a phrase that surely must be an oxymoron) is that they are always shifting, and a person who may be above one person one day could very well find himself below said person the next.

Many years ago, while I was working for a well-established literary magazine, the editor had been wooing a certain young author but had, until then, rejected all of his stories. For whatever reason— perhaps she was too busy?—the editor asked me to call him to let him know that although we wouldn't be taking either of his two latest stories, she'd like for him to continue submitting work to her.

Even as I picked up the phone, I had a bad feeling. I didn't want to be the one who made this call, but I was a grunt worker at the magazine, so call him I did.

I could tell instantly that he was perturbed.

"So, are you taking one of the stories or not?" he asked after I explained who I was and how much we enjoyed his stories.

"Well, no. But we really want to see more work."

"I normally talk to H——. Who are *you*? Why isn't *H——* calling me?" he asked, his voice becoming more shrill.

"She's busy today. She asked me to call you."

"Who are you?"

I told him again who I was.

"I don't understand why H—— didn't call me. Normally, H—— calls me."

I said nothing. We'd already gone over this.

"Have you published anything?" he asked. "How old are you?"

Allow me to pause here to talk about subtext. *Have you published anything? How old are you?* I knew from this writer's bio that he had recently graduated from an MFA program and had published a few stories in decent literary magazines. What he was doing here was forcing my hand to reveal where I stood on the hierarchy in relation to him. Should he temper his tone, or was he justified in his condescension? I wish I could accurately capture the snottiness in his voice. I also wish I could accurately capture the *whine* each time he said, *Why isn't H—— talking to me?*

This conversation took place over fifteen years ago. The writer has gone on to publish two novels during those fifteen years—not a bad career, but I doubt it's the career he thought he was on the brink of. What did he gain from his attitude? Nothing from me. Perhaps it worked better on someone else, though I somehow doubt it. Would I ever include him in one of my anthologies? Would I ever invite him for a reading at my university? Would I ever do anything to support this writer's career? No, no, and, uh . . . no.

In the summer of 1989, for its special fiction issue, *Esquire* published a supposed hierarchy of writers in the form of a pyramid made out of Post-it notes stuck on the back of an office door. What's funny is how different, twenty years later, the hierarchy would look. What goes up must come down. During the more than twenty-five years that I've been taking writing seriously, I have watched reputations soar and then plummet. I've witnessed innumerable shifts in the so-called hierarchy. There's the cliché that you better be nice to those on your way up because you may just pass them on your way down. Boy, is it true in writing! And the writing world is a small one. I often tell people that if there's a writer or editor I don't know, I'm sure I know someone who knows him or her. It's a profession where there are, at most, two degrees of separation. So, tread lightly, my friends. And don't forget your manners.

On Being Humble

A few years ago, I had a student who would come up to me before turning in his story to tell me how brilliant the story was. "I think it's really quite brilliant," he'd say without a trace of irony. Unfortunately, his stories were far from brilliant. I wish I could say that he was the only student of mine who's ever trumpeted his self-declared genius, but it's begun happening with more frequency, especially these last few years. Sadly, each year brings fewer students who want the sort of feedback that might make them better writers. What they want instead is affirmation that their parents and grade-school teachers were correct. They want me to say, *Yes, they were right, every last one of them—you're a genius!*

The age of humility is over. It's been gone so long that I was starting to forget that it had even existed . . . that is, until I started reading the translator's note in Thomas Mann's *The Magic Mountain* the other day. H. T. Lowe-Porter, whose translation appeared in 1927, wrote, "The translator wishes to thank, in this place, a number of scholars, authorities in the various special fields entered by *The Magic Mountain*, without whose help the version in all humility here offered to English readers, lame as it is, must have been more lacking still."

How refreshing it is to read the words of someone who isn't standing on a mountaintop and bellowing, "Oh, but look at how *brilliant* I am!"

Or take John Steinbeck's journal entry as he neared completion of *The Grapes of Wrath*: "I only hope it is some good. I have very grave doubts sometimes. I don't want this to seem hurried. It must be just as slow and measured as the rest but I am sure of one thing—it isn't the great book I had hoped it would be. It's just a run-of-the-mill book. And the awful thing is that it is absolutely the best I can do."

If John Steinbeck felt this way about *The Grapes of Wrath*, I think we could all, each and every one of us, stand to be more modest when we talk about our work.

Dealing with Fame

Recognition almost always has an effect on the writer who receives it; this is inevitable. But what effect will it have on you, should you be so lucky (or cursed) to experience the kind of recognition that comes with fame?

As previously mentioned, I worked as a freelance media escort for a few years, which meant that I sometimes spent a good part of the day with an author, picking her up from the airport, taking her to interviews, walking her from the hotel to the bookstore, sometimes having meals with her. One writer I was lucky enough to escort was David Sedaris. At the time, *Me Talk Pretty One Day* was on the *New York Times* bestseller list, and he'd already been doing interviews on TV shows like the *Late Show with David Letterman*. He was a bona fide celebrity. The good news is that he didn't act like one. Sedaris chatted with me, asking what I did, and when I told him that I'd just had my first book come out, he offered several tips, many of which had to do with how to treat people. That morning, over breakfast, he took the time to write thank-you cards to various people from his previous stop: booksellers, interviewers, hosts. He told me that he shows up to his readings an hour early to sign books so that people don't have to wait in line afterward. Not that he minded the long lines afterward, he assured me. But sometimes the signings went on for several hours, and he just wanted to make sure that anyone who wanted a signed book got one. And sure enough—he showed up early to his reading that night to chat with the people filling up the seats and to sign their books. After his talk, he continued signing, even taking up an invitation by some fans to go with them to a local pub, but before he left for the night, he bought a copy of my book and had me sign it for him.

David Sedaris, who could have been a royal jerk and probably gotten away with it, was, in a word, gracious. The next day, on our way back to the airport, he regaled me with stories about writers who weren't particularly gracious and how booksellers went out of their way to talk customers out of buying their books.

Fame can show one's mettle. So, what's it going to be? Do you want to be known as the arrogant jerk, or do you want to exhibit grace and generosity?

You've Published a Book—Now What?

I used to wonder why an author who had published several books suddenly, inexplicably disappeared. I sometimes didn't even realize that they had disappeared until unpacking one of their books after a move or seeing a sun-bleached and dusty copy on the shelf of a second-hand bookstore or, worse, at the Goodwill.

I used to wonder, but I don't anymore. You know the cliché: It's easy to fall in love; it's harder to keep a marriage going. That first book, the one you labored over for however many years, is your love affair. But once it's published, the realities of publishing kick in: low book sales, disappointed publishers, dashed hopes, the desire for a quick follow-up. It's easy to forget why you had begun writing in the first place.

Sometimes writers disappear against their will. Their first book is published, but then they can't get a second one published. Maybe the first book received good reviews—maybe even *great* reviews—but the sales weren't enough to justify a paperback, let alone another book. Or maybe this happens after their fifth book. The publisher—or a series of publishers—clings to the hope that this writer will write a book that breaks them out of the dreaded midlist, but the dark realization eventually settles in: It's not going to happen—or so the publisher believes.

Sometimes writers disappear because they throw in the towel. Being a writer isn't an easy life, and, hell, maybe it's actually a relief to give it up, especially if what you're getting out of it doesn't even come close to what you're putting into it.

And sometimes a writer disappears because they've said all they want to say. Perhaps they had just the one book in them. Or two books. Or five. But then there's nothing else to say.

I don't care what art you pursue—music, film, writing—it's extraordinarily difficult to keep the creative juices flowing over an extended period of time. There are a number of astonishing examples to the contrary—Joyce Carol Oates, Stephen King, T. C. Boyle, Margaret Atwood, David Lodge—writers who keep putting out the books, one after the other, some better than others, but who can blame any of them for an occasional clunker? When you think about the difficulty of writing *one* good book (yes: *one*), you have to stand in awe before the body of work of any one of these writers.

The paradox of this profession is that most writers don't hit their stride until their forties or, in some instance, their fifties, right around the time many people are winding down, or, at the very least, beginning to look more seriously at their retirement portfolios. Let's face it. Most of us in our forties and fifties don't have the energy we did when we were in our twenties, but when most of us were in our twenties, we weren't disciplined enough to sit down every day or experienced enough to write with as much depth as we would have hoped for. *Most* of us. There are, of course, exceptions.

The older I get, the crazier my chosen path seems to me. And so it's no surprise to me anymore when I pull a book off my shelf and wonder what's become of this writer or that. The surprise is always when I see a newly released book by a writer who's been at this for a long time, especially a writer who hasn't yet achieved the prominence her work deserves. *Good for her!* I think. Against all odds, here is a writer who has persevered.

It's easier to stop writing than it is to keep going, and I don't blame the writer who quits, either. I read somewhere that the heart of every mystery is this maxim: "Everyone has their reasons." Well, every writer does, too. And at least, if even briefly, you were "in the arena," as Teddy Roosevelt would have said. At least your place shall never be with those cold and timid souls who knew neither victory nor defeat.

Notes

I posed the question "What's the best advice you have for an aspiring writer?" to several authors. The following were kind enough to answer via e-mail: Sherman Alexie, Julianna Baggott, Joseph Bathanti, Geoffrey Becker, Janet Burroway, Ron Carlson, Elizabeth Crane, Michael Czyzniejewski, Darren DeFrain, Sherrie Flick, Lisa Gabriele, Ray González, Dave King, Lee Martin, Jonathan Messinger, Judith Claire Mitchell, Mary Helen Stefaniak, and Ayelet Waldman. Their quotes can be found throughout this book.

Ten Rules to Keep near You

These are my rules.
Feel free to use these or come up with your own.

1. Write every day. No excuses.
2. Don't fixate on rejection. Remember: The publishing world's decisions are rarely logical.
3. Spend less time on the Internet.
4. Don't let your day job become an excuse not to write.
5. Don't spend more time talking about writing than actually writing.
6. Make writing a habit, but don't let it consume your life.
7. Keep other projects on the side. If you get stuck on one, work on another.
8. Keep your eye on the big picture. When you're trying to write a book, don't get sidetracked with a thousand small writing projects. The onslaught of small projects is often the reason big projects die.
9. Spend time browsing bookstores. Read books.
10. Find some joy in the act of writing. If you cease to find joy in it, it's probably time to do something else.

My Five Favorite Movies about Writers

I love movies. Movies can serve as a shot of adrenaline, a quick fix for the writer's slump. I highly recommend having on hand several movies that inspire you to write. Here are five that never fail to send me back to the writing table.

Barton Fink
Henry and June
Orange County
The Squid and the Whale
Wonder Boys

Recommended Reading

The following list is by no means comprehensive. It's a highly subjective list of books and other publications that I have found interesting and useful. Some, like John Gardner's *The Art of Fiction* and *On Becoming a Novelist*, have been my constant companions ever since I decided to take writing seriously; others, like Flannery O'Connor's *The Habit of Being*, I'll open at random to read a few pages at a time. Some of these, like *The Rhetoric of Fiction* and *Aspects of the Novel*, are old-fashioned, but I love them nonetheless and make no apologies for their inclusion on this list; others are so new they may not stand the test of time, but I've grown fond of them in the short time we've spent together. A few of the books are out of print, so you may have to scour used bookstores, go to your local library, or search online for them.

I have broken the items on this list down to correspond with the sections of this book that seem the most applicable, but many of them could just as easily be moved to another section. I'm including this list here, idiosyncratic though it is, with the hope that you'll find something useful on it.

Part One: The Decision to Become a Writer
Caldwell, Erskine. *Call It Experience*. New York: Duell, Sloan and
  Pierce, 1951.
Gardner, John. *On Becoming a Novelist*. With an introduction by
  Raymond Carver. New York: Harper and Row, 1983.
Keyes, Ralph. *The Courage to Write: How Writers Transcend Fear*. New
  York: Owl Books, 1995.
Manguel, Alberto. *A History of Reading*. New York: Viking, 1996.
Welty, Eudora. *One Writer's Beginnings*. Cambridge: Harvard
  University Press, 1998.

Part Two: Education and the Writer
Addonizio, Kim. *Ordinary Genius: A Guide for the Poet Within*. New
  York: Norton, 2009.
Addonizio, Kim, and Dorianne Laux. *The Poet's Companion: A Guide
  to the Pleasures of Writing Poetry*. New York: Norton, 1997.

Bernays, Anne, and Pamela Painter. *What If? Writing Exercises for Fiction Writers.* 3d ed. New York: Longman, 2009.

Booth, Wayne. *The Rhetoric of Fiction.* 2d ed. Chicago: University of Chicago Press, 1983.

Burroway, Janet, and Elizabeth Stuckey-French. *Writing Fiction: A Guide to Narrative Craft.* 8th ed. New York: Longman, 2010.

Chapman, Robert L., and Barbara Ann Kipfer. *American Slang.* 2d ed. New York: Harper Perennial, 1998.

Forster, E. M. *Aspects of the Novel.* London: Penguin, 1976.

Gardner, John. *The Art of Fiction.* New York: Knopf, 1984.

Hacker, Diana, ed. *A Writer's Reference.* 6th ed. Boston: Bedford/ St. Martin's, 2009.

Hemley, Robin. *Turning Life into Fiction.* 2d ed. St. Paul: Graywolf, 2006.

Holman, Amy. *An Insider's Guide to Creative Writing Programs: Choosing the Right MFA or MA Program, Colony, Residency, Grant or Fellowship.* Upper Saddle River: Prentice Hall, 2006.

Huddle, David. *The Writing Habit.* Lebanon: University Press of New England, 1994.

Hugo, Richard. *The Triggering Town: Lectures and Essays on Poetry and Writing.* New York: Norton, 1992.

Kealey, Tom. *The Creative Writing MFA, Revised and Updated Edition: A Guide for Prospective Graduate Students.* 2d ed. New York: Continuum, 2008.

King, Stephen. *On Writing: A Memoir of the Craft.* New York: Scribner, 2000.

Lukeman, Noah. *A Dash of Style: The Art and Mastery of Punctuation.* New York: Norton, 2007.

Madden, David. *Revising Fiction.* New York: Plume, 1988.

Masih, Tara, ed. *The Rose Metal Press Field Guide to Writing Flash Fiction: Tips from Editors, Teachers, and Writers in the Field.* Brookline: Rose Metal Press, 2009.

O'Connor, Frank. *The Lonely Voice: A Study of the Short Story.* Cleveland: World Publishing Company, 1963.

Pack, Robert, and Jay Parini, eds. *Writers on Writing: A Bread Loaf Anthology.* Lebanon: University Press of New England, 1991.

Perl, Sondra, and Mimi Schwartz. *Writing True: The Art and Craft of Creative Nonfiction.* Boston: Houghton Mifflin, 2006.

Prose, Francine. *Reading Like a Writer.* New York: Harper Perennial, 2007.

Root, Robert L., and Michael Steinberg. *The Fourth Genre: Contemporary Writers of/on Creative Nonfiction.* 5th ed. New York: Longman, 2009.

So, Is It Done? Navigating the Revision Process. DVD. Directed by Jotham Burello. Chicago: Elephant Rock Productions, 2005.

Stern, Gerald. *Making Shapely Fiction.* New York: Norton, 1991.

Woodruff, Jay, ed. *A Piece of Work: Five Writers Discuss Their Revisions.* Iowa City: University of Iowa Press, 1993.

Writers on Writing: Collected Essays from the New York Times. New York: Times Books, 2002.

Writers on Writing, Volume II: More Collected Essays from the New York Times. New York: Times Books, 2004.

Tom Kealey, author of *The Creative Writing MFA*, also maintains a website worth checking out:

http://creative-writing-mfa-handbook.blogspot.com/.

You should read the *Paris Review*'s "Writers at Work" interview series, whether in the magazine itself or in its many anthologies of interviews. These are terrific interviews that focus on the craft of writing.

I highly recommend reading any of these annual anthologies:

The Best American Essays
The Best American Mystery Stories
The Best American Nonrequired Reading
The Best American Poetry
The Best American Science and Nature Writing
The Best American Short Stories
The Best American Travel Writing
Best of the Web
Prize Stories: The O. Henry Awards
The Pushcart Prize: Best of the Small Presses

Part Three: Getting Published

Farson, Richard, and Ralph Keyes. *The Innovation Paradox: The Success of Failure, The Failure of Success.* New York: Free Press, 2003.

Henderson, Bill, and André Bernard. *Pushcart's Complete Rotten Reviews and Rejections: A History of Insult, A Solace to Writers.* Wainscott: Pushcart Press, 1998.

Herman, Jeff. *Jeff Herman's Guide to Book Publishers, Editors, and Literary Agents.* 20th ed. Naperville: Sourcebooks, 2009.

Keyes, Ralph. *The Writer's Book of Hope: Getting from Frustration to Publication.* New York: Owl Books, 2003.

Korda, Michael. *Making the Bestseller List: A Cultural History of the American Bestseller, 1900–1999.* New York: Barnes and Noble Books, 2001.

Lukeman, Noah. *The First Five Pages: A Writer's Guide to Staying Out of the Rejection Pile.* New York: Fireside, 2005.

———. *How to Land (and Keep) a Literary Agent.* http://www.landaliteraryagent.com/.

Submit! The Unofficial All-Genre Multimedia Guide to Submitting Short Prose. DVD. Directed by Jotham Burello. Chicago: Elephant Rock Productions, 2005.

Writer's Digest Books publishes annually reference books for submitting creative work to magazines, publishers, and agents:

Children's Writer's and Illustrator's Market
Guide to Literary Agents
Novel and Short Story Writer's Market
Poet's Market
The Writer's Market

Subscribe to *Poets & Writers*.

Subscribe to *The Writer's Chronicle*, a publication of the Associated Writing Programs.

Part Four: Publicity

Deval, Jacqueline. *Publicize Your Book! An Insider's Guide to Getting Your Book the Attention It Deserves.* New York: Perigee, 2008.

Elliott, Stephen. "The D.I.Y. Book Tour." *New York Times Book Review*, January 14, 2010. http://www.nytimes.com/2010/01/17/books/review/Elliott-t.html.

Weber, Steve. *Plug Your Book! Online Book Marketing for Authors, Book Publicity through Social Networking.* Weber Books, 2007.

Part Five: Employment for Writers

For jobs in higher education, subscribe to the *Chronicle of Higher Education*.

Also, join the Modern Language Association, which gives you access to their Job Information List, a weekly listing of jobs available in higher education.

For daily listings of jobs in publishing, subscribe to the website *Publishers Marketplace*, www.publishersmarketplace.com.

Here's an interesting wiki, used primarily by those looking for jobs: http://academicjobs.wikia.com/wiki/Academic_Jobs_Wiki.

Part Six: The Writer's Life

Arana, Marie. *The Writing Life: Writers on How They Think and Work*. New York: PublicAffairs, 2003.

Dillard, Annie. *The Writing Life*. New York: Harper Perennial, 1989.

O'Connor, Flannery. *The Habit of Being: The Letters of Flannery O'Connor*. Edited by Sally Fitzgerald. New York: Farrar, Straus and Giroux, 1979.

Singleton, George. *Pep Talks, Warnings, and Screeds: Indispensable Wisdom and Cautionary Advice for Writers*. Cincinnati: Writer's Digest Books, 2008.

Steinbeck, John. *Working Days: The Journals of "The Grapes of Wrath."* Edited by Robert DeMott. New York: Penguin Books, 1990.

Wolfe, Thomas. *The Letters of Thomas Wolfe*. Edited by Elizabeth Nowell. New York: Scribner, 1956.

Bibliography

Barth, John. "Doing the Numbers." In *The Friday Book*. New York: Perigree Books, 1984.

Brod, Max. *Franz Kafka: A Biography*. New York: Schocken Books, 1963.

Caldwell, Erskine. *Call It Experience*. New York: Duell, Sloan and Pierce, 1951.

Carver, Raymond. "The Paris Review Interview." In *Fires: Essays, Poems, Stories*. New York: Vintage, 1984.

Chayefsky, Paddy. Interview with John Brady. *American Film* 7 (December 1981): 60–64.

Crace, John. "Ballard Proves You Should Live a Bit Before Writing." *Books Blog. The Guardian.* http://www.guardian.co.uk/books/booksblog/2009/apr/21/jgballard-fiction.

D'Amato, Barbara. "Persistence." In *The Outfit: A Collective of Chicago Crime Writers*. http://theoutfitcollective.blogspot.com/2007/07/persistence.html#156024424606589089.

García Márquez, Gabriel. *One Hundred Years of Solitude*. Translated by Gregory Rabassa. New York: Harper and Row, 1970.

Gardner, John. *The Art of Fiction*. New York: Knopf, 1984.

———. *On Becoming a Novelist*. With an introduction by Raymond Carver. New York: Harper and Row, 1983.

———. *On Writers and Writing*. Edited by Stewart O'Nan. With an introduction by Charles Johnson. Reading: Addison-Wesley Publishing Company, 1994.

Gornick, Vivian. *The Situation and the Story*. New York: Farrar, Straus and Giroux, 2001.

Irving, John. Interview by Ron Hansen. *Paris Review*, no. 100 (Summer/Fall 1986): 74–103.

Joyce, James. *A Portrait of the Artist as a Young Man*. New York: Penguin, 1976.

Keillor, Garrison. Letter to Andy. "Don't Inhale Too Deeply." In *Post to the Host*. A Prairie Home Companion. http://www.publicradio.org/columns/prairiehome/posthost/2008/07/14/dont_inhale_too_deeply.php#comments.

Kelly, Mary Pat. "Almost the Last Temptation." In *Martin Scorsese: A Journey*. New York: Thunder's Mouth Press, 1996.

King, Stephen. "C.V." In *On Writing: A Memoir of the Craft*. New York: Scribner, 2000.

———. *The Stand: The Complete and Uncut Edition*. New York: Viking, 1990.

Leaming, Barbara. *Orson Welles: A Biography*. New York: Viking Penguin, 1985.

Mann, Thomas. *The Magic Mountain*. Translated by H. T. Lowe-Porter. New York: Modern Library, 1952.

McCarthy, Cormac. Interview with John Jurgensen. "Hollywood's Favorite Cowboy." *Wall Street Journal*, November 20, 2009. http://online.wsj.com/article/SB100014240527487045762045745297035 77274572.html.

Mutter, John. "Nancy Olson, Quail Ridge Books, Raleigh, N.C.: Bookseller of the Year." *Publishers Weekly*, May 7, 2001. http://www.publishersweekly.com/article/CA74853.html.

Nabokov, Vladimir. *Lectures on Literature*. Edited by Fredson Bowers. With an introduction by John Updike. New York: Harcourt Brace Jovanovich, 1980.

O'Brien, Tim. Interview with Steve Kaplan. *Missouri Review* 14 (Winter 1991): 93–108.

O'Connor, Flannery. "The Nature and Aim of Fiction." In *Mystery and Manners*. Edited by Sally and Robert Fitzgerald. New York: Farrar, Straus and Giroux, 1969.

Offutt, Chris. "Getting It Straight." *SFWP: A Literary Journal*, October 15, 2002. http://sfwp.org/archives/22.

Petty, Tom. Interview with David Fricke. *Rolling Stone*, no. 1093 (December 10, 2009): 70–75, 101.

Pinter, Jason. "Does Social Networking Kill the Author Mystique?" *Huffington Post*, December 16, 2009. http://www.huffingtonpost.com/jason-pinter/does-social-networking-ki_b_392747.html.

Rosenberg, L. M. "Introduction." In *MSS*. Winter/Spring 1984.

Russo, Richard. Commencement Address. Colby College, 2004. http://www.colby.edu/news/detail/488/.

Silverman, Kenneth. *Edgar Allan Poe: Mournful and Never-ending Remembrance*. New York: HarperCollins, 1991.

Solotaroff, Ted. "Writing in the Cold: The First Ten Years." In *A Few Good Voices in My Head*. New York: Harper and Row, 1987.

Steinbeck, John. *Working Days: The Journals of "The Grapes of Wrath."* Edited by Robert DeMott. New York: Penguin Books, 1990.

Weller, Sam. "Dark Carnival." In *The Bradbury Chronicles*. New York: William Morrow, 2005.

Wolfe, Thomas. *The Letters of Thomas Wolfe*. Edited by Elizabeth Nowell. New York: Scribner, 1956.

Wroblewski, David. Interview with Jenny Shank. *New West: Books and Writers*. http://www.newwest.net/topic/article/an_interview_with_david_wroblewski/C39/L39/.

Acknowledgments

This book would not exist without Holly Carver, director of the University of Iowa Press. She has been consistently supportive, good-natured, and patient throughout this process. I'm lucky to have worked with such a smart and generous editor. I am also grateful to Charlotte Wright and James McCoy for reading an earlier draft of this book and offering invaluable suggestions. It's a thrill to work with the University of Iowa Press again after so many years, and I would be remiss in not thanking the entire staff. I'm also indebted to all the writers and editors I called upon, many of whom helped me to be less myopic in my opinions; I take full responsibility for any remaining myopia. As always, my best editor is my wife, Amy Knox Brown, who helped me rein in my hyperbole, cut down my profanities, and curtail my redundancies. It's a vastly improved book because of her.

Index

Capote, Truman, 93, 135
career path, 19–22
careerism, 20
Carl Djerassi fellowship: awarded by Wisconsin's Institute for Creative Writing, 21
Carlson, Ron, 224
Carver, Holly, 204, 224
Carver, Raymond, 34, 88, 179, 228, 229, 230
Cathedral (Carver), 179
Cather, Willa, 164
Cat's Cradle (Vonnegut), 228
Chabon, Michael, 214
chance. *See* luck
Chaon, Dan, 158
Chaplin, Charlie, 3
Chappell, Fred, 160
Chase, Joan, 40
Chattahoochee Review, 84
Chayefsky, Paddy, vi
Cheever, John, 30, 74, 231–232
Chelsea, 84
Chercover, Sean, 121
Chicago Bulls, 219
Chicago Public Radio, 188
Chicago Reader, 156, 174
Chicago Sun-Times, 174
Chicago Tribune, 174; Printer's Row Book Festival, 166
Chico State University. *See* California State University–Chico
Clancy, Tom, 102
Clark, Martin, 195
Clarke, Will, 94–96
Clinton, Bill, 65
Coe Review, 20
Coetzee, J. M., 214
Coffee House Press, 126, 163
Cold Mountain (Frazier), 160
Colorado Review, 84, 119
Columbia, 119
Columbia College Chicago: English Department, 35; Fiction Writ-

ing Department, 35–36, 50; and poetry writing, 35
Columbia Pictures, 95
Columbia University, 49
columns: writing for newspaper, 183
Comic-Con, 165
commercial presses, 103–105
Commonwealth Writers' Prize, 41
competition: writing as, 236
composition theory, 71–72
Confederacy of Dunces (Toole), 102, 135
conferences. *See* writers' conferences
Conroy, Frank, 26, 30, 135
Coover, Robert, 228
Cornell University, 123
Counterpoint, 124, 199
cover letters, 5, 86–89; sample, 86–87
Crace, John, 11–12
craft: and learning it, 25–27, 68
Crane, Elizabeth, 223
Creasy, John, 121
creative writing degrees, 32–45
critics and criticism, 235. *See also* book reviews
Cunningham, Michael, 170
Cutbank, 81
Czyzniejewski, Michael, 222

Da Capo Press, 154
Daily Southtown, 174
D'Amato, Barbara, 121
Davis, Bette, 45
Davis-Gardner, Angela, 160–161
Dean Martin Show, 237
DeFrain, Darren, 77
degrees. *See* creative writing degrees
Delacorte, 199
DeLillo, Don, 214
DeMaio, Christine, 95–96